ADULT FOSTER HOMES

ADULT FOSTER HOMES
Their Managers and Residents

John M. McCoin, Ph.D., M.S.S.W.

Social Worker
Veterans Administration Medical
Center, Battle Creek, Michigan

 *HUMAN SCIENCES PRESS, INC.*
72 FIFTH AVENUE,
NEW YORK, N.Y. 10011

Printed in the United States of America
3456789 987654321

Library of Congress Cataloging in Publication Data

McCoin, John M.
    Adult foster homes.

    Includes bibliographical references and indexes.
    1. Mental retardation facilities—United States—
History. 2. Group homes—United States—Management—
History. I. Title.
HV3006.A4M35   362.4'0485'0973   LC 82–6083
                                          AACR2

ISBN 0–89885–087–8

To my siblings in the order of their birth:

Ruby McCoin Billings
Robert Andrew McCoin
Hassell Lee McCoin
Cecil Kyle McCoin

CONTENTS

LIST OF TABLES

ACKNOWLEDGMENTS

Mentioning all of the contributors to this book would be impractical, if not impossible. Therefore, only those people and organizations consi- dered to have made the most significant positive contributions will be named. However, this is not to negate the contributions of critics, especially in the formative stages in the evolution of this book. Indeed, their contributions would have to be ranked on a near or equal footing with the supporters.

Acknowledgment of financial grant #0900-4023 in the prere- search phase of the study is extended to the National Institute of Mental Health. To Max Richter, A.C.S.W., former chief social worker, F.D.R. Veterans Administration Medical Center, Montrose, New York, appreciation is extended for his being the first person to suggest that I do my doctoral dissertation on adult foster care; this was in 1975. Subsequently, my doctoral committee was much more conciliatory than previously, possibly because of my experience as a clinical social worker in adult foster care. Gratitude is extended to the Chairperson of my doctoral committee, Professor Beulah Compton, School of Social Work, University of Minnesota, Minneapolis. Her support and en- couragement in the early phases of the study were invaluable. Also, I am indebted to her for introducing me to the "nesting syndrome" concept. Also from the University of Minnesota, I extend my gratitude to Professors Don Martindale, sociology; Clarke Chambers, history; and Donald MacEachern, psychological foundations, for valuable support and consultation in the early phases of the study. Also for early consultation, I am indebted to Dr. Lewis Chartock, School of Social Work, Yeshiva University, New York.

In the middle and final phases of the study, I acknowledge the support and suggestions of Norma Fox, vice president and editor-in-chief, Human Sciences Press. Noteworthy is that five other publishers in the human sciences were not interested in publishing a book on adult foster homes. Also in the middle and final phases of the study, acknowledgment of support and encouragement is extended to Dr. Natalie Trager, former director, School of Social Work, Grand Valley State Colleges.

To John Wiley and Sons and Janice Proctor, N.H. Department of Health and Welfare, acknowledgments are made for permission to use long quotations in Chapters 2, 9, respectively. Also I am indebted to many other authors, publishers, and universities for materials used, especially those universities that provided M.S.W. theses and Smith College for a doctoral dissertation. Lastly, University Microfilms, International provided a valuable service.

The many people contributing to Chapter 4 warrant special attention. From the F.D.R. Veterans Administration Medical Center, Montrose, New York, appreciation is extended to the social work staff, research committee, many of the outpatients, and most of the adult foster home managers for participating in the study. Noteworthy also is the courage of that center's administrative officials in authorizing me to assess manager-authoritarianism, especially when considering the fact that three other facilities/hospitals refused such a request. Also for Chapter 4, acknowledgment is made for the consultative assistance of several people with statistics and data analysis. These are (1) Patricia Chartock, Croton-on-Hudson, New York; (2) Dr. Ronald Marks, associate professor, business administration, University of Wisconsin, Oshkosh; and (3) Darlene Wnukowski and Scott Coryell, computer programmers, University of Wisconsin, Oshkosh. Appreciation is also extended to Teachers College, Columbia University and the University of Wisconsin, Oshkosh, for the use of computer facilities.

Numerous people also contributed to Chapter 6. Acknowledgment is made to Dr. Reginald Carter and Dave Ferguson, Evaluation

Division, Michigan Department of Social Services for their guidance, direction, and support. From the Kent County Department of Social Services, Grand Rapids, Michigan, appreciation is extended to several people. These are: (1) Evert Vermeer, director; (2) Dave Thiele, supervisor, Adult Community Placement Services; and Gary Stahl, home finder. Also, I am most indebted to the participating managers and residents from the Kent County Adult Foster Home Program.

For the materials utilized in Chapters 5, 7–10, I am most appreciative to contributing officials, who deal with adult foster care throughout the United States. Altogether, responses were received from 49 states, the District of Columbia, Puerto Rico, and the Veterans Administration. Such a high response rate, to form letters primarily, is indicative of their high level of dedication to adult foster care.

Concluding the acknowledgments would be incomplete without recognizing the tremendous contributions of the typists. Typing all but two chapters, Sandra Sheldon, Minneapolis, Minnesota, is also a scholar and friend. Nancy Crittenden, Grand Rapids, Michigan, also made a significant contribution to the typing of the manuscript. Both have the great skill and ability to transform my longhand writing into a finished product, which is no mean task. Finally, readers are encouraged to submit any questions, suggestions, or criticisms to me at 4231 West Dickman Road, #1-D, Battle Creek, Michigan, 49015; telephone 616–964–3684 (evenings). I assume complete responsibility for all of the contents of this book, the contributions of many others notwithstanding.

John M. McCoin
Battle Creek, Michigan

Chapter 1

INTRODUCTION

THE PROBLEM

Seemingly having always been problematic for humanity are mental illness, mental retardation, and the dependent aged. It is assumed that the reader can differentiate between these three problem areas. However, a brief refresher will be presented. As used in this book, mental illness means a severe, chronic functional mental illness in which the exact causes are unknown, e.g., schizophrenia. Mental retardation essentially is below normal intellectual functioning, as measured by standardized IQ tests, ordinarily ranging from 0–67, with range 68–83 being borderline (American Psychiatric Association, 1968). By way of comparison, an average IQ would be 100. In this book the dependent-aged concept will be utilized to refer to people aged 60 or over who have a long history of functional mental disorder and/or organic brain or other physical disorders, who are unable to function independently but who are not sufficiently disabled as to require placement in a nursing home or to require continued hospitalization.

Since adult foster care has a long history of providing services for the functionally mentally disordered, the primary focus of this book will be on adult foster home care for this category. However, some attention will also be given to foster care for the mentally retarded and dependent aged, since these categories of people are being placed in adult foster homes in increasing numbers, especially in the last decade.

In less civilized times, the mentally ill, mentally retarded, and dependent aged were probably abandoned and left to die or sometimes put to death. More recently, they have been treated in various ways, influenced by changing philosophies, ideologies, and technologies. In my opinion, the most influential factor in our Western culture has been that of economics. It is widely known that the poor receive second-rate mental health services. With limited funds and emotional resources, they are often unable to adequately fulfill what Henry (1963) calls the first and second "Commandments" of the economic marketplace, i.e., "Thou shalt consume" and "Thou shalt create more desire" (p. 20). Henry blames science for these commandments, i.e., the scientific emphasis on newness leads to "human obsolescence" or to a "social junk yard" (p. 406). There are probably many people today who would agree that the chronically mentally ill, mentally retarded, and depen- dent aged are all too frequently placed in social junk yards. More recent critics have accused society of abandoning these categories of people by warehousing them in custodially oriented facilities, e.g., back wards of mental hospitals, boarding houses, and welfare hotels, to name but a few. Some critics would also place many adult foster homes in the warehouse category.

Hippocrates, who lived from 460–377 B.C., is acclaimed as the father of Western medicine. He theorized that madness was caused by a mixing of different "biles." Moreover, his bile theory as the etiology of mental illness replaced the demonic theory (National Association of Social Workers, 1971, p. 774). Deutsch (1949) indicates, however, that the poor mentally ill in Greece and Rome were often put to death. With the advent of the Middle Ages, the spirit of inquiry from the Greeks was dead. Apparently the Moslems provided the most sophisticated care for the mentally ill during the period and also probably built the first hospitals (Deutsch, 1949). However, in the Western countries the mentally ill were usually depicted as possessed by evil spirits in the early Middle Ages. For this reason and probably also due to the dormancy of the medical profession, attempts to help the mentally ill emanated from religious groups. Moreover, cloistered religious groups were about the only people with the intellectual wherewithal to undertake such a task in the Middle Ages.

At times during the Middle Ages, the mentally ill were viewed with veneration because it was believed they possessed supernatural powers. At other times they were depicted as witches and burned at the stake. One bright spot during the Middle Ages is that the adult foster home program had its genesis around 600–700 A.D. in Gheel, Belgium, under the auspices of the Roman Catholic Church. More will be said about this in Chapter 2.

Deutsch (1949) indicates that the mentally ill were probably first treated in a hospital in the late fourteenth century in England's infamous "Bedlam" hospital (p. 15). However, the widespread use of medical treatment for the mentally ill was centuries away.

In the colonial United States the mentally ill poor were undifferentiated from other groups of needy and sick people. The mentally ill from affluent families were often imprisoned in the cellars and strong rooms of their own homes. The poor mentally ill and other undesirable categories of people were customarily auctioned to the lower bidder, who was required to provide for them but, no doubt, often exploited them. Some mentally ill persons were placed in private residences at public expense during this period (Deutsch, 1949). This practice could be conceived as a precursor to the adult foster home program in the United States which developed centuries later.

With the advent of almshouses in the colonial United States in the late 1600s, the mentally ill were kept in them, undifferentiated from other categories of poor, dependent, and sick people. Finally, with the development of the first mental hospital in Williamsburg, Virginia, in the late 1700s, the mentally ill began to be viewed as a separate category (Pumphrey & Pumphrey, 1961). However, even then, the mentally ill were often viewed as "wild beasts" who had to be "tamed," sometimes by convicts who were serving as hospital attendants (Deutsch, 1949, p. 80). The reader should bear in mind that this was generally the period of Benjamin Rush, who is considered the father of American psychiatry.

Gradually, however, a more humane concept for treating the mentally ill emerged, called "moral treatment" (Miller & Blanc, 1967, p. 66). The originator of this concept is considered to be Philippe Pinel of France who struck the chains from some mentally ill people there in 1793 (National Association of Social Workers, 1971). Pinel's humane approach was adopted in England and eventually in the United States around 1810 (Miller & Blanc, 1967). These same authors report that the concept was widely practiced in the United States from about 1810 until after the Civil War. Moral treatment was derived from moral philosophy, the precursor of the profession of psychology. Moral treatment deviated from earlier treatment approaches in that religion was only an adjunct to treatment. The most important concepts were humanistic and optimistic approaches to treatment, coupled with a caring attitude and frequent contacts with patients. Work therapy was strongly encouraged. The early moral therapists were educated laymen, often Quakers, who eschewed the harsh practices of the past. Usually the therapist was of the same socioeconomic class as the patient, thus facilitating communication. The mental institutions of the period were called asylums, usually owned and operated by religious or private organizations. In addition to the mentally ill, asylums also kept people with mental retardation and epilepsy. Apparently 65 such asylums existed in 15 states by 1838 (National Association of Social Workers, 1971). Physicians then gradually took over as therapists and administrators as the Association of Medical Superintendents was founded in 1848 (Deutsch, 1949). Also, it was at about this period that state hospitals began to proliferate under the courageous and dynamic leadership of Dorothea Dix. Although some contemporary authors dispute the high claims of cures and remissions from the moral therapists, others think the figures are accurate and note that they compare favorably with statistics today (Kaufman, 1976; Miller & Blanc, 1967).

Concomitant to the proliferation of state hospitals in the United States during the latter half of the nineteenth century was the demise of moral therapy, replaced by the organic brain disease concept as the cause of mental illness. Instead of the optimism of the moral therapists, pessimism was now prevalent, resulting in few discharges and the frequent breaking of ties between patients, their families, and communities. Kaufman (1976) considers the period from 1885–1907 to be the period of "custodial orientation" (p. 33). Moreover, Kaufman indicates that this custodial orientation, coupled with economic and social pressures, precipitated the United States adult foster home movement from within and without the hospitals. Thus, the adult foster home movement floundered until the Great Depression of the 1930s. During the 1930s and 1940s several states adopted official policies for adult foster home programs for the mentally ill. In 1946 the National Mental Health Act was passed which recognized mental illness as a major health problem. With its enormous hospital system, the Veterans Administration served as a boon to the adult foster home movement by establishing an adult foster care policy in 1951. In 1955

Congress passed the Mental Health Studies Act which prescribed a review of the mental health system. Finally, the advent of tranquilizer drugs in the 1950s probably greatly enhanced the movement toward adult foster home placements.

In the 1960s the movement toward placing mental patients and the mentally retarded in the community gained momentum under the leadership of President Kennedy and the passage of the Community Mental Health Centers Act of 1963. Also probably influencing the movement were the "right to treatment" cases of the 1960s, wherein hospitals were legally required to prove that they provided more than custodial care. Otherwise, if the patient were not considered danger-ous to himself/herself or others, and could manage in the community, the patient could not be hospitalized against his/her will. The passage of the Community Mental Health Center Amendments of 1975 further discouraged prolonged hospital care.

Zweben (1977) reports that from 1961–1974, the number of men-tal hospital patients dropped from 427,799 to 237,692 for a 44% decline. Moreover, he reports that the number of elderly patients in mental hospitals dropped from 135,322 to 59,685 between 1969–1974 for a 56% decrease. Wolff (1970) claims that 30% of all first admissions to mental hospitals are aged 60 or over and that 45% of the people in most United States psychiatric hospitals are over age 60. Butterfield (1976) reports that the mentally retarded population in hospitals drop-ped by one-third from 1950–1971. Although difficult to interpret, statistics show that a large percentage of these three groups were transferred to adult foster homes. More will be said about this later.

PURPOSE OF STUDY

The general purpose of this study was to do a qualitative assess-ment of the adult foster home program in the United States, including its past and present.

More specifically, a thorough review of the literature was con-ducted, including all the known doctoral dissertations on the subject from 1955–1979. This review was conducted to give the reader an appreciation of the development of the program over a 1200–1300 year period and to show readers how research methodology has adv-anced in the social sciences, especially in the past two decades. The literature review was also intended to give readers a greater appreciation of the impact of wars, politics, and economic factors upon social movements, particularly the adult foster care movement. Generic terminology was largely used in Chapter 2 in an effort to simplify comprehension and to help in conceptually refining the terminology. The reader should keep in mind that various authors during various periods used diverse terminology, but to follow all the exact terminology used by the authors would be impossible, if not undesirable. Finally, for Chapter 2, insofar as is feasible, the professional discipline of the authors was reported. Though this may appear somewhat redundant, it was thought necessary to show the contributions, or lack of them, by certain disciplines at various times, especially social work and psychiatry.

Chapter 3 was promulgated to assist researchers, policy makers, administrators, social workers, and other interested people to develop a boarder comprehension of the latest theoretical thinking in the field. Hopefully, Chapter 3 will also stimulate further inquiry. Chapter 4 summarizes the results of the field testing of some of the theoretical thinking in the field and should be of interest to researchers, scholars, and others.

A review of current programs in the United States was presented in order to, hopefully, stimulate more interest in the adult foster home movement and add to conceptual refinement in the field. Hopefully, such an accomplishment would not only be of great value to policy makers and researcheres but to line social workers, not to mention managers and residents of these homes. Next, case examples of some managers and residents of adult foster homes are given in an effort to help present managers and residents as human beings and to give readers some idea on what they are like as people.

Chapter 7 discusses the relevance of the adult foster home program as a mode to help meet the needs of increasingly large numbers of patients who are being placed into the community but not with their families. Chapters 8 and 9 discuss the successes and failures of adult foster care, including my own observations of a program which I worked for 7 years on a part-time basis at the Franklin Delano Roosevelt Veterans Administration Hospital, Montrose, New York. It is believed that such a procedure will help bridge the communication barriers between clinical practitioners and researchers. The future prospects for the adult foster home movement are delineated in order to stimulate dialogue and, hopefully, further research. Finally, Chapters 10–12 are presented summarizing the adult foster care movement and future prospects, and certain conclusions are drawn. Again, the purpose is to generate more interest, dialogue, inquiry, research and, hopefully, to stimulate further thinking in the field.

Since social work has been the primary professional discipline involved in implementing the adult foster home programs since the 1930s, further elaboration on the purpose of social work is deemed necessary. Pincus and Minahan (1973, p. 9) conceptualize the purpose of social work as to:

1. Enhance the problem-solving and coping capacities of people.
2. Link people with systems that provide them with resources, services, and opportunities.
3. Promote the effective and humane operation of these systems.
4. Contribute to the development and improvement of social policy.

The profession of social work has always been concerned and involved with the population groups in our society which have been vulnerable to abuse and control. Throughout most of the history of social work, the profession has searched for more effective treatment modes for the mentally ill, including helping them return to and remain in their communities as coping people. As members of professional treatment teams in mental hospitals, social workers observed firsthand the negative impact of prolonged hospitalization for many patients. Therefore, it seems only natural that social workers should be at the forefront of the mental health professionals who are interested in another treatment alternative to prolonged hospitalization. One such mode is the adult foster home program, which is the focus of this book.

DEFINITIONS

The literature abounds with a macrocosmic disarray of terms in describing adult foster homes. Nowhere is this more prominent than in the terms used to describe the homes and the people who operate them. As for the people residing in these homes, exclusive of management, the term *resident* seems fairly well accepted, though some are still referred to as patients, boarders, or guests. The term resident seems to be an appropriate one, as used above, for regular use.

Some of the terms extant in the literature which seem to be analogous to the phrase *adult foster homes* are *personal care homes* and *family care homes*. Of course, the phrase adult foster homes is also used in the literature. From the literature it is not often readily apparent what differentiates adult foster homes from boarding homes and board and care homes. However, from Segal and Aviram (1978) one gets the impression that in California, board and care homes may be replacing adult foster homes and, moreover, that board and care homes are developing rapidly in an ad hoc manner. Generally, one gets the impression that boarding homes and board and care homes provide a marginal level of services in all areas, while adult foster homes are considered to provide better quality services. Also, one gets the impression that adult foster homes are more closely scrutinized by licensing bodies and professional staffs.

Adding to the confusion is the fact that the terms adult foster homes, family care homes, personal care homes, board and care homes, group homes, halfway houses, homes for the aged, and sometimes even nursing homes are subsumed under one umbrella term, e.g., such as community care homes, personal care residence programs, shelter care facilities, and community-based residential facilities. Even within the Veterans Administration hospital complex, there is variation in the terminology used. One Veterans Administration hospital uses the generic term "Community Care Homes" to include "personal care homes" (analogous to adult foster homes), boarding homes, and "special homes" (McCoin, 1977, p. 55). Another Veterans Administration hospital uses an umbrella term "personal care residence program" under which are listed adult foster homes and halfway houses (Kaufman, 1976, p. 73).

Often, the generic and specific terminology is used interchangeably so as to make data interpretation extremely difficult. Reporting agencies apparently often are unable or unwilling to break down data for the specific programs, instead reporting data simply on all the programs that fall under the generic programs. Thus, by now, it is fairly obvious that each state largely determines its own policy on terminology. As previously mentioned, the Veterans Administration does not have a uniform policy on terminology. Apparently there are a total of 11 federal agencies which determine policy in the area of community living facilities for the categories being considered here (McCoin, 1979).

For the sake of conceptually refining the terminology in the field, capitalizing on the rich history of adult foster homes and showing historical linkages between foster homes for children and adults, some of my own thinking is now posited. These terms are not original with me, but perhaps they have not been used so explicitly before in the area of adult foster homes.

The phrase adult foster homes obviously contains three words. In this book the word *adult* simply means any person who is 18 years or older. The word *foster* is rather tricky, so a contemporary dictionary definition is proffered: "Affording, receiving, or sharing nurture or parental care though not related by blood or legal ties. . . . To promote the growth and development of . . ." (*Webster's New Collegiate Dictionary,* 1977, p. 459).

This definition seems fairly adequate for our purposes, except that the phrase "parental care" would be more appropriate for children's foster homes than adult foster homes. However, despite the shortcomings of this definition, the term foster seems more conceptually accurate than many other terms now in use. For example, the term *care* is often used in lieu of foster. A perusal of dictionary definitions for care indicate such terms as watchful attention, caution, and custody. These terms appear to be more patronizing, when applied to adults, than foster. At the risk of sounding old-fashioned and in line with the reasoning of Henry (1963) to the effect that science courts the new and shuns the old, another definition of foster is proffered: "Affording, receiving, or sharing nourishment, nurture, or sustenance, though not related by blood, or, figuratively by ties of nature, citizenship, or the like" (*Webster's New Collegiate Dictionary,* 1953, p.327). With all due respect to science and the new, this definition seems more relevant to our needs in the book.

As for the word *home,* this theoretical concept, or word, probably needs little elaboration when it is used in conjunction with the other two words in the phrase *adult foster home.* The entire phrase essentially refers to a private home, wherein the manager(s) usually own and manage the home, which has been assessed and approved by a state licensing agency (or local facility, often a hospital) for the purpose of housing, feeding, and supervising certain categories of handicapped adults. Of course, it can easily be argued that a number of community-based residential facilities for handicapped and dependent adults would correspond to this definition. This is precisely why more conceptual refinement is needed. For example, if a uniform national policy were formulated to standardize terminology, the preceding definition could be used as a general frame of reference upon which to begin a more uniform national policy on adult foster homes. This would impact heavily on state policy formulation through the federal control of monies. Only through a procedure such as this can we begin to bring some order out of the chaos. All programs not meeting the statutory requirements for adult foster homes could aspire to have their homes upgraded to meet the standards or else they would be closed. However, this would require a reasonably uniform statewide licensing policy, and this is not yet a reality.

The preceding definition of adult foster homes needs explication because one vital link has been excluded; that is, the person, or people, who operate adult foster homes. Most frequently, they own the home. Miller (1977) notwithstanding, the operators of these homes could not be considered professionals in the strict sense of the word; usually they are lay people. Sometimes they go into the field as a part-time occupation; others do so on a full-time basis. However, these should not be considered professionals, unless they have professional educational qualifications from relevant fields in the human services, e.g., licensed social worker, psychologists, or registered nurses. Defining professionalism, however, is also complex and is beyond the scope of this book. Parenthetically, numerous states still do not certify or license social workers.

In the literature, people who operate adult foster homes have been referred to variously as caretakers, staff, proprietors, and foster parents, to name only some of the terms. The word *caretaker* conjures up an image of someone caring for a cemetery or the grounds of an estate. The term *sponsor* implies that the sponsoree has an almost sycophantic relationship with the sponsor. If adult foster homes are supposed to help rehabilitate handicapped people, then the term *sponsor* could be misleading.

In my opinion, the more logical and humane term to apply to people who operate adult foster homes is simply *manager*. An abbreviated contemporary definition of manager is simply, "one who conducts business or household affairs" (*Webster's New Collegiate Dictionary*, 1977, p. 697). This is certainly a more unifying conceptual term than the other terms extant in the literature.

SUMMARY

An introduction to the history of differing treatment philosophies for mental illness has been presented. The primary purpose for writing this book has been elaborated upon, which is chiefly to stimulate thought, dialogue, and a renewed spirit and dedication to scientific inquiry, Henry's (1963) negative viewpoints on science notwithstanding. For essentially the same reasons as delineated above, efforts have been made at conceptually refining the common terminology extant in the field, therefore, hopefully being of practical use to researchers, policy makers, administrators, clinical social workers, and others interested in the field. With its table of contents and indexes, this book should prove to be a ready reference source for the above disciplines and other interested readers who are concerned about more efficient and humane treatment and care for the mentally ill, mentally retarded, and dependent aged. Hopefully, a large percentage of people will be so concerned.

It is hoped that this book will generate a greater understanding and appreciation of the negative impact of economic factors on the treatment and care of the three populations in question.

Prospects for the future for the adult foster care program seem mixed at this point. The whole concept of the program seems to be based upon the premise that a family environment is healthy for nurturance, stimulation, companionship, and supervision. Yet, the extended family of grandparents, parents, and children is now all but passé. Even the nuclear family of parents and children often seems to be in jeopardy. However, perhaps the troubles of the nuclear family are caused by factors external to it, as opposed to inherent weaknesses. Though criticizing science and economics, Henry (1963) praised the family when he indicated: "The economic system causes hostility, fear, and suspicion; it is within the family that these feelings must be worked through and subordinated in love" (p. 128). If we can share Henry's optimism about the family, perhaps we can transfer this positive attitude to our surrogate families—those people who reside in and manage adult foster homes.

Chapter 2

HISTORY OF ADULT FOSTER HOMES

The materials reviewed in this chapter are reviewed chronologically as much as possible, i.e., within the year in which they were written. The rationale for this approach is to show the increasing momentum of interest in adult foster homes in recent years and the probable influence of policy changes on the movement. For the early and middle periods, reliance was placed upon secondary sources because of the paucity of journal articles and books in the United States during those periods.

   Interpreting data, which are oftentimes contradictory and repetitious, from the publications is no mean task. Lamb (1976) alludes to the "Persistence of Barnumism in America" (p. xi), or what could also be categorized as faddism. The literature extant on adult foster homes certainly forces one to question Barnumism and faddism as contributory factors adding to the confusion in the murky waters of the adult foster home program. In an effort to bring some semblance of order to the chaos and to prevent redundancy, I have used the generic terms of *adult foster homes, managers,* and *residents,* instead of the plethora of other terms extant in the literature. Briefly, the term adult foster home will be given further elaboration in this chapter. Managers are the operators (usually also owners) of these homes. In the literature managers are frequently called *caretakers* or *sponsors*. Residents are the people who live in these homes.

This chapter focuses heavily on psychiatric patients who became residents of adult foster home programs. The rationale for this is that this type of resident has been studied longer and more intensively than other types. Nevertheless, foster homes have been utilized for mentally retarded adults for many years. As the 1970s passed into history, articles on foster home placement for the aged began to proliferate. Moreover, some articles on children's foster homes are reviewed because of many similarities between them and adult programs. Interest in the administrative and policy aspects prompted me to include some articles in these and related areas.

Evidence of historical linkages between foster homes for children and adults abound (Fenske & Roecker, 1971; Magner, 1961; Ullman & Berkman, 1959; Wohlford, 1968). Contrary to the opinion of many, foster home care for adults antedates foster home care for children.

600–1852 Era

Since much of the early history of the adult foster home movement is legendary, there is some variation on its roots. Kilgour (1936) places the origin at 600 A.D., while Dumont and Aldrich (1962) place the beginning at 700 A.D. While the exact date of the roots of the adult foster home movement may have been lost to antiquity, there is unanimity among authors that the location of the movement was Gheel, Belgium.

The legend goes that the establishment of Colony Gheel can be attributed to the beautiful Irish Princess Dymphna. The daughter of a Catholic mother and pagan father, who was also King of Ireland, Dymphna is reported to have resembled her beautiful mother very much (Kilgour, 1936). Dympha's aspirations of becoming a nun were interrupted by the untimely death of her mother. Heartbroken and lonely from his wife's death, the King directed his subjects to search out a woman who most closely resembled his late wife. As none could be found, he proposed marriage to Dymphna; parenthetically, incest was not uncommon among pagans. However, Dymphna being Catholic, was horrified by her father's proposal. After seeking solace from her priest, Father Gerbern, they both decided to flee for their own safety, feeling that her father was insane to make such a proposal. Hastily, they fled to Belgium. Soon, however, her father and his entourage overtook them at Gheel. The King was so outraged that he ordered his subjects to slay Dymphna and the priest. Following orders, the priest was slain but the subjects refused to slay the beautiful Dymphna. This task the King promptly did himself (Goldenson, 1970).

Unaccustomed to such madness, the legend continues, the people of Gheel were so curious and awe-struck that they preserved Dymphna's body. The body began to attract visitors who began to attribute saintly powers to her for what was considered the triumph of wisdom and chastity over the lust and impurity of her father's alleged insane desires toward her. Gradually, Dymphna's remains became invested with magical powers to cure the mentally ill. Dumont and Aldrich (1962) report that over the next few hundred years visits to Dymphna's remains became a pilgrimage for many of the mentally ill, who were then considered spiritually ill. So Dymphna eventually became a saint of the Roman Catholic Church. At that time, mental illness was considered a spiritual matter because its sufferers were considered to be "possessed" (p. 116). Dumont and Aldrich indicate that records date to 1250 A.D. which contain the names of pilgrims who visited St. Dymphna's remains. Alongside the names it is said is often written the words "and the evil spirit departed" (p. 116). Eventually, the Church and the annex containing Dymphna's remains became too small to accommodate all the pilgrims so citizens in the community began taking in pilgrims. The Roman Catholic Church assumed overall responsibility for the pilgrims, and nuns provided nursing supervision. Furthermore, Dumont and Aldrich indicate that the demise of the influence of the Roman Catholic Church on Colony Gheel was caused by Napoleon's antichurch policy in the early nineteenth century. However, after the boundaries of Belgium were reestablished, Colony Gheel was maintained by the municipal government until 1852 when it was placed under state control but under medical direction (Kilgour, 1936).

Meanwhile in the colonial United States, mentally ill paupers, along with an admixture of other poor people (both children and adults), were sometimes housed with private families at public expense (Morrissey, 1967). With the advent of almshouses, however, in the late 1600s the practice of placing the poor and mentally ill in private homes was discontinued. In the almshouses the mentally ill were kept undifferentiated from other types of needy people. Not until the first mental hospital was built in Williamsburg, Virginia, in the late 1700s (Pumphrey & Pumphrey, 1961) were the mentally ill singled out as a special category of unfortunate people.

1853–1935 Period

Dominating this period was the state and medical profession. Pollock (1945) claims that by 1867 Scotland had begun to compete with Gheel for worldwide attention in the adult foster home arena. Scotland then had over 1637 former psychiatric patients in adult foster homes.

By the midnineteenth century, state hospitals began to proliferate in the United States, due chiefly to the courageous and pioneering efforts of Dorothea Dix. Historically, this period marked the beginning of the widespread differentiation of mental patients from society's other misfortunate people. By the midcentury point, various leaders from the United States had visited Scotland and Gheel's adult foster home programs and were attempting to sell the concept in the United States. In 1855 Massachusetts became the first state to adopt a policy of adult foster care for mental patients in the United States but did not actually place its first patients into adult foster homes until 1882. In 1914 Rhode Island became the second state to so place patients, but this did not become official state policy until 1940 (Pollock, 1945). Maryland's Springfield State Hospital had a primitive type of adult foster home program in 1916–1917, supervised by nursing service, but it was short lived and did not become official state policy until 1938 (de Alvarado, 1955).

Chronologically, New York became the second state to officially adopt an adult foster home program in 1935. Utah followed suit the same year (Morrissey, 1967). By the mid-1930s there was a paucity of publications on adult foster care save for a few relatively obscure publications (Crockett, 1934; Sandy, 1935).

1936–1959 Time Frame

During this period the literature was dominated mostly by psychiatrists, many of whom praised the therapeutic potentialities of the adult foster home program (Bigelow & Schied, 1939; Kilgour, 1936; Molholm & Barton, 1941). The first book-length publication on adult foster care was published in 1944 (Crutcher) and the author was a social worker. She was rather inconsistent in using the terms *foster care* and *family care* interchangeably. Muncie (1945), a psychiatrist, delineated three case histories in which he felt adult foster home placement had been therapeutic for his patients.

Concrete examples of the interest exhibited by psychiatry in adult foster homes can be found in the *American Journal of Psychiatry* from the 1940s until the mid-1960s. During those years, brief articles appeared in the January issue on family care and related topics. Stycos (1951), a psychiatrist, stressed the need for more research and believed the reason for the slow growth of the movement was due primarily to the United States tradition of "rugged individualism" (p. 304).

Although not the first organization to initiate adult foster homes in the United States, the Veterans Administration has been one of heaviest users since officially establishing a uniform policy for adult foster homes in 1951 (U.S. Veterans Administration, 1971). However, there is evidence that some Veterans Administration hospitals were utilizing adult foster homes earlier, e.g., the St. Cloud VA Hospital since 1948 (V.A. Hospital, St. Cloud, Minn., n.d.) and VA Hospital, Bedford, Massachusetts, since 1949 (Redding, 1963). At any rate, the VA has left more precise data on its adult foster home program since 1951, thus helping to bring some semblance of order in the field.

The first masters or doctoral thesis on adult foster homes appears to have been produced by de Alvarado (1955). Her study was an ex post facto study of 900 residents from Springfield State Hospital, Maryland, covering the period from 1935–1950. The author emphasized the custodial nature of the program, in contrast with most early authors, who had expounded upon the alleged therapeutic benefits.

In a search for indicators for successful placements in adult foster homes, a psychologist-social worker team (Ullman, Berkman, & Hamister, 1958) concluded that hospital routine and number of years of hospitalization were better indicators than psychological reports. That project was conducted at the Palo Alto Veterans Hospital in California. From the study emerged the Hamister Post Hospital Adjustment Scale which seems to still have some practical utility in predicting a person's successful placement in an adult foster home. However, at least in the published literature, it appears to have been little used.

By 1959, Norway reportedly had 29% of its severely mentally ill population in adult foster homes (Barton, 1959). A psychologist-social worker team attempted to classify patients by devising "criterion groups" for placement in adult foster homes by using such terms as "sitters, jumpers, goers, trippers," and "failures" (Ullman & Berkman, 1959, p. 74).

In his a masters, thesis Parks (1959) seems to be the first researcher to assess the personalities of adult foster home managers, using the Edwards Personal Preference Schedule. Parks compared the personality profiles of managers and psychiatric nurses. Furthermore, he found the nurses to be rather "domineering and aggressive" and the adult foster home managers to be rather "subservient and timid" by comparison (p. 27).

A 5-year ex post facto study was performed at the Northport New York Veterans Administration Hospital (Cunningham, Bowitnick, Dolson, & Weichert, 1959). The authors categorized the residents as either successful or unsuccessful, depending on whether or not they were able to be sustained in adult foster homes for the 5-year period studied. They found that those residents who were successful in placement averaged 51.4 years, while the unsuccessful ones averaged only 36 years. Also, they found the mean years of hospitalization for the successfuls was 10.7 and for the unsuccessfuls it was 5.3.

A survey of the literature on mental retardation for this period indicates that by the late 1950s institutional care was becoming less fashionable. Brown, Windle, and Stewart (1959) thought that foster home placement was the logical extension of institutional care for the mentally retarded.

Morrissey (1967) indicates that several states officially adopted adult foster home programs between 1936–1959. According to him these states are: Maryland and Pennsylvania, 1938; Rhode Island, 1940; California, 1941; Michigan and Illinois, 1942; Ohio, 1945; New Jersey, 1948; New Mexico, 1951; Indiana and Wisconsin, 1955; Alabama and Idaho, 1958; and Missouri, 1959. Adding those 14 states to the 3 from the 1935–1939 period would place the number of states with approved adult foster home programs in 1959 at 17. Morrissey (1967), furthermore, indicates that Puerto Rico officially adopted an adult foster home program in 1950. However, he cautions that different authors have cited different dates for the establishment of programs, and he thinks that some of the confusion may be due to the fact that some reporting organizations subsume all community-based residential placements under the adult foster home category, e.g., including nursing homes and halfway houses data. Furthermore, he believes that some confusion may be caused by the fact that some states unofficially began the program before officially adopting same. Another possible area of confusion mentioned by Morrissey is that some states adopted official policy for the establishment of programs at different times for the mentally retarded and mentally ill, e.g., New York's official adoption of a program for the mentally retarded is given as 1931 and for the mentally ill, 1935 (Morrissey, 1965a).

Finally, closing out this period, especially the 1950s, would be incomplete without reference to the likely impact that the advent of the widespread use of ataractic and antidepressive drugs had on policy changes and the amelioration of attitudes toward the mentally ill. Though the administration of these drugs have critics, there is no doubt in the author's mind that they had a strong impact on alleviating many undesirable psychotic symptoms whereby the patients could be tolerated in the community.

1960 DECADE

The advent of the 1960s witnessed the continued decline in the quantity of articles by psychiatrists on adult foster homes. Also, this period marks the first time that social workers dominated the human service professions in the number of published articles on the subject. Concomitantly, this period indicated a decided trend toward more research sophistication (Giovannoni & Ullman, 1961; Magner, 1961; Morrissey, 1967; Smitson, 1967; Steffy, 1963). The probable contributing factors to the proliferation of articles during this period are many. Possibly the program was coming of age and possibly the social work profession was also coming of age and was becoming more research orientated. Then, too, the 1960s were turbulent times, due chiefly to the Vietnam war and to the fact that turbulent times tend to generate more introspection and innovation. Then, there can be little doubt that the interests of President Kennedy and his family in the areas of mental retardation and mental illness influenced federal legislation in the early 1960s. Concrete examples can be found in the Joint Commission on Mental Illness and Health report (1961) and the passage of the Mental Health Centers Act of 1963 (P.L. 88-164). Both of these provided greater impetus toward placing long-term psychiatric patients into the community.

Since the quantity of published literature on adult foster homes proliferated in the 1960s, it will be evaluated in two sections, i.e., 1960–1964 and 1965–1969.

1960–1964

In 1961 two social workers (Lyle & Trail) studied the outcome adjustment patterns of residents from the Veterans Administration Hospital, American Lake, Washington. The study included 77 residents, two-thirds of whom had schizophrenic diagnoses. Among their findings was that erratic behavior was definitely linked with failure to remain in the homes. Furthermore, they found that older residents who had longer periods of hospitalization were more likely to be successful in adult foster homes. They also found that residents became less withdrawn in the homes than they were in the hospital. Finally, they learned that residents were significantly more likely to remain in the homes if they liked the manager. The implications of these findings are many but would be fairly easy to assess.

Giovannoni and Ullman (1961), a social worker-psychologist team, indicated that the presence of both sexes among managers helped structure and refine relationship roles for all concerned, but especially for the residents. More specifically, they found that 67% of the male residents who were placed in homes where there were both male and female managers made "relatively desirable" adjustments, whereas only 21% of the residents placed with a female manager made relatively good adjustments. The authors observed that the widespread tendency to place residents with female managers only is hard to justify, except that the mentally ill in our society are viewed with considerable confusion.

Magner (1961) produced a doctoral thesis in which he categorized 44% of the homes he studied as rehabilitative. This leaves the majority of them as being custodial, which is contrary to the views of earlier authors who tended to view them as largely therapeutic. While Magner focused on the casework process, personality development, and psychopathology, he largely neglected the role of the community in successful programs. Some psychiatrists continued to publish on adult foster homes in the early 1960s (Barton, 1963; Barton & St. John, 1961).

Two other psychiatrists evaluated Colony Gheel, one of them having gone there to make an in-depth study (Dumont & Aldrich, 1962). They indicated that the residents came mostly from Belgium, but there were some from many parts of the world, including the United States. Moreover, they found that about one-third of the residents were women and that some had been there for 50 years or longer. Some young children were also in residence. They found that 55% of the residents were diagnosed as mentally retarded, 29% schizophrenic, and there was a varied assortment of other diagnoses. Most of the residents were state supported. The authors further reported that the program was custodial rather than rehabilitation oriented. Colony Gheel reached the apex of its resident population in 1940 when there were 3,700 residents. By 1962, the population had decreased to 2,400. Finally, the authors expressed their belief that the residents improved in the Colony by becoming more actively alert and interested in their environments, not to mention improved posture and verbal communication skills. The Colony was then under the direction of three psychiatrists who freely prescribed medication and were required to make rounds once a month.

There has been considerable discussion in the literature about difficulties in assessing the suitability of psychiatric patients for foster home placement and of monitoring their symptomatology during placement. Overall and Gorham (1962) describe a scale that would seem to have practical utility for such purposes, i.e., the Brief Psychiatric Rating Scale (p. 799). The interviewer completes the 16-item scale in a structured 20 minute interview. Interrater reliability ranged from .62 to .87, which gives a reasonably reliable indication of the person's symptomatology. A subsequent reviewing of more current literature reveals that the scale has been utilized to evaluate some residents' adjustment in some homes.

Researching community attitudes toward adult foster homes, a social worker-psychologist team (Bowen & Fischer, 1962) found that 28% of those returning questionnaires reported positive attitudes toward keeping nonrelative mental patients in their homes. Furthermore, they found that four-fifths of those returning questionnaires had known someone in a mental hospital. Another interesting finding they reported was that the age range 35–54 was more likely to have altruistic motives for keeping patients, while those over age 55 were more likely to be motivated more by financial remuneration expectations.

Cherry (1963) did a masters thesis on why 30 adult foster homes in California were closed over a 27-month period. She thought that one-third of those homes which were closed should have never been opened because of the managers' inability to effectively communicate with agency personnel. The author of another masters thesis (Steffy, 1963) studied the adult foster home program at the VA Hospital, Danville, Illinois. Steffy used some sophisticated testing instruments and statistical procedures including correlational analysis and part of the Minnesota Multiphasic Personality Inventory, Custodial Mental Illness Ideology Scale, and the Health Engendering Scale. However, she did not find any significant correlation between managers' personalities and residents' adjustment patterns. She did find that the managers ranged in age from 26–78, with the mean being 56.7. The mean resident age was 48.6 and the average number of years of hospitalization was 9.6. Furthermore, Steffy found that an honest, open approach from managers and that younger-aged managers seemed to be associated with residents' improvement.

Reporting in 1963 (Barton), a psychiatrist indicated that Norway had one-half of its mental patients in adult foster homes and that Canada had a total of 1466 so placed. Moreover, he indicated that in 1963 there were 40 veterans hospitals utilizing adult foster homes and he thought the decline of Colony Gheel could be due to a decreasing belief in the powers of St. Dymphna and the fact that Belgian psychiatrists were not enthusiastic over the program.

Switching now to later efforts at devising an effective instrument for selecting residents for placement in adult foster care, we turn to Lee (1963), a social worker. Many authors found that length of hospitalization was an important criterion for selection for placement. Lee thought that the amount of time residents spent out of the hospital was also an important variable in selecting patients for placement. Thus, he devised the Departure Index (p. 565), symbolized as

$$D = \frac{T + 1}{M}$$

In the index, the T represents the number of times the patient was on convalescent leave since the last admission. Conceivably, this could be 0. Thus, a constant of 1 was added to make division possible in such instances. The M represents the number of months the patient has spent in the hospital since the last admission. Although this index appears logically sound, it has had little or no empirical testing according to the published literature.

Another social worker, Redding (1963) examines the importance of the patients' early life experiences in the selection process. Several case histories are presented of schizophrenic residents and their reactions to placement. Some good diagnostic indicators for successful placements are given. For example, many residents should be placed in homes with managers who have different personalities from their siblings and parents. Also, the social worker needs a great deal of empathy and a sound comprehension of the residents' personality dynamics, particularly as influenced by the residents' early parental and sibling relationships. Moreover, the social worker needs a firm comprehension of the primitive symbolic communication patterns of schizophrenic residents, not to mention their complex defense mechanism systems. Moreover, Redding indicated that the social worker needs skills in recognizing and dealing with residents' anxiety over leaving a known hospital environment for the unknown one—having to negotiate new relationships with surrogate family members.

Schwartz and Schwartz (1964) suggest a form of "graded stress" to help rehabilitate residents moving into the community. In essence, the residents should be given gradually increasing amounts of responsibility so as to mobilize their coping strengths, thereby helping to enhance their level of social functioning and integration into the community.

Miller (1964), a social worker, compiled data on 137 managers in California. She concluded that less than one-half went beyond the tenth grade and this category had annual incomes of less than $5200. Moreover, the majority of the managers had lower-class value systems, indicating that they perceive more concretely than, for example, their middle-class social workers, who would be more inclined to think abstractly. Possibly, these class differences produce communication problems. Williams and Neilson (1964) compiled data on residents of adult foster homes in California. They found the best indicators for successful placements to be men with chronic brain syndrome diagnoses, women with psychotic diagnoses, and any type of patient with over 10 years hospitalization.

1965–1969

Apetekar (1965), a social worker, explained that adult foster homes keep essentially three groups of people, i.e., mental patients, mentally retarded adults, and the elderly. This seems to be one of the first references in the literature to the aged in foster care, and the author mentions this as a comparatively recent development. Aptekar lamented the fact that, despite its long history, the program was relatively unknown in 1965, i.e., outside the Veterans Administration. He noted that the Veterans Administration had a 22% increase in foster home placements between 1959–1960. The author indicated that adult foster homes have an inherent contribution to make for certain patients because of the benefits of living with a family as opposed to continued hospitalization.

Finally, Aptekar indicated that France's adult foster home program dates to 1892, Switzerland's to 1909, Germany's to 1911, and the Providence of Ontario, Canada, dates to 1933. McNeel (1965), a psychiatrist, stated: "A quick review of the recent literature suggests that articles on Family Care for the mentally ill are being replaced by articles, scattered through a variety of journals, on halfway houses, hostels, and other forms of community care for special groups . . ." (p. 701). Continuing, McNeel indicates that functionally there is no clear line between hostels, halfway houses, and foster homes. However, he does indicate that many foster homes, like hostels and halfway houses, are also used as transitional facilities. That is, they are not meant to be permanent residences. However, many of them do wind up to be custodial facilities. McNeel further pointed out that foster homes are private residences, while hostels and halfway houses are administered and staffed by a hospital or supporting agency. Finally, McNeel gave one reason for the decline of Colony Gheel in Belgium as being that the majority of applicants were too mentally ill to be cared for in the Colony.

During the mid-1960s the most prolific writer on adult foster homes was Morrissey (1965a, 1965b, 1967), a social worker. His publications will now be reviewed chronologically.

Morrissey (1965a) comments that, with the exception of the Veterans Administration, reliable data on the adult foster home program are unreliable. From a survey he learned that 23 states, Puerto Rico, and Washington, D.C. had programs for adult foster care in 1965. Moreover, he added that Colorado, Kentucky, and Hawaii officially adopted programs in 1962, 1962, and 1963, respectively. Though he does not say so explicitly, one gets the impression that perhaps numerous states did not respond to his survey. Morrissey, furthermore, indicates that Maryland, New York, Utah, Pennsylvania, California, Illinois, and

Michigan had 83% of the residents in placement in the United States (exclusive of the Veterans Administration), for a total of 11,000 in placement in 1965.

Continuing, Morrissey (1965a) thinks the relatively slow growth of the program may be due to a variety of factors, including professional apathy, legal difficulties (e.g., zoning laws), irrational fears, and conflict between the ideologies of institutional versus noninstitutional care. Also, he indicated that perhaps parents of the mentally ill were becoming overly defensive as a consequence of their having been blamed by professionals for their alleged causative role in mental illness. Morrissey (1965a) emphasizes the need for research on the managers of homes and better assessment plans for selecting residents for placement.

What appears to be the last lengthy publication on adult foster care was accomplished by Morrissey (1967). This appears to be the most sophisticated and comprehensive assessment of the adult foster home program extant to date. The greatest contributions of the publication are his development of the history of the program, the assessment of the research in the field, and the theoretical formulations. The author claims the program has been treated like a "bastard child" (p. 13), possibly one reason being that mental illness breeds fear which causes resistance. Another possible reason given for resistance to the program was the prevailing psychiatric belief that the mentally ill could best be treated in institutions, which could simultaneously protect the public from the patients by providing strict measures of social control over them. Other reasons for resistance given are the lack of professional and legislative leadership, probably the key to the resistance phenomenon.

Further elaboration on Morrissey's chapter on theory seems warranted. His development of theoretical concepts on the causative elements of schizophrenia are stimulating, especially as it is generally conceded that the majority of the population in adult foster homes have this diagnosis. That schizophrenic people may have difficulty assimilating precepts is postulated. As a consequence, they may adopt bizarre defense mechanisms in efforts to ward off deluges of intolerable thoughts. Thus, with unorthodox methods of coping with reality, the schizophrenic person may become frustrated and his/her family may become likewise because of communication and other problems. As a consequence, they may develop an "emotional allergy" to each other (p. 42). In such situations, the movement of the patient away from the family may be one of the few remaining avenues of ameliorating the strain between the patient and family, save continued hospitalization. Also, the author indicates that psychotic persons frequently have "rebirth" fantasies and that placing them with surrogate families might fit positively into these fantasies (p. 43). The statement the author makes, about which I have the greatest reservations is his belief that, properly placed, 80% of the adult foster home patients should be able to graduate to independent living within 2 years. Finally, Morrissey (1967) postulates the following theoretical assumptions:

> The patient relives some meaningful experiences assumed to be related to his illness; that is, he undergoes a partial peripheral rebirth. He learns to respect other individuals and himself, to trust and relate to people, with discretion. His perceptual field is rehoned; enlarged if it is constricted, sharpened if it is muddled. A major goal is to help the patient focus on the process of assessing reality . . . viewing the world and people as largely gray rather than black or white. Also efforts are geared to helping a patient effect a present-future orientation rather than a past-present one. (p. 50).

Presented next is the doctoral dissertation of Smitson (1967) because, like Morrissey, he presents some theoretical formulations on the causes of schizophrenia, although in a psychoanalytic context. However, Smitson admits there are no well-developed theoretical formulations on adult foster care. Regarding schizophrenia the author notes:

> As clinicians know, many adults fail to progress along the developmental course . . . [of life]. Limitations in object relationship functioning almost invariably accompany intrapsychic disorder. The conventional location of pathology as expressing points of fixation or regression also serve to describe relationship functioning. It is no accident that Freud initially described psychoses as a narcissistic illness. (p. 21)

Following the psychoanalytic line of reasoning postulated by Smitson, one is led to believe that schizophrenia is a narcissistic illness whereby the patient's personality is functioning inadequately through either fixation at an early developmental level or, of once having attained a mature level of development, the person's personality regresses to an early narcissistic level.

Continuing to follow the psychoanalytic line of reasoning, Smitson tested foster home managers from the Bedford, Massachusetts Veterans Administration Hospital by the use of the Custodial-Humanistic Ideology Schedule and an interview schedule. He categorized their personality types as "pre-oedipal, Oedipal," and "post-oedipal" (p. 62). Moreover, he classified 63% as preoedipal; 23% as Oedipal, and 15% as postoedipal, indicating that he considered the majority of them emotionally immature. Furthermore, he thought the preoedipal group became managers more out of needs to replace dependent children than for altruistic or financial reasons. Also he suggests complementary roles between the immature preoedipal managers and the narcissistic residents. Finally, he admits that little is known about the role of foster parenting but proffers the assumption that a good prognostic indicator for effective foster parenting would be to locate managers who had provided good role models for their own children.

In a comprehensive review of the literature on foster parenting for children, Taylor and Starr (1967), who were social workers by credentials, delineated some observations which are reminiscent of many shortcomings already alluded to earlier in this chapter when referring to adult foster homes. For example, in foster parenting for children there has been little systematic study of the roles of foster parents, little effort to build a knowledge base from published studies, and wide differences of opinion exist among clinicians and researchers and certainly differences exist between administrators, researchers, and clinicians. Some researchers think that foster parents for children are chiefly motivated out of needs to solve their own problems; others believe they are seeking "secondary psychological gains" (p. 373). Also there are differences of opinion on the importance of matching the child and foster parent. One study showed that foster parents whose motivation was primarily altruistic did better with high-risk children, while all foster parents did well with low-risk children.

Taylor and Starr cited studies which indicate many foster parents for children came from a segment of the population having minimal education and income levels. Moreover, many were in the 70–89 IQ range on verbal skills, and reading levels were often below the ninth grade level. Moreover, other studies showed that many of them were more family-church focused as opposed to being community focused.

This could present communication problems with middle-class, community-focused social workers. Furthermore, Taylor and Starr think it is unrealistic to expect foster parents to function as semiprofessionals, given their generally low educational levels of attainment. A study is cited wherein a 2-year certificate was offered by the University of Pittsburgh for child care workers. The authors conclude their report by the statement:

> Perhaps foster care is an outmoded social response to situations that have more adequate alternatives; in many ways our field is a captive of structures and systems that were designed for other purposes and in other times. Perhaps foster care is an appropriate social response to many current situations. (p. 383)

Titmuss (1968a) criticizes the haphazard development of social and medical policy in England and elsewhere in the 1960s. He questions the trend toward community-based facilities for the mentally ill and asks the question:

> Have we, in fact, produced a new instrument of community care policy or are we in the process of developing inadvertently, new 'chronic wards' in the community because of the rejection of this 'chronic role' by mental hospitals conscious of the need for a productivity rapid turnover? (p. 4)

Elsewhere Titmuss (1968b) conceded that transforming mental hospitals into truly therapeutic institutions would be a monumental task. However, he continued to be extremely skeptical about community-based care because he viewed this as a step backward since it was transferring the care from trained staff to untrained personnel, who also are ill equipped in terms of physical facilities, to carry out the great task of community care for the mentally ill.

Now we shift our focus to what appears to be a new development in adult foster care, i.e., where the supporting agency is a welfare department (Wohlford, 1968). This project was begun in 1967, sponsored by a 3-year federal grant. Essentially the purpose of the project was to extend the existing foster home program for children in Winnebago County, Wisconsin, to include foster care for the aged. The residents, who came from the county hospital, nursing homes, and independent living arrangements, were officially called "guests" (p. 225). The attitude of the managers was the most important variable, i.e., they must show motivation to help others feel more worthwhile. Most of the residents preferred homes where there were no children.

Reporting in 1969 (Michaux, Katz, Kurland, & Gansereit) conducted an extensive study in which discharged psychiatric patients were assessed for their first year out of the hospital. Though the study did not focus exclusively on adult foster care, a scale was developed which would seem to have some practical utility for selecting and monitoring residents, i.e., the Katz Community Adjustment Scale. At least one subsequent publication reveals this scale has some practical utility in adult foster home programs. Now, let us turn our attention to the next decade.

1970 DECADE

Since so much material was published in the 1970s, this decade will be divided into three sections. In the 1970s a plethora of journals on social work specialties came into being. Some of these were clinical practice, administration, research, health, and the aged. Also, there were more doctoral dissertations by social workers than before, including more on adult foster home programs. Published were several books on community-based shelter care, in which adult foster homes are included, often under different names such as boarding homes, board and care homes, family care homes, group homes, personal care homes, and community care homes. Such a proliferation of terms, in my opinion, beclouds the issue, making it more difficult for all concerned to conceptualize what really is an adult foster home. As a general rule, the journals seem to have accepted the concept of adult foster homes, while books tend to ascribe other terms, as described previously. Worthy of note is that the 1971 and 1977 issues of the *Encyclopedia of Social Work* did not contain a section on adult foster care. Could this oversight be symptomatic of social work's ambivalence towards its "bastard child"?

1970–1973

The results of a study, in which 463 aged, mentally retarded patients were evaluated for community placement, were reported

(O'Connor, Justice, & Warren, 1970). Of the total number considered, 74% were considered eligible for placement in adult foster homes or nursing homes. The authors thought that self-exposure and passivity could preferably be better tolerated in foster homes than in hospitals or nursing homes, and they thought passivity would be an asset for foster home placement. A case example was given of a 69-year-old woman with an IQ of 30 who had been hospitalized for 46 years and who was successfully placed in an adult foster home as an "unpaid family worker" (p. 359).

Getting back now to adult foster homes for the mentally ill, two social workers described how a large adult foster home program functioned with part-time social workers who lived in the communities in which the homes were located (Richter & Ostlund, 1970). The setting was the F.D.R. Veterans Administration Hospital, Montrose, New York. The part-timers held other full-time jobs and working with the veterans was, therefore, only a secondary position. Some of the rationale for this practice was that the managers and residents had easier access to the workers, which presumably enhanced communication.

Noteworthy is the fact that the *Encyclopedia of Human Behavior* (Goldenson 1970) had a brief section on adult foster homes.

Writing on therapeutic housing, Richmond (1971) presented a confusing array of terms. However, he admits this and indicates that many of these terms are used interchangeably. Moreover, he indicates:

> The term used to describe a particular type of residence, whether it be foster home, boarding home, or family care home, depends either on the definition of the state or local licensing authority, if there is one, or if the home is not licensed, on the whim of the caretaker-owner. (p. 123)

Were there a centralized national policy or a title for adult foster care, or even given that there is not, it seems conceivable to me that all of the terms used above by Richmond could be subsumed under the term adult foster homes. Excluded, of course, would be halfway houses, because they are under the direct control of the sponsoring facility, including their staff. However, in adult foster homes the facility staff provides only consultation and some supervision for managers, who actually operate and usually own the private homes in which they keep residents.

Lamb and Goertzel (1971) produced one of the most ex-
perimentally focused articles extant in the literature in the area of
community-based shelter care for the mentally ill. For the experiment,
they randomly assigned patients being discharged from state hospitals,
who for various reasons could not return to their own homes, to
experimental and control groups. In effect, the experimental group
was the high-expectancy group and the control group was the low-
expectancy group. The high-expectancy group was assigned to high-
prestige halfway houses, which are usually rehabilitation oriented and
the control group was assigned to low-prestige boarding homes or
foster homes, which are usually custodially oriented. As is the typical
modus operandi for halfway houses, the high-expectancy group was
subjected to an intensive rehabilitation regimen, while the low-
expectancy group was permitted to live in the manner often typical of
custodial facilities, i.e., to remain rather passive, having few structured
activities. The high-expectancy group exhibited more erratic adjustment patterns, e.g., required more frequent hospitalizations than the
low-expectancy group. Yet, the high-expectancy group members were
hospitalized for briefer periods than the low-expectancy group members requiring rehospitalizations. The authors, moreover, contended
that: "The level of functioning and integration in the community is
higher after both six and eighteen months (for the high expectancy
group) than it is for the low expectation environment" (p. 31). Furthermore, the authors contended essentially that the low-expectation
group's being in the community was only illusionary because these
residents were living in environments which were similar to mini-
psychiatric wards which had simply been moved into the community.
By inference, these observations could be interpreted as a slight on the
foster home program. For example, who can say that if the low-
expectation group had been subjected to the same intense rehabilitation efforts as the high-expectation group, that its members too would
not have shown equally high levels of community integration?

Reporting on how another demonstration project functioned
under the auspices of a welfare department, Fenske and Roecker
(1971) indicated the project was authorized by Section 1115, Title XI,
of the Social Security Act but was sponsored by the Washington State
Division of Public Assistance. Like the project referred to earlier in
Winnebago County, Wisconsin (see 1968 section, this chapter), the
staff used inactive children's homes in Seattle for the project. Although

they admitted there is considerable correspondence between foster homes for children and adults, they cautioned of some differences. Generally, adults do not like to be treated as children, and managers of adult foster homes do not need to be as physically agile.

Murphy, Pennee, and Luchins (1972) conducted qualitative studies of 50 adult foster homes in Canada. As in the United States, they are called a variety of names there, e.g., "foster homes, approved boarding homes," and "family care units" (p. 1). One of their guiding assumptions was that "normal" family settings should counteract the "sick role" the residents learned in hospitals (p. 4). However, their findings indicated that generally the residents were not accepted into the usual household routines or community affairs. There was a noticeable lack of interaction between residents and managers and between residents. Moreover, the managers often had double standards for themselves and residents, i.e., the managers eating alone and the residents eating by themselves. The researchers noted that residents' inappropriate behavior was usually not handled directly but was usually handled by environmental manipulation instead. Moreover, some managers seemed to have authoritarian personalities. Though many professionals believe that smaller homes are more therapeutic, the researchers found that there was more rivalry and generalized hostility in smaller homes. In larger homes, i.e., those with over six residents, more interaction was found between managers and residents. In referring to the residents and the managers' handling of them the authors indicate:

> ... if one thinks of them [residents] as requiring resocialization in the way that a child requires socialization, they were not being given the encouragement and punishment, the opportunity to make mistakes and to try again, that constitute the normal socialization process. (p. 13)

Some recommendations from the study were more formal training for the managers and deference for more "unconventional" managers in rural settings (p. 17). The authors concluded that expecting residents to be treated as family members and to become integrated into the communities was unrealistic without more staff input.

A pragmatic how-to-do book by a physician-nurse team (Schrader & Elms, 1972) contains some realistic suggestions on management of adult foster homes. The authors were generally complimentary of the program, indicating: "This type of care might well be called the 'Cinderella' of the mental health field, for it has been so sadly neglected as a resource and its potential has never been fully developed" (p. 9). Moreover, the authors present a strong argument for the implementation of uniform licensing procedures for adult foster homes. Parenthetically, progress has been made in this area and will be alluded to briefly later in this chapter and in more depth in another section of this book. Moreover, it seems worthy to note that even with its large adult foster home program, the Veterans Administration has no uniform licensing procedure. While the central authority of the Veterans Administration is in Washington, D.C., the central office delegates authority and responsibility to local hospitals for implementaton of the various programs (U.S. Veterans Administration, 1971).

Buxbaum (1973), a social worker, questioned whether or not a dangerous precedent is not being established by placing so many patients in the community because of a dearth of technological expertise in the field of mental illness/health.

1974–1977

Supported by a grant from the National Institute of Mental Health and after careful planning, in 1968 the Missouri Institute of Psychiatry and St. Louis State Hospital implemented an innovative project in foster community living for psychiatric patients (Keskiner & Zalcman, 1974). The most innovative feature of the project was the direct and continued involvement of community members in the planning and supervision of the project.

Two small towns within an hour's drive from St. Louis were selected, this idea having come from the ancient Colony Gheel concept in Belgium (Gheel is about an hour's drive from Antwerp). After much planning and organizing by staff and indigenous community members, legally sanctioned corporations were formed in both communities. The corporations set quotas that mental patients coming into the communities would not exceed 1% of the population. Indigenous community members were employed as staff members, replacing social workers in many functions. After careful screening and resocialization efforts by the hospital, referred patients were screened by the corporations and, if approved, were accepted into the communities.

The patients were given a choice of living in apartment complexes or foster homes. The authors noted that women were somewhat more acceptable by the communities, possibly because the rural communities could more easily tolerate women being unemployed than they could men.

Arnhoff (1975), a psychology professor, cautions that the shifting emphasis from mental illness to mental health and the concomitant shift from hospitalization to community placement for many psychiatric patients may produce more psychological and social disturbances than it ameliorates. Furthermore, Arnhoff criticizes the quantification of mental health to include all behavior ranging from the commonplace to the extremely disturbed. The author thinks that chronic, psychotic persons' functioning should be qualitatively differentiated from other forms of psychological functioning. Moreover, the author explains how opinions change over time about mental illness and its treatment. Finally, he chastises the medical profession for being too much influenced by "social philosophy, moral suasion, and belief under the guise of medicine" (p. 1278) and having not been adequately influenced by scientific contributions.

A business administration professor posits some challenging questions and presents some suggested answers about the levels of payments and how they influence the law of supply and demand on the availability of foster homes for children (Simon, 1975). As an example, he indicated that doubling the amount of payment to managers would increase the availability of homes from 50–100%. Perhaps this line of reasoning could be transferred to recruiting adult foster home managers.

Cautley and Aldridge (1975), a social work professor and college lecturer, helped select and did follow-up studies on 145 managers of children's foster homes. An attempt was made to discern variables which might predict successful placements for school-age children. Among their findings was that social workers should spend considerable time preparing children for placement and that more experienced workers were more successful than inexperienced ones. Furthermore, they thought that the foster mothers should be among the oldest in their sibships, because there was a positive association between this variable and being a successful foster mother. High religiousness in foster parents was correlated negatively with success. Also, more democratically functioning parents were found to be more successful, as was also a positive attitude from the foster parents toward social work supervision.

That the Community Mental Health Centers Act of 1963 was not structured to meet the clinical needs of long-term mental patients is reported by Shadoan (1976). However, he indicates that Congress attempted to remedy that problem by passing the Community Health Centers Amendments of 1975 (P.L. 94-63). Among the seven new services of the amendments was one to strengthen community living programs as alternatives to continued hospitalization. Moreover, the author mentions that the hard-won legal fights on the "right to treatment" may also help the long-term psychiatric patient survive in the community (pp. 56–57).

Edelson (1976) discusses alternative living arrangements for long-term mental patients, conceptualizing them on a continuum from "high envelopment" to "low envelopment." Examples of high-envelopment facilities would be hospitals or "therapeutic residential centers," which are essentially closed facilities and are intensely supervised on a 24-hour basis. Moreover, the author categorizes "mid range envelopment" homes as "board and care" homes (apparently analogous to adult foster homes). These midrange envelopment facilities are intended to be custodial homes in the low-expectation philosophy (pp. 36–37). At the other end of the continuum the author places "low envelopment" facilities which include a variety of transititional facilities, e.g., "satellite housing" (pp. 39–41), residential hotels, and so forth. Satellite housing may involve group living in an apartment complex or single family dwellings, leased by the residents, agency, or both. Many graduates of other programs, such as halfway houses, are referred to satellite housing, which is considered the therapeutic housing that comes closest to normal community living. Thus, satellite housing is considered to meet the high-expectation philosophy. To mitigate against low morale for managers in community-based shelter care, the author recommends following the precedent set in some children's foster home programs, i.e., pay managers for nonfilled beds in order to ensure needed vacancies. Finally, Edelson comments on the "mental health ghetto" phenomenon (p. 50) in which large numbers of patients (sometimes up to 500) are placed in communities in old residential hotels.

Switching now from the mentally ill to the mentally retarded,

Butterfield (1976) indicates that mentally retarded residents in public facilities peaked in 1967. Since 1969 the number of mentally retarded residents placed in residential community facilities has increased. Butterfield, moreover, indicates that this trend toward removing the retarded from institutions is a national trend, save for New Jersey and 10 Southern states. However, he predicts that they too will latch onto the trend. By 1971 the number of retarded residents in public institutions was down by one-third from 1950.

Using sophisticated statistical procedures, Kaufman (1976) conducted a quantitative-descriptive study of adult foster homes and halfway houses from the Brockton, Massachusetts Veterans Administration Hospital. Utilizing a socioecological frame of reference, the researcher examined certain intrapersonal and situational factors. The factors evaluated were the organizational climate and structure of the settings, personal characteristics of managers and residents, managers' attitudes about mental illness, manager and residents' perceptions of the settings' psychosocial environment, and the residents' attitudes toward themselves and the settings. Findings suggested that situational factors in the settings may account for much of the success or failure of residents in becoming rehabilitated. Nearly one-third of the settings were categorized as being rehabilitation oriented. In these settings the managers treated residents more like adults. In the middle-range category residents were treated more like siblings and in the low-range category managers treated residents more like children. Kaufman recommended urban settings, as opposed to rural settings, a couple of reasons being the opportunity for more professional supervision and closer proximity to work opportunities. Also, he recommended younger managers over older ones, more training and education for managers, regular discussion group meetings between residents and managers, the elimination of negative incentives for managers (e.g., keeping a full house), and the rewarding of managers for the successful rehabilitation of residents. Also, he recommended that residents' funds be more equally distributed.

Commenting on the often contradictory and confusing results of extant publications on adult foster care, Evans (1976) completed an interesting study on the programs at Bedford and Brockton, Massachusetts VA Hospitals. Her concern for the adult foster home movement in general is expressed thus:

> It would appear that, in spite of ninety years of experience with community family care in this country (not to mention centuries of European experience . . .), we are still floundering in the very initial exploratory stages of systematizing our knowledge. (p. 32)

Evans' theoretical considerations, about what types of people are likely to make the most effective managers, are thought provoking; for example, that typical managers come from rural backgrounds, which is thought to produce people with attitudes oriented toward more open types of family systems. By way of contrast, urban environments are thought to produce people with more closed types of family orientations. However, data analysis on the results of the study in this area were inconclusive. Though numerous references can be gleaned from the literature on the importance of the managers' personalities, little actual empirical work has been done in this area. Evans tackled this thorny problem. Using interaction theory, she attempted to show how the residents and managers influence each other personality-wise. She recommended recruiting managers who are "submissive and affectionate," adding that:

> Such sponsors would not fully complement the patient role; rather they would reinforce socially acceptable corresponding affectionate behavior while forcing patients to assume more dominant, responsible, independent roles in order to reciprocate sponsors' submissiveness. (p. 235)

Finally, Evans could find no significant differences in resident adjustment patterns depending upon whether or not there was a female manager only or both male and female managers in the homes.

A quantitative study of adult foster homes in three providences in Canada (Murphy, Engelsman, & Tcheng-Laroche, 1976) revealed a substantial decrease in symptoms but improvement in social functioning was virtually nil after 18 months in the homes. The researchers used some sophisticated instruments (referred to earlier in this chapter), i.e., the Brief Psychiatric Rating Scale and the Katz Community Adjustment Scale. The authors concluded that an active therapeutic regimen, such as that utilized in many psychiatric hospitals may be more "symptom-provoking" than "symptom-reducing," at least in the short run (p. 183). Moreover, the authors indicated that an undemanding setting such as an adult foster home appears to be conducive to symptom-reduction in the short run. In essence, the authors recommended more professionally directed centers for semichronic patients. An example of this might be a high expectation environment such as a halfway house. Then, if they cannot tolerate such a setting, they should be transferred to settings such as adult foster homes.

Brook, Cortes, March, and Sundberg-Stirling (1976) report on a study of an alternate system to intensive psychiatric hospitalization in Denver. Briefly, in lieu of hospitalization, acutely disturbed psychiatric patients are placed in adult foster homes. The managers are required to have accepting attitudes toward mental illness. Some supports suggested for managers are evening meetings, staff meetings held monthly in a different home, a salary was guaranteed for 24-hour availability of beds, regardless of whether or not they are used, and managers are urged to take 30 days paid vacation annually. Residents averaged 10 days stay in the homes, usually followed by a stay of up to 3 months in a supervised apartment setting. The authors thought that 10 beds in the community was adequate for the southwest Denver population.

Reporting on a study conducted at Veterans Administration Hospital, Northport, New York, Zweben (1977) attempted to ascertain whether the social environment in the adult foster home provided a viable alternative to continued hospitalization. Evaluating the level of manager-restrictiveness, including areas in which residents were excluded from normative living activities in the homes, Zweben classified only 15% of them as restrictive. These homes could be categorized as custodial. Managers who had previously been employed in custodial settings, e.g., back wards of state hospitals, scored significantly lower on levels of excluding residents from the normative living patterns in the homes than managers from other work experiences, thus indicating that the former group may be more rehabilitation oriented. Also, he found that younger managers were more restrictive than older managers, indicating that perhaps older managers may be in the business more out of a desire for companionship than anything else. Furthermore, the author indicated that the Veterans Administration had 10,243 residents in adult foster homes in 1974, while New York State had 6,987 so placed in 1973.

Finally, Zweben colorfully describes adult foster care by the following paragraph:

> In short, family care homes might be described as a "mongrel" having features of opposing types of settings, namely, a human relations or familial type of arrangement as well as an authoritarian type of dwelling. Such a situation is not usually observed in other settings dealing with the mentally ill where there seems to be a more uniform approach to patient care. (p. 148)

Attempting to show an association between high manager authoritarianism and high resident alientation, McCoin (1977) was unable to demonstrate this in a quasiexperimental study. This study was grounded in Sullivan interpersonal theory, a precursor of interaction theory used by Evans (referred to earlier under 1976), and was conducted at the F.D.R. Veterans Administration Hospital, Montrose, New York, where the researcher also worked several years as a social worker with the adult foster home program there. Reported from data analysis was a statistically significant association between high manager authoritarianism and religiosity. Also associated with high manager authoritarianism was certain ethnic groups, e.g., Italians, many of whom were from the "old country." A negative association was found between high levels of manager education and authoritarianism. Residents who had been in the foster home program for long periods (up to 15 years) scored significantly lower on alienation and social isolation than residents who were being prepared to be placed in homes from the hospital.

Reporting on the results of a study conducted at the Danville, Illinois, Veterans Administration Hospital, Miller (1977) indicated the modal age group for managers was 61–65. He indicated the majority of the managers were easy-going, religious, and most were high school graduates. Recruitment was mostly by word-of-mouth, and he indicated that no reliable ways have been devised for selecting managers, save for the intuitive efforts of staff. One criticism he proffers is that the diets are overly laden with carbohydrates.

Segal, Baumohl, and Johnson (1977) define the concept of "social margin" and explain its interrelationship with mental disorder.

> Social margin refers to the set of resources and relationships an individual can draw on either to advance or survive in society. It consists of relations, friendships, possessions, skills and personal attributes that can be mortgaged, used, sold, or bartered in return

for necessary assistance. Social margin aids advancement and pro-
tects, or softens the fall of the downwardly mobile. (pp. 388–389)

The authors give a person's reputation as an example of whether
or not a person has social margin in the area of personal attributes.
That social margin and mental illness are often associated can be found
in the poor person who has a tarnished reputation and low financial
resources plus mental illness. These factors are likely to decrease their
level of social margin because potential benefactors are less likely to
invest time, energy, and financial resources in them. Thus, often the
mentally ills' level of social margin is low or relatively nonexistent.
Moreover, the authors give examples of emotionally disturbed young
street people who are low on social margin, even in the street culture.
The authors predict that this group will ultimately become candidates
for sheltered living environments, e.g., adult foster homes. The social
margin concept sounds logical and offers guidance for future research
on mental illness.

Evaluating 572 male patients who were referred for adult foster
care by five Veterans Administration hospitals, Linn and Caffey (1977)
observed that 14% were aged 60 or over and were most likely to have
chronic brain syndrome diagnoses, while the younger veterans were
more likely to have schizophrenic diagnoses. The 572 patients were
dichotomized into an experimental and control group by random
assignment. The experimental group was prepared for foster home
placement and the control group received continued hospitalization.
Seventy percent of the experimental group was placed in foster homes.
Compared to the control group, those from the experimental group in
foster homes exhibited less social dysfunction and better overall adjustments, with there being no difference between the older and younger
experimentals' adjustments in the homes. The authors concluded that
foster home placements for older psychiatric patients are underutilized and are a viable alternative to continued hospitalization.

Commenting on the dearth of published reports on the aged in
foster care, Newman and Sherman (1977) surveyed 100 managers of
adult foster homes in New York. That state sponsors two programs for
adult foster care. One comes under the Department of Mental
Hygiene, which usually accepts responsibility for mental patients from
the state hospitals. The other state-sponsored program is under the
control of the State Board of Social Welfare/Department of Social

Services. Forty percent of these residents were likely to have come from their own homes to the foster homes and a high percentage of them were elderly. The researchers studied the managers of 50 homes from each of the two programs. They found that 58% of the managers were married and that 29% of them afforded residents an opportunity to become socially involved with the family, but much of this "familism" appeared to be maternalistic, or similar to foster parenting for children (p. 439). Seventy-five percent of the residents were female. The authors think foster parenting for those 50 and over can provide a meaningful role for the managers' later lives.

Sherman and Newman (1977) allude to the paucity of published reports on foster home care for the elderly as a viable alternative to continued hospitalization. Furthermore, they think that foster home placement can prevent or delay nursing home placement. The authors also express concern over the problem of properly classifying health and residential care facilities because they have evolved in such an illogical manner as to defy rational analysis. Moreover, the authors state that adult foster homes are so ill-defined and state regulations are so fragmented that a uniform evaluation of adult foster care is impossible. The Department of Mental Hygiene limits new homes to 6 residents but some older homes have 7–10. And about one-fourth of residents are elderly. The State Board of Welfare/Department of Social Services share responsibility with local social service districts, usually for homes for two to four residents. These homes are certified. Local social service departments supervise homes with only one resident but these homes are not certified. A third major program in New York, though not under state jurisdiction, are those homes under the supervision of VA hospitals. In 1974 nationwide figures indicated that one-fourth of all VA psychiatric patients in its foster home program were over age 60 and 70% of the VA's medical-surgical patients in foster care were over 60. Parenthetically, the VA officially began placing mental patients in foster care in 1951 and medical-surgical patients in 1962. Managers from all three systems in New York expressed a desire for more training workshops and more provisions for respites from their demanding jobs.

In a critique of the preceding Sherman and Newman article, Brody (1977) questions whether keeping 10–15 residents, e.g., if VA-approved foster homes are really family-focused homes. (I have known a few such homes which kept 20 residents in New York state.) Brody thinks these homes may be more analogous to "mom and pop" board-ing homes, mostly without the "pop," or unlicensed nursing homes.

1978–1979

We now move into the final phase of the chapter on history of the adult foster home movement. Numerous authors who were active during the preceding period continued to publish in 1978–1979, with Segal, Sherman, and Newman being the most notable.

California has required licensure for shelter care facilities, includ-ing adult foster homes since 1971 (Segal & Aviram, 1978). Also licensed in California are board and care homes and halfway houses. (California's categorization of *family care homes* is apparently analogous to what I am categorizing as adult foster homes.) Part of the statistics from Segal and Aviram are:

> Family care homes account for 26% of the facilities in California and serve 14% of the population in shelter care. Halfway houses, which have by far received the greatest attention from mental health professionals, constitute only 2% of facilities and serve only 3% of the population in sheltered care. Board and Care homes, which have developed in an unplanned ad hoc manner, service 82% of the California sheltered care population and comprise 72% of the state's facilities. The extent of services now provided by board and care facilities leaves little doubt that an entirely new residential-care system for the mentally ill is emerging. The more familiar and well-defined facilities—halfway houses and family care homes—have only a minor role in the new system. (p. 106)

Albright (1978) reports that Wisconsin has required licensure of community-based residential facilities, including adult foster homes, since July 1, 1978. A follow-up on the pilot foster home program in Winnebago County, Wisconsin (reported earlier under 1968 section, this chapter) indicates that the program is now part of the regular departmental structure of the county department of social services (Adult Foster Care Handbook, n.d.).

It would appear that recent federal policy may be an impetus to a proliferation of licensing adult foster homes in most states. This policy states in part:

Effective October 1, 1977 . . . state or local authorities [will] establish, maintain, and insure the enforcement of standards for . . .
foster homes . . . in which . . . a significant number of recipients of
Supplemental Security Income . . . benefits residents are likely to
reside. (*Federal Register,* January 31, 1978, p. 4020)

This policy presents an interesting question about whether VA
hospitals will be required to undergo licensure in order to comply with
the policy, especially when considering the fact that a sizable proportion of veterans residing in foster homes are recipients of Supplemental Security Income.

The syndicated columnist, Jack Anderson (1978), reported that
psychiatric ghettos were being created in Chicago as a consequence
of the "purge" of mental hospitals in the area. Anderson indicated
the patients are being placed in boarding homes with minimal supervision.

McCrary and Keiden (1978), reporting on a nationally televised
program, blamed the dumping of large numbers of psychiatric patients into communities on a recent U.S. Supreme Court decision
making it unlawful to keep patients hospitalized if they can be maintained in the community. McCrary and Keiden, furthermore, indicated that there is no uniform policy on shelter care; actually they
indicated federal policy in this area is shared by 11 federal agencies.
Moreover, they referred to these patients as the "ideal victims" because
they have little preparation for leaving the institutions and few follow-
up services.

Switching now to 1979, we discuss the topic of the resettlement of
mentally retarded adults into the community (Birenbaum & Re, 1979).
The authors did a longitudinal study for nearly 4 years of 63 mentally
retarded adults from three state schools who were placed in a managed
community residence (apparently similar to a halfway house). At the
end of the study 42 of the original 63 were still in the residence. They
were found to have maintained steady involvement in sheltered workshops and to have maintained some relations with peers. However,
they participated less in community leisure time activities and were
more constricted in the decision-making process of the residence than
when first placed.

Segal (1979) indicated that between 1964–1973 the percentage of
people over 50 residing in community-based facilities in California was

46%. The author differentiates between being "psychologically disturbed" and "psychologically distressed" (p. 49). In describing the
distressed he seems to be describing those with more acute psychological problems, while by disturbed he seems to mean those with more
chronic psychological problems. Recommended for the distressed
were halfway houses; for the disturbed the equivalent of adult foster
homes were suggested. The author contends that the latter group
accepts a position of powerlessness in exchange for a protective environment because the reestablishment of normal social roles is too
threatening for them.

Examining the interaction between social workers, managers, and
residents in a foster home program for the elderly, Sherman and
Newman (1979) describe two major types of adult foster homes in New
York. One type is the "family type" home for the dependent and infirm
who require personalized services in addition to lodging and board.
These are under the jurisdication of the State Board of Social Welfare/
Department of Social Services and supervised by the Division of Adult
Residential Care of the State Department of Social Services. The other
major program provides services under the auspices of the State Department of Mental Hygiene. The latter category of homes were visited
weekly to monthly by a staff member 80% of the time, while for the
other category this was only 28%. An average of two-thirds of the
managers from both groups requested more direction from the supervision organizations, indicating they did not even receive printed materials.

Zeil (1979) reported that Michigan has licensure for the aged
under the State Department of Public Health. For the nonaged disabled, licensure emanates from the State Department of Social Services.

Bernstein (1979) reports that the Texas Department of Health
presently "certifies" some types of residential community facilities for
the mentally retarded and is currently implementing licensure for
"personal care homes," which provide shelter, food, and some assistance with problems in daily living. Moreover, he indicates that the State
Department of Human Resources licenses what he categorizes as
"adult foster care homes" for up to three residents.

So it now seems obvious that licensure for adult foster homes, in
these few states sampled, is a complex matter, often involving more
than one major state agency. At this point my guess is that most states

do not yet have licensure. Further elaboration on this dilemma will follow in a subsequent chapter.

Summary

Though adult foster care dates to 600–700 A.D., it has been slow in developing. The literature in the field, while proliferous, is often repetitious, contradictory, not solidly grounded on human behavior and social science theories, and the research methodology employed often makes replications of studies difficult. The proliferous representation of many professional disciplines in the literature is encouraging. The slow beginning of social work in this area poses interesting introspective questions for the profession. It seems unrealistic to expect managers to provide a high-expectancy environment when many professionals have not been very successful at rehabilitating the mentally ill. While frequent references are extant in the literature to such terms as *boarding homes, personal care homes,* and *board and care homes,* I have yet to find adequate definitions or explanations of these terms. It could be that the ancient concept of adult foster homes is disliked by idealists who think the term is too infantalizing for adults because of the similarity to the concept and children's foster homes. In my opinion, if this assumption is valid, it is unwarranted and a unifying concept such as *adult foster homes* is sorely needed to help clarify the murky waters of adult foster home care. Finally, since the social work profession inherited primary responsibility for implementation of adult foster home programs, it behooves us as a profession to take a hard look at ourselves. For example, references cited in this chapter sometimes refer to the adult foster home program as "bastard child" or either the "Cinderella" or the "mongrel" of the mental health field. Why do professional authors have to desperately grasp such theoretical concepts in efforts to explain the program or to sell their wares? Perhaps they were becoming desperate because we have not been listening.

Chapter 3

THEORETICAL CONSIDERATIONS

INTRODUCTION

Why study the theoretical aspects of adult foster home care? Some of the more important considerations to this question are that theoretical study facilitates further inquiry and facilitates communication. Moreover, the practical utility of theory was aptly stated by an author whose name alludes me when he stated, "Nothing is so practical as a good theory."

Notwithstanding the practicality of sound theoretical thinking, some human service clinicians and administrators eschew theory as too abstract to be applied to the empirical, or "real" world. Academicians, on the other hand, sometimes accuse practitioners of being so preoccupied with dealing with the real world that they virtually ignore theory. Due to this apparent hiatus between theory and practice, it seems incumbent upon some of us to serve as a linking function between the two groups. Such is the purpose of this chapter.

Assuming that social work, and possibly other human service professionals, are "soft scientists" (as is sometimes claimed in the scientific community), some explanation seems indicated. Wax (1968) notes that social workers are primarily value oriented, while physicians and administrators are inclined to be factually oriented. Researchers would generally be somewhere in between these two extremes since they would be more likely to adhere to a scientific knowledge-building approach to problem solving. Lastrucci (1967) has defined science as " . . . basically an objective, logical, systematic, and verifiable method of analysis" (p. 29). Moreover, Lastrucci indicates that science is a method, not a philosophy. As such, science is not committed to any theory or philosophy but is committed to truth in knowledge building.

The necessity of theory in knowledge building is widely accepted in the scientific community. However, defining theory is difficult. One way to begin is by attempting to define concepts. An unknown author described concepts as "the building blocks of knowledge." A way that I explain concepts is to differentiate between theoretical and empirical concepts. Theoretical concepts can be viewed as abstractions which have been reduced to the lowest possible level of knowledge that can be communicated. Examples of theoretical concepts would be schizophrenia, alienation, personality, and home. In other words, comprehending theoretical concepts requires cognitive effort. However, this definition of theoretical concept would seem to be more in line with Lastrucci's explanation of the term *construct,* which he states " . . . is often employed to refer to abstract or purely synthetic formulations . . ." (p. 77). By way of contrast, empirical concepts are generally conceived as requiring little, if any, cognitive effort to most people to comprehend. Examples of empirical concepts would be house, man, woman, or tree. One accepted method of operationalizing theoretical concepts is to devise scales, or other measuring devices, to empirically validate or refute them. However, this is usually a prolonged, difficult process. Thus, knowledge building in science is a cumulative time-consuming process.

Viewed within the preceding context then, theory is defined simply as " . . . a logical explanation of the interrelationships of a set of facts that have been empirically verified" (Turner, 1974, p. 4). Selltiz, Wrightsman, and Cook (1976) define theory essentially as " . . . a set of concepts plus the interrelationships that are assumed to exist among these concepts" (p. 16). Thus, scientific research can begin by utilizing more or less established theories, or theory can be generated from data analysis of empirical data. The process is considered "grounded theory" (Glaser & Strauss, 1967, pp. 4–6). Another way of theory development is to do so hypothetically, by utilizing abstract referents with few, if any, connections in the empirical world. This chapter attempts to utilize all three methods in theory building.

In the social sciences there is a hierarchy of research designs which depend primarily on the purpose of the research. At the pinnacle of research designs would be the experiment whereby an experimental group is given some "treatment" while the control group is held constant. This type of design is not popular in social work, apparently because it has been so misused on human subjects by some other professional groups. Nevertheless, our hesitancy to employ more sophisticated research designs may be one reason why we are considered soft scientists in the scientific community. Thus, if the experiment could be considered at the pinnacle of research designs, the descriptive design would fall considerably lower in the hierarchy. Evans' (1976) criticism of the lack of scientific rigor in studies on adult foster care notwithstanding, this book could be considered as a descriptive study. Lastrucci (1967) indicates the primary purpose of descriptive studies is: " . . . the accurate and systematic portrayal of what is. Descriptive studies try to answer the question of who, what, where, when, how much and the essential function is largely reportorial." (p. 107).

Viewed within this context, therefore, it is hoped that this chapter will generate further scientific inquiry, including the formulation and testing of hypotheses about the predictability of the theories and concepts delineated in this chapter.

THEORIES

While there is disagreement in the social sciences about what constitutes social theory, many theorists contend that numerous social theories do qualify as low- to middle-range theories. In the hierarchy of theory development, a law would be at the apex. An example from economics would be the law of supply and demand; even then, considerable explanation is necessary due to the complexities of human nature. Most, if not all, of the theories in the social sciences are far less developed than the law of supply and demand. Some humanists argue against the development of high-level theories in the social sciences, claiming that such a practice is too mechanistic and unhuman. The

history of science, however, argues in favor of rigorous theory development. An example of this would be in medicine where little progress
was made in ameliorating the ravages of disease until after the discovery and explication of bacteria theory.

The best known theory discussed in this book is psychoanalytic
theory, used by Smitson (1967) in attempting to describe the etiology of
schizophrenia and in categorizing managers of an adult foster home
program. Smitson contended essentially that schizophrenic people
apparently become fixated or regress to a childlike level of psychosex-
ual functioning, thus making it very difficult for them to relate to
adults on a peer level. Moreover, Smitson operationalized the above
theoretical framework by categorizing the adult foster home managers
in his study as "pre-oedipal, Oedipal," and "post-oedipal" (p. 77). Of
his sample of 40 managers, Smitson classified 25 as preoedipal, 9 as
Oedipal, and 6 as postoedipal. In psychoanalytic parlance, preoedipal
would indicate a level of psychosocial functioning not unlike that of a
child. The Oedipal group would be considered neurotic and the post-
oedipal group would be considered essentially normal. Parenthetically,
it should be noted that psychoanalytic theory has fallen into disrepute
by many social scientists, essentially because it is claimed that the theory
is so abstract that it does not lend itself to being adapted to empirical
testing. McCoin (1977, 1979) utilized interpersonal theory in an effort
to explain what happens in the evolution and continuation of the
schizophrenic process. Furthermore, McCoin attempted to operationalize interpersonal theory by assessing alienation patterns of men
with schizophrenic diagnoses in a large adult foster home program.
Essentially, interpersonal theorists indicate that the schizophrenic person has suffered a breakdown in the ability to communicate effectively
with others on an interpersonal level. Harry Stack Sullivan, the de-
veloper of interpersonal theory, is also considered one of the founders
of interaction theory, used by Evans (1976) in her study of two adult
foster home programs. Essentially, Evans used interaction theory to
help explain interaction patterns between the managers and residents.
Evans, furthermore, thought that humans tend to organize their interaction patterns into a vertical hierarchy whereby some tend to be
dominant and others tend to be submissive. An example of this would
be in adult foster homes where the dominant manager dominates the
passive, submissive residents.

Utilizing some more contemporary theoretical thinking, Kaufman
(1976) employed a "social ecological" frame of reference to help ex-

plain the interaction of the social and physical environments in two adult foster home programs. Both Kaufman and Zweben (1977) seem to believe that human behavior cannot be studied apart from its environmental context. Social systems theory would, no doubt, substantiate this claim. Parenthetically, social systems theory is becoming increasingly more widely used in social work in lieu of the once popular psychoanalytic theory of Freud. Some of the findings of Murphy, Pennee, and Luchins (1972) and Murphy, Engelsmann, and Tcheng-Laroche (1976) would also support the claim of the importance of the physical environment in adult foster care.

Cupaiuolo (1979) implicitly used conflict theory as a framework to assess community interaction with managers of adult foster homes throughout the VA system. He found that communities of moderate density were more likely to be resistive than rural or urban communities. Resistance was more intense in communities categorized as in the high socioeconomic bracket. Generally, resistant community members tended to eschew open conflict with managers. Instead, they tended to use a form of institutionalized conflict by charging alledged zoning violations.

Utilizing social exchange theory, Whorley (1978) found that intimate behavior between managers and residents in a VA adult foster home program may be therapeutic for residents, provided that high manager-resident interdependency is present. Moreover, he found that intimate social exchange patterns between residents was likely to mitigate against resident distress. Whorley, moreover, indicated that there is " . . . theoretical convergence between symbolic (interaction theory) and (social) exchange theory" (p. 131). Furthermore, he advocates more synthesis between the behavioral and symbolic interaction models, i.e., the development of a "synergetic (behavioral-interactionist) model" (p. 164). Whorley denotes that interactionists stress cognitive learning through "role-taking," while behaviorists concentrate on overt behavior; within the framework of socialization theory, these viewpoints are considered as complementary. Moreover, Whorley indicates that both managers and residents are marginal groups who may be forming a symbiotic relationship which helps maintain both groups in the community. Whorley, however, thinks that this would apply mostly to elderly managers, i.e., those who may be candidates for institutional or community-based residential placement themselves. Needless to say, Whorley's theoretical thinking bears further inquiry and empirical testing.

Theoretical Concepts: Residents

Schizophrenia

The literature review indicated that the largest single diagnostic category in adult foster homes is schizophrenia. For our purposes, schizophrenia is a theoretical concept which has been widely studied but is still little understood except symptomatically. McCoin (1977, 1979) indicates that interpersonal theorists contend essentially that the etiology of schizophrenia begins in infancy, caused essentially by a poor relationship with the mothering person. Interpersonal theorists contend that the preschizophrenic child, having had a poor relationship with the mothering person, may avoid overt schizophrenia if successful in forming an intimate relationship with a same-sex peer in preadolescence. Moreover, interpersonal theorists contend children who are unsuccessful in these endeavors are likely to develop schizophrenia in adolescence or young adulthood. Furthermore, interpersonal theorists denote that schizophrenia is essentially a collapse of the self-system. That is, it is believed that the schizophrenic person's self-concept is so damaged that the person lacks the confidence to effectively assert himself/herself in interpersonal communications. This conceptualization places tremendous responsibilities on helpers who work with schizophrenic people. Generally, it is believed that these helpers should be emotionally mature people who can be flexible in a relationship. Empirical research indicates that a sizable proportion of adult foster home managers may be lacking in this regard, i.e., they may have preoedipal (Smitson) or authoritarian-type personalities (McCoin).

Following an ego psychology theoretical framework, Marcus (1976) thought that schizophrenia is caused by a breakdown in ego boundaries, resulting in the loss of personal identity. Furthermore, Marcus indicated that the end result in schizophrenia is the person's inability to accurately perceive, memorize, synthesize, integrate, comprehend, and to organize his/her thought patterns.

The American Psychiatric Association (APA) (1968) implies that schizophrenia may be caused by a physical condition. Moreover, the APA indicates that schizophrenia is characterized by disturbances in mood, thinking, and behavior. The APA further indicates that alterations in concept formation in schizophrenia may lead to misinterpretations of reality and to delusions and hallucinations. Other symptoms listed by the APA are withdrawn, bizarre behavior, mood changes including inappropriate emotional responses, and "loss of empathy for others" (APA, 1968, p. 33). Finally, the APA lists 11 different categories of schizophrenia, each with somewhat different symptoms.

A currently popular hypothesis on the causality of schizophrenia is that the condition may be caused by biochemical imbalances in the body and that these disturbances may have a genetic base (Lukton, 1976). The leading proponents of this school of thought are Hoffer and Osmond (1966). They also essentially contend that a genetic defect may trigger biochemical imbalances that can produce vitamin deficiencies which can possibly precipitate, or aggravate, the schizophrenia. To counteract the vitamin deficiencies, Hoffer and Osmond recommend large doses of vitamins, known as megavitamin therapy. This school of psychiatry has become known as the orthomolecular school of psychiatry. In some places orthomolecular psychiatry is practiced in conjunction with self-help groups called *Schizophrenics Anonymous,* an organization which is patterned closely after the Alcoholics Anonymous self-help organization. If these authors are correct in their biochemical imbalance hypothesis, one must question the genetic deficiency hypothesis. For example, most of the information that I have points toward personality as being learned and not genetically predetermined. Thus, it seems conceivable that people with different personality types have differing emotional responses to both internal and external stimuli and that some emotional responses could be a precipitating factor in these adduced biochemical imbalances. Such is believed to be the case in the development of stomach ulcers, for example.

In summary, this section on schizophrenia is, by no means, all-inclusive. There are many other excellent references on that subject. However, my thinking on the subject has been strongly influenced by several years of clinical experience with this category of people. Thus, the possibility of bias (as well as insight) exists.

Mental Retardation

Evidence of subnormal intelligence, as measured by standardized intelligence tests, is generally accepted as bona fide evidence of mental retardation. Below normal intellectual functioning is often associated with learning impairment and social maladjustment.

Although there is more agreement on what is mental retardation than what is schizophrenia, the American Medical Association (AMA)

(1965) reports that over 200 causes of mental retardation have been identified. This information notwithstanding, the AMA indicates that determining causation is complex, often involving multiple factors that interact in a complex manner. That is, a considerable amount of mental retardation is believed to be caused by a complex interaction of biological, psychological, and sociocultural factors. Crucial to understanding mental retardation is the person's psychosocial adaptation and his/her interaction with others in the environment. Some people with subnormal intelligence make relatively normal psychosocial adaptions, while others with similar IQs do not. The American Medical Association (1965) reports that three out of four mentally retarded people have significant medical problems, e.g., seizures, speech handicaps, poor vision, and hearing problems are but a few.

Whether mental retardation is caused by multiple factors or by one single factor, the AMA reports that a diagnosis of mental retardation is appropriate only if made before age 17. The causative factors in some mental retardation have been traced to physical and/or chemical damage to the unborn fetus. Some of the better known primary causes of mental retardation are the mother's contracting German measles during the first trimester of pregnancy, maternal toxemia during pregnancy, or mechanical damage during the birth process. Some other conditions, which are considered as primary causes of mental retardation, include genetic abnormalities, e.g., Tay-Sachs disease and phenylketonoria (APA, 1968, p. 17). Both these conditions are believed to be caused primarily by a single recessive gene. Down's syndrome, or mongolism, another primary cause of mental retardation, has been determined to be caused by an abnormal number of chromosomes. Bernard (1978) indicates that mental retardation may be caused by maternal deprivation and poor diet in developing infants. Postnatally, other primary causes of mental retardation include physical or chemical trauma and infectious diseases which cause high temperatures for prolonged periods of time. Finally, some contemporary research, emanating primarily from the media, indicate that mothers who overindulge in alcohol, coffee, or tobacco pose a threat to the fetus.

In summary, mental retardation is a syndrome presenting many biological, psychosocial, and sociocultural problems. They suffer many problems in common with people with schizophrenia, especially difficulties in communicating and relating to others. Also, they share a problem in common with the dependent elderly in that both groups have a high percentage of physical problems.

Dependent Elderly

While it seems relatively safe to say that a large percentage of people with schizophrenia and mental retardation spend a considerable proportion of their lives in institutions, Bernard (1978) reports that worldwide only 5% of the people over age 65 require custodial care. However, this does not mean that the other 95% are healthy. Wolff (1970) indicates that about 38% of all patients in mental hospitals in the United States are over age 60. In an empirical study of a hospital population McCoin (1978) found that 23% were over age 60.

From the literature search and empirical observations, it appears that many residents in adult foster homes have had prolonged periods of psychiatric hospitalization, often for schizophrenia. As clinicians frequently observe, schizophrenia tends to "burn out" with advancing age, i.e., the symptoms often subside to the point where psychiatric medication is no longer required. However, after long periods of hospitalization the elderly person is likely to have become quite dependent and to have largely broken ties with family members and the community. Thus, it seems logical that many would be candidates for adult foster homes.

Theories on aging abound, but there is less agreement on the causative factors in aging than, for example, on mental retardation. One of the more popular theories on aging seems to be disengagement theory (Bernard, 1978). In effect, disengagement theory means that the aging person gradually withdraws from social and family roles. Though not utilizing the term *disengagement theory,* Wolff (1959) seems to be implying such when he indicated the elderly, who have successfully aged, have avoided prolonged stress situations in life such as prolonged conflicts with authority figures.

Field and Bluestone (1968) emphasize the importance of the elderly maintaining a competive spirit, which would seem to be in consonance with activity theory (Bernard, 1978). Basically, activity theory would seem to be the opposite of disengagement theory. Wolff (1970) refers to the "mutation theory" of aging (p. 20). That is, the body cells gradually accumulate deleterious genes which cause a gradual deterioration in the human organism. Bernard (1978) indicates that socioenvironmental theory seems to partially account for the aging process. That is, social expectation influences the attitudes of the elderly toward themselves, others, and society.

It seems safe to assume that a relatively high percentage of the dependent elderly in adult foster homes suffer from organic brain syndromes. Moreover, psychotic reactions are often associated with organic brain syndromes. The APA (1968) indicates that some of these are senile dementia, several types of alcohol-induced psychoses, psychoses associated with infection, brain trauma, cerebral arteriosclerosis, and other cerebrovascular disturbances. Bernard (1978) indicates that cholesterol gradually accumulates in the arteries with advancing age, thus decreasing blood circulation. This decreased blood circulation, especially to the brain, may help account for the deterioration of about 10% of the brain cells in the cerebral cortex by age 75. Lidz (1976) indicates that senile and arteriosclerotic changes can cause the blood vessels to become obstructed, causing a rupturing of an artery to the brain. This is commonly known as a stroke. Some of the symptoms of the elderly with organic brain syndromes are self-centeredness, acting childish, experiencing difficulty in assimilating new experiences, and poor memory for recent events. Also disorientation for time, place, and person are not uncommon.

As with schizophrenia and mental retardation, the process of aging presents new sociological and psychological problems. This is not only true for society but also for the aging themselves. For example, Wolff (1959) claims that for many aged people, " . . . retirement (from employment) seems like a compulsory divorce from a beloved spouse" (p. 32). Other sociological problems for the aged are living on reduced incomes, adjusting to the death of a spouse, societal lack of appreciation for the aged, and a paucity of defined social roles. Wolff (1970) indicates that some of the memory loss in the aged may be due to psychological factors such as a loss of interest in living. Thus, by disuse, the brain power gradually deteriorates, not unlike unused muscles.

In conclusion, as with schizophrenia and mental retardation, it appears that many variables are operative in the aging process. Moreover, it appears that many of these variables overlap in the three groups under study in this book while some are unique to the group under consideration. Further elaboration follows.

Social Margin

Segal, Baumohl, and Johnson (1977) describe social margin as "...
the set of resources and relationships an individual can draw on ... to
survive in society" (p. 388). Viewed from within this context, it seems
conceivable that many people in the three groups under consideration
in this book may be lacking in social margin. For example, many people
in these groups suffer from tarnished reputations, due to such factors
as irrational behavior and a lack of competitiveness in the job market.
In cases of schizophrenia, particularly, the schizophrenic person and
family members may develop an "emotional allergy" to each other
(Morrissey, 1967, p. 42). Furthermore, it seems possible that an emotional allergy could also develop between some mentally retarded and
elderly people and their families, thereby further depleting their supply of social margin. Moreover, Segal (1979) indicates that financial
security is an indication of social margin.

Segal (1979) indicates that social margin may be conceived as a
"credit" and "debit" account that each person possesses (p. 47). Furthermore, Segal notes that people requiring long-term shelter care in the
community often have few credits in their social margin. Besides a
good reputation and financial resources as indicators of social margin,
Segal also considers being married as a credit. For example, he notes
that in California in 1970, only 5% of the people in community-based
residential care were married. By way of comparison, he indicated 70%
of the general population in California were married.

Viewed from within the framework of credits and debits, it is not
difficult to discern numerous debits which the groups under study in
this book have. For example, they are frequently chronically dependent. Levinson (1964) indicates that chronic dependency can lead to
alienation from relatives and people in the community. Another debit
which Segal (1979) mentions is the fact that people with long histories
of mental illness often take large doses of psychoactive medication
which reduces their level of social functioning, thereby helping to
deplete their social margin. Still another debit listed by Segal (1979) is
that people with long histories of hospitalization tend to develop "institutional neuroses" (p. 52) which can stifle their willingness to risk
developing new social roles. In other words, they tend to accept positions of powerlessness in exchange for the protection of a structured
environment.

Another way of viewing social margin is to apply Henry's (1963) frame of reference. That is, the first "commandment" of the economic marketplace is, "Thou shalt consume" (p. 20). Without the financial wherewithal to buy goods and services, the groups under study in this book may be socially considered as humanly obsolete and be relegated to "social junkyards" (Henry, p. 406). If one conceives of mental hospitals and community-based shelter care facilities as social junkyards, then the confinement of people in them could be conceived as an attempt by society to prescribe a minimal amount of credits toward their social margins. That is, these dependent groups are at least marginally reinstated in the social and economic marketplace, albeit in a tenuous and dependent manner.

The theoretical concept of social margin would seem to have practical utility in assessing people for placement in adult foster homes. That is, the concept would seem to be relatively easy to operationalize in the empirical world of social work practice. Whorley (1978) uses the term "socially bankrupt" (p. 141) which seems to be similiar in meaning to social margin.

Alienation

The theoretical concept of alienation has been widely studied by theorists. The concept has an added advantage by having been operationalized extensively in the empirical world.

Torrance (1977) states that the ideological theme of alienation can be traced to ancient Jewish and Christian mythology wherein man was considered to be alienated from God because of man's transgressions against God. That is, man was supposed to renounce certain powers to God in return for salvation. Marx believed that workers were alienated from the products of their labor (Lukes, 1977). Lukes also indicates that Durkheim believed that man's emotions were largely unregulated in industrial societies and, therefore, these emotions must inevitably conflict with the larger interests of society.

The concept of alienation has metamorphosed considerably since the nineteenth century. Indeed, different disciplines seem to alter the concept to suit their own needs. For example, a medical publication considered alienation to be, "A syndrome which reflects psychological arrest in growth and maturity" (*Dollard's Illustrated Medical Dictionary*,

1957). The same publication refers to a psychiatrist as an "alienist." More recently, a psychotherapist used alienation as a theoretical framework with which to treat psychiatric patients with paranoid symptomatology (Aaronson, 1977).

Of all the disciplines, sociologists have done the most to operationalize the concept of alienation. In recent years social workers have begun to study the concept, e.g., Teeter (1972) and McCoin (1977, 1979). Alienation can be conceived as global, situational, interpersonal, or intrapersonal. Using an interpersonal or situational approach would seem to be the favored approach in the study of residents in adult foster homes. Viewed within this context, Hajda's (1961) definition would seem to suffice:

> Alienation is an individual's feeling of uneasiness or discomfort
> which reflects his exclusion or self exclusion from social and cultu-
> ral participation. It is an expression of non-belonging or non-
> sharing, an uneasy awareness or perception of unwelcome contrast
> with others. . . . (p. 752).

McCoin (1977, 1979) used the Dean Alienation Scale to operationalize alienation with residents in an adult foster home program. Dean (1961) operationalized alienation as consisting of powerlessness, normlessness, and social isolation. Briefly, Dean considered powerlessness to the individual's belief that his/her behavior could have little or no influence in determining the outcomes sought. Essentially, Dean considered normlessness to be the individual's belief that he/she cannot use socially approved means to achieve goals which are sought. Dean considered social isolation to be the individual's belief that he/she is separated from the standards of the group, or from the group itself.

In a subsequent chapter, more elaboration will be given on the operationalization of alienation with a group of residents in an adult foster home program. McCoin (1977, 1979) and Teeter (1972) found former psychiatric inpatients to have higher mean alienation scores than those reported in the literature for normals. Also, McCoin (1978) found that the hospitalized elderly in a large hospital scored higher on alienation than any other age group. As far as I can determine, the concept of alienation remains to be operationalized with the mentally retarded.

Nestling Syndrome

This section is being presented last in the theoretical concepts about residents for several reasons. First, it is polemic in that is suggests humans have not evolved as far from the lower animals as we would like to believe. Moreover, theoretical concepts which give some indication of a possible instinctual basis for human behavior are becoming unpopular, ostensibly because they are difficult to operationalize. One of the best examples would be psychoanalytic theory. Another reason for presenting the section on the nestling syndrome here is because it is considered a companion to the *nesting syndrome,* proferred next as a theoretical explanation as to why some managers may elect to become managers.

Proponents of interpersonal and interaction theories underscore the importance of human interactions on behavior. Accepting this premise, therefore, it would seem that the norm of reciprocity is operative in all human interactions. In her study of adult foster homes, Evans (1976) commented, "In general, patients tended to complement their sponsors' Dominance-Affectionate interpersonal behavior types by being predominately Submissive and Affectionate" (p. 211).

Based upon Evans' reasoning above, therefore, it seems that a plausible explanation is needed as to why residents would be submissive to dominant managers. The nestling syndrome (Ellenberger, 1960) offers one explanation. Ellenberger apparently deduced this hypothesis after lengthy study of wild animals in zoological gardens and comparing their responses with patients in mental hospitals. Further elaboration on this follows.

Ellenberger observed that wild animals, especially the more intelligent, older ones, underwent strong reactions when deprived of their natural habitats, i.e., when they were caged. For example, he noted that they frequently underwent severe bouts of what appeared to be agitated depressions. During these episodes they would frequently refuse to eat and manifested otherwise self-destructive behavior. However, Ellenberger indicated that most of them became acclimated to their cages, thereby transforming their cages into their new individual territory. Moreover, he noted that after internment, they would often refuse to leave their cages, or would voluntarily return to them if they did leave. By analogy, Ellenberger compares their transforming their cages into new territory with mental patients' reaction processes after becoming hospitalized. In other words, the animals and mental patients tend to "nestle" in their respective new territories, not unlike young birds which tend to nestle in their nests until literally being pushed out by their mothers. Parenthetically, in my social work practice, I have frequently observed that many mental patients and/or their relatives were extremely resistive to the patients' reentry into the community via adult foster care home placement.

If the preceding observations can indeed be transferred to hospital settings, it would seem to be but a small step for residents to repeat the nestling syndrome when placed in foster homes. If the nestling syndrome is operative in mental patients, ascertaining whether it is culturally induced or instinctual would be no mean task.

THEORETICAL CONCEPTS: MANAGERS

Nesting Syndrome

A perusal of the literature and empirical observations indicate that many adult foster home managers are female, or many of the homes appear to be headed by female-dominated couples. Steffy (1963) found the mean age of managers to be 56.7, well past the childbearing age. Zweben (1977) indicated that older managers often stated that the reason they wanted to be managers was to mitigate against feelings of loneliness as a consequence of their children's having left home. Deykin, Jacobson, Klerman, and Solomon (1966) indicate that the "empty nest syndrome" may be a contributory factor toward depression in some middle-aged women (p. 1422). Moreover, the authors expound on changes in family life in twentieth century America which make it more difficult to accept an "emotional divorce" from grown children (p. 1423). Furthermore, the authors believe that the empty nest syndrome may be more prevalent among European-born and first-generation United States women. Also, the authors found that the majority of their sample came from the lower middle class. McCoin (1977, 1979) found that a large percentage of his sample were European-born or first-generation United States residents. Several authors refer to managers' having limited education and being from the lower socioeconomic status groups. Bernard (1978), however, does not seem to place much credence in the empty nest hypothesis. Neither does he ascribe it primarily to females, and he thinks that most parents are happy to see their offspring leave home, provided the parents have sufficient cultural concerns and avocational interests.

Glickman (1957) indicates that the empty nest syndrome is often the primary motivation for wanting to become managers of children's foster homes (p. 181). Babcock (1965) goes as far as to refer to the "biology of nestbuilding" (p. 492). Thus, she seems to consider the syndrome to be instinctual in humans. A more recent publication, however, indicates that the syndrome is probably learned by humans through the socialization process of becoming human (Goldenson, 1970). Supporting the nesting hypothesis are the works of Fanshel (1966) and Evans (1976), who suggest that female managers of children's foster homes are able to express their femininity more as mothers than as wives. This could be indicative of their becoming foster home managers, i.e., as an outlet for their own unmet sexual and emotional needs.

Bernard's (1978) failure to attribute the nesting syndrome exclusively to women and my own empirical observations lead me to think that the syndrome may also be prevalent among men. For example, many men are quite concerned about their homes and children. Also numerous middle-aged men have been known to reject their wives and marry younger women, possibly due in part to a biological and/or psychological urge to replenish the empty nest.

As mentioned earlier in the section on the nestling syndrome, the nestling syndrome and the nesting syndrome are considered complementary. As with the nestling syndrome, operationalizing the nesting syndrome would appear to be easier because the feelings and thoughts of managers could conceivably be obtained relatively easy from managers with respect to having companionship in the home.

The Family

The family is a concept which has been widely studied by many disciplines. Smalley (1950) claimed the family to be one of the greatest social institutions ever devised for the socialization of the young. Since 1950, however, the family in the United States has undergone considerable change. Except among a few subcultures, the extended family of grandparents, parents and children is all but passé. Indeed, the nuclear family of parents and children appears to be declining in popularity, as experimental alternatives to conventional marriage are becoming more explored. The reader could rightfully ask, "That's true, but what has the decline in the influence of the family got to do with adult foster care?" A simplified response to this rhetorical question is that the foundation for the adult foster care program rests upon the assumption that the substitute family is the treatment of choice for many dependent and disabled groups such as those under study in this book. If the family is the great socializer for the young, who like the groups under study in this book are quite dependent, why would not the substitute family be an effective socializer for some of our troubled adults?

McBroom's (1970) work would seem to offer a partial answer to the above question in her conceptualization of socialization theory. Furthermore, she denotes that socialization occurs primarily through the social interaction between people who are considered significant to each other. Moreover, McBroom indicates, " . . . the socialization process involves reward and punishment by a socializing agent who adopts the role of teacher and becomes an active model for imitation" (p. 319). McBroom borrows from the concept of feedback from social systems theory whereby feedback is utilized to help others learn socially acceptable behavior. Though McBroom places considerable emphasis on teaching, it can be easily argued that so do families, especially in socializing the young. Here it should be emphasized that one of the chief criticisms from the study by Murphy et al. (1972) was that adult foster home managers provided little or no feedback to residents.

Assuming that socialization theory is relevant to enhancing comprehension of adult foster homes management, the question arises as to what would be the best type of setting in which to implement the theory. Currently, what are considered adult foster home programs have between 1–20 or more residents. It seems that large adult foster home programs may be based upon the large, extended family model which seems to be becoming extinct in the United States. Therefore, people with experience with the extended family model are becoming rarer. The question arises as to whether a formalized educational program for adult foster home managers, especially for large homes, is not needed. While criticizing the large extended family as being male dominated and authoritarian, Evans (1976) also depicts large families as being more open and better oriented to the realities of life because the primary emphasis is on cooperative group effort as opposed to the closed individualistic emphasis of smaller families. Murphy et al. (1972) found more rivalry and hostility between residents in smaller homes. However, it could be argued that rivalry and hostility are a part of real life. However, another study by Murphy et al. (1976) revealed no substantial improvement in social functioning between residents in large and small homes. In their 1972 study Murphy et al. recommended more "unconventional" homes in urban settings to mitigate against resident loneliness and to provide greater anonymity for residents so they could live down the deviant or "sick roles" they had acquired.

Finally, adult foster home living is considered "less restrictive" than hospitalization by a number of authors including Morrissey (1967), Miller (1977), and Zweben (1977). This in itself would appear to be a good argument in favor of adult foster homes. However, much more research is needed on the family and especially on substitute families before many of the lingering questions on adult foster care can be answered.

Authoritarianism

The first empirical study on authoritarianism seems to have been accomplished by Adorno, Frenkel-Brunswick, Levinson, and Sanford (1950). A precipitating factor in the studies was the Nazi atrocities of the Second World War, especially those directed toward Jews. Though based upon psychoanalytic theory, the authors deviated somewhat from Freud's deterministic view that the psyche was largely under the control of the individual, at least as far as people with authoritarian personalities are concerned. Adorno et al. seriously considered the individual's potential for behavior when influenced by leaders whose leadership had considerable psychological meaning. That is, people with certain type personalities, presumably submissive, would gravitate toward dominant or aggressive leaders. Put another way, they would gravitate toward authoritarian leaders.

Ellman (1972) indicated that authoritarianism is a syndrome resulting from faulty personality development. Numerous references are extant in the literature on the importance of healthy personality development in adult foster home managers. Moreover, the literature search indicated that many adult foster home managers are considered to have authoritarian personalities. It is believed that people with authoritarian personalities have not internalized social anxiety, or have inadequately developed consciences. As such, it is believed that they tend to rely on outside authority in lieu of internalized social anxiety. Jones (1954) indicated that authoritarians harbor a great deal of hostility and are more preoccupied with aggression than egalitarians. Gregory (1957) indicated that authoritarians are compulsive, religiously orthodox, and tend to project responsibility for their own actions onto others. Other authors report that authoritarians are likely to conceive in deterministic terms, tending to deny or ignore the shades of gray in an issue (Christie & Jahoda, 1954). Kates and Diab (1955) indicate that authoritarians desire more total control of others, are less introspective, and are more preoccupied with the power motif than are egalitarians.

Authoritarianism has been operationalized by several scales. However, the most widely used one is the California F Scale which emerged from the study by Adorno et al. (1950). This scale has high reliability and validity and was used by McCoin (1977, 1979) in his empirical study of managers in a large adult foster home program. The scale purports to measure authoritarianism, or antidemocratic potential in an individual's personality. The scale consists of 30 items, grouped into 9 attitudinal categories. More will be said about operationalizing authoritarianism and the attitudinal categories in the next chapter.

Normalization

The theoretical concept of normalization forms the theoretical base for adult foster care in Michigan and several other states (Sheerin & Sheerin, 1977). Although no effort was made by me to discern the theoretical base used by the states, it could be that this concept is the most widely used one. Moreover, Sheerin and Sheerin contend that the concept is difficult for managers to comprehend, ostensively because it has two meanings, i.e., one is statistical where normative means "typical" or "conventional" (p. 17) and the other is sociological, which essentially means the process of learning and conforming to societal norms. The authors, furthermore, state that the concept has had little empirical validation and has limited practical utility. For example, managers who have had training in which normalization was emphasized had practically no better comprehension of it than managers who had not been so trained. To me, the concept seems misleading because it connotes normality for disabled populations, which may be an unrealistic goal. Nevertheless, the concept warrants further research, with one strong reason being that it is already in use in several states. An idealistic concept, such as this one, could conceivably provide some inspiration for the adult foster care movement in that it could be an ideal goal for which to strive. Still, adult foster care is not a very idealistic business. Further reference will be made to normalization in subsequent chapters.

Chapter 4

FIELD TESTING OF THEORIES OF ADULT FOSTER HOMES

This chapter deals with the empirical testing of some of the theoretical concepts delineated in Chapter 3. The material presented in Chapter 4 emanated from research conducted from 1975–1979. However, 21 social workers from the setting assisted in data collection. The primary references for this chapter are McCoin (1977, 1979). The data, used in both studies, were the same and were collected in 1976–1977. However, different research designs and data analysis procedures were utilized in the 1977 and 1979 studies, generally referred to later in this chapter simply as the 1977 or 1979 study.

STUDY SETTING

The setting was the Franklin Delano Roosevelt Veterans Administration Medical Center, Montrose, New York, where I worked as a clinical social worker in the late 1960s and part of the 1970s. During all of that time, I worked part time with the adult foster home program there.

Located about 38 miles north of New York City, on the Hudson River, the center's primary mission is the diagnosis and treatment of inpatient and outpatient military veterans whose primary problems are psychiatric. The center's catchment area includes New York City and parts of New Jersey and Connecticut. Presently, the inpatient population is about 1100 and the outpatient population is about twice that amount. Of the approximately 2200 outpatients, about 600 are in the center's adult foster home program. An umbrella term, however, is employed; the program is called the *Community Care Program*. This program includes personal care homes, nursing homes, and special homes. For the purpose of this study, personal care homes will be considered analogous to the adult foster homes, which are intended to keep between 1–20 veterans.

The center's adult foster home program began in 1953. By 1973, 1,644 veterans of both sexes and 193 managers had participated in the program. The vast majority of veterans affiliated with the center receive either service-connected compensation of nonservice-connected pension checks from the VA. As of 1978, checks for service-connected disabilities ranged from $48.00–$754.00 monthly for a single veteran. Also in 1978, nonservice-connected veterans received between $5.00–$315.00 monthly. Both groups of veterans often receive additional Social Security disability benefits and nonservice-connected veterans often receive Supplemental Security Income (SSI) benefits. Generally, managers are paid for their services from the veteran's income. This arrangement results in considerable financial savings for the VA, which defrays the entire cost of hospitalization when the veteran is hospitalized.

As Cupaiuolo (1979) indicates, the F.D.R. Veterans Administration Medical Center's adult foster home program is designed primarily for the ". . . . older, sicker, or more regressed patient" (p. 56).

RESEARCH DESIGNS

In the 1977 study the quasiexperimental "Recurrent Institutional Cycle" design was utilized (Campbell & Stanley, 1966, p. 57). Hypotheses were tested which dealt with manager authoritarianism and resident alienation.

An exploratory research design was utilized in the 1979 study for several reasons. One of these was that many of the findings of the 1977 study were not statistically significant at the established level. Moreover, the purpose of the 1979 study was exploratory. Kahn (1960) and Sellitz, Wrightsman, and Cook (1976) indicate essentially that exploratory designs are relevant in areas in which theory development has been limited, which is certainly the case with adult foster home programs. Furthermore, exploratory studies often provide new insights into seldom-explored phenomena. As such, exploratory studies help generate hypotheses for empirical testing which can help enhance theory development.

As previously mentioned in Chapter 3, this book essentially follows a descriptive design.

INSTRUMENTS

The Dean Alienation Scale was used to test resident alienation and to test alienation in patients being prepared for placement into the adult foster home program. The Dean scale purportedly measures the theoretical concept of alienation and three components of alienation which are: (1) powerlessness; (2) normlessness; and (3) social isolation. When the component scores are added, the total score comprises the alienation score. However, Dean (1961) indicates that the component scores can be treated as separate variables. Essentially, powerlessness means that the individual lacks confidence in the ability to deal effectively with controlling societal forces. Basically, normlessness means that the person lacks sufficient normative values to help guide or regulate the person's life. Social isolation means essentially that the person feels socially isolated from others. (See Chap. 3 for a more thorough explanation.)

Sellitz et al. (1976) indicate that any measurement in the social sciences is likely to include other characteristics in addition to what the researcher wants to measure. In efforts to reduce these error terms, the instruments should be as reliable and valid as possible. Robinson and Shaver (1973) report that the Dean scale has an overall reliability of .78 but that the scale has not yet had adequate application to be empirically validated. The Dean scale is a Likert-type scale, commonly accepted as measuring at an ordinal level. In measurement hierarchy, a nominal level of measurement is at the bottom, followed in ascending order by ordinal, interval, and ratio levels of measurement. Generally, the higher the level of measurement, the more powerful are the statistics which can be used. Some scales seem to fall between an ordinal and interval level of measurement. These are considered "ordered-metric" (Nie, Hull, Jenkins, Steinbrenner, & Bent, 1975, p. 6). Moreover, Labovitz (1970) indicates that there are numerous statistical advantages to treating ordinal levels of measurement as interval. Not the least of these advantages would be the application of well-developed multivariate statistical procedures, e.g., multiple regression analysis which was used in the 1979 study. Accordingly, the Dean scale would be considered as meeting the requirements for an ordered-metric level of measurement. A self-administering questionnaire was also utilized in data collection from resident-patients. More will be said about this later.

The California F Scale (Adorno, Frenkel-Brunswick, Levinson, & Sanford, 1950) was used to operationalize manager authoritarianism. Like the Dean scale, it is also considered to measure at an ordered-metric level. The F scale purports to measure the extent of authoritarianism, or antidemocratic potential, in a person's personality. Robinson and Shaver (1973) indicate that the F scale has an average reliability of .90 and a validity of .73 when correlated with the California Ethnocentrism Scale. Furthermore, the F scale has nine attitudinal categories which can be considered as variables in the authoritarianism syndrome. The combined scores from the nine categories represent the authoritarianism score.

Briefly stated, the nine attitudinal categories of authoritarianism will now be explicated: (1) conventionalism, or the tendency to adhere to conventional values; (2) authoritarian-submission, or the tendency to idealize in-group authority figures; (3) authoritarian-aggression, or the tendency to reject and condemn those who violate conventional values; (4) antiintraception, or the tendency to oppose subjective, imaginative thinking; (5) superstition and stereotypy, or the tendency toward rigid thinking and the belief that faith primarily determines one's course in life; (6) power-toughness, or a preoccupation with dominance and submission; (7) destructiveness-cynicism, or a generalized hostility toward people; (8) projectivity, or the tendency to project one's unconscious feelings outwards and onto other people; (9) sex, or overconcern about sexual occurrences (Miller, 1970).

A self-administering questionnaire was also utilized to collect data from the managers which were thought to be conceptually related to the study. More will be said about this later.

SAMPLING

In both the 1977 and 1979 studies the A group of residents represented a random sample of males with schizophrenic diagnoses who had been in the adult foster home program up to 15 years. All of the A group members were living in adult foster homes in which the manager was also participating in the research project. The rationale for limiting the resident sample to schizophrenic males was because of the use of Sullivan interpersonal theory, which was developed by Sullivan while working with this type of population (Sullivan, 1962).

By virtue of their sex, diagnoses, and length of time in the adult foster home program, $n = 390$ residents were eligible for inclusion in the A group. From the eligible population, a random sample of $n = 48$ was selected for the A group. In some instances, one participating manager had one resident participating in the A group, and in other instances one participating manager had up to three residents who were in the A group.

The remaining residents (patients) included 97% of the schizophrenic males from the setting who were being prepared for placement in the adult foster home program; the other 3% remained hospitalized, or refused to participate in the project. All of the participating residents-patients were later placed in the adult foster home program. In the 1977 study, the B group was dichotomized into the B_1 and B_2 subgroups of $n = 20$ each, and a C group of $n = 30$ was added as a contrast group. In the 1979 study, the B and C groups were collapsed and redesignated as the B group, consisting of $n = 70$.

The eligible manager population was $n = 90$. That is, only managers from homes keeping male veterans with schizophrenic diagnoses were considered eligible. Of the 90 eligible managers $n = 77$ completed the California F Scale and questionnaire. Data from 12 managers were not utilized in the study because they did not have a schizophrenic male participating in the study.

DATA ANALYSIS

In the 1977 study the mean differences between resident groups were tested on alienation and alienation components by the parametric t test. A χ^2 nonparametric test was utilized to test other data, primarily data obtained from residents' and managers' questionnaires. However, the χ^2 test was also utilized to test the association between manager authoritarianism and resident alienation. The Fisher Exact Test and descriptive statistics were also utilized. A significance level of .05 was established as the maximum level at which the null hypotheses could be rejected. The statistical tests were two-tailed. Data analysis for the 1977 study was conducted at Teachers College, Columbia University, using the Burroughs SPSSG computer system. For the 1979 study, data were analyzed at the University of Wisconsin, Oshkosh, utilizing the IBM SPSSH computer system.

A perusal of social work journals in recent years indicates that the use of multiple regression statistical analysis is proliferating (Berger & Piliavin, 1976; Fanshel, 1977; Fischer & Hudson, 1976). Berger & Piliavin describe the multiple regression model as ". . . . a linear combination of variables, called independent variables or predictors, that best accounts for the observed variation in some dependent or predicted variable" (p. 208). With the advent of computer technology and more reliable and valid data collection instruments, multiple regression analysis is becoming increasingly important in prediction. As Kogan (1960) indicates, ". . . . the long run objective of scientific research is to develop principles which will account for what has already been observed in the empirical world and predict what has not yet been observed" (p. 89).

Resident data were obtained from the questionnaire and the Dean Alienation Scale, including its components of powerlessness, normlessness, and social isolation. These four variables comprise the dependent, or predicted variables. The independent, or predictor variables, were obtained from clinical and demographic data. For managers, the California F Scale scores were the dependent, or predicted variable, and the independent, or predictor, variables were obtained from the demographic data on managers, obtained from the questionnaire. Table 4–1 is now promulgated to show the list of resident independent and dependent variables in the 1979 study.

From Table 4–1 it can be observed that, with the exception of ages, the independent variables would not meet the measurement requirements for regression analysis by virtue of their being nominal levels of measurement. Therefore, it became necessary to treat them as either dichotomies or dummy variables before they could be inserted into the regression analysis. Nie et al. (1975) indicate that a dichotomy consists of a variable with only two possible outcomes. According to convention, a 1 is usually assigned to the characteristic being measured and a 0 is assigned if the characteristic is absent. For example, from table 4–1, financial status (100% service connected) was treated as a dichotomous variable and assigned a 1 while being nonservice connected was assigned a value of 0 as the reference category, or the reference point with which the other category is compared. Also from Table 4–1, being competent or incompetent was likewise treated dichotomously.

The creation of dummy variables is somewhat more complex. As Fanshel (1977) indicates:

> Dummy variable coding involves successively dichotomizing a nominal scale so that each category is used to create a variable that distinguishes the category from the remaining categories. . . . it is unnecessary to create the final dichotomous variable. . . . because (it) becomes the reference group for the other (categories). . . . (p. 7)

Table 4–1.   List of Resident Variables in Study

Dependent Variables	Independent Variables
Alienation	Age
	Religion
	Education
	Ethnicity
Normlessness	Financial status
	Marital status
	Clinical diagnosis
Powerlessness	Legal status
	Extent of impairment
Social Isolation	Amount of hospitalization

Thus, from the above explanation, it can be observed that the creation of dummy variables is an extension of the concept of the dichotomies. Kim and Kohout (1975) give another explanation of the creation of dummy variables:

> ... the nominal variable religion, with categories Catholic, Protestent, Jewish and Other, can be conceived as four separate dichotomous variables. All can be assigned arbitrary scores of ... 1 or 0 on all four of these variables. A Catholic would be scored 1 on all of the dummy variables standing for Catholic and 0 on all others. ... The newly-created dummy variables are called dummy variables because their scores have no meaning ... other than standing for a particular category in the original variable. (p. 374)

Thus, from this reference it can be observed that there would be four dummy variables for the nominal variable of religion. Again, reference is made to Table 4–1. Since the exact age of residents was known, that variable was treated as an interval variable. Therefore, no dummy variables had to be created for resident age. As previously mentioned, financial status and legal status were treated as dichotomies; the remaining independent variables were treated as dummy variables. Thus, it became necessary to create several dummy variables for each of these independent variables. Notice that all but age were nominal variables, obtained from the self-administering questionnaire and face sheet information form.

Table 4–2 is now presented to show the manager variables in the 1979 study. Observe that all of the independent variables are at a nominal level of measurement with the information having been obtained from the self-administering questionnaire.

No dichotomous variables were used in data analysis for managers. However, several dummy variables were created for each of the independent variables, including age, since only the approximate ages were known, e.g., 50–54.

In the tabular presentations to follow, the r, referred to as multiple r, represents the correlation coefficient, and the r^2 represents the coefficient of determination. Both the r and r^2 are useful in helping to determine the strength of predicting on the dependent variables from the independent variables used in the analysis (Nie et al. 1975). For example, the amount of variation in the dependent variable alienation

Table 4–2.   List of Manager Variables in Study

Dependent Variables	Independent Variables
Authoritarianism	Age
Conventionalism	
Authoritarian-submission	Education
Authoritarian-aggression	
Anti-intraception	Religion
Superstition-stereotypy	
Power-toughness	Ethnicity
Destructiveness-cynicism	
Projectivity	Marital status
Sex	

can be explained by linear dependence upon the 10 independent variables from table 1 operating jointly. The same claim is posited about the dependent variable authoritarianism and the five independent variables in Table 4–2 for managers. In other words, the coefficients of r and r^2 give the relative strength of the relationship between the dependent and independent variables. For example, if all of the variance between variables is 1.0, then $1 - r^2$ would represent all the unexplained variance in the equation. The remaining variance, r^2, would represent all of the explained variance in the equation. Thus, the r^2 is the more straightforward interpretation. However, both the r and r^2 are unstandardized regression coefficients.

To aid in data interpretation, standardized regression coefficients are utilized in some of the following tabular presentations. These coefficients, called β weights, are standardized so that such difficult problems as different independent variables being measured on different units can be controlled (Nie et al., 1975). An example would be income, which is measured in dollars, and education, which is measured in years. In the tabular presentations to follow from the 1979 study, the weights are given directionally. The sign of the β indicates the direction of the relationship between variables. A negative sign does not denote a poor fit, but rather, an inverse relationship. That is, as the independent variable increases, the dependent variable becomes smaller. In this case it could be claimed that the dependent variable is a decreasing function of the independent variable. A more specific example would be that as manager education increases, authoritarianism decreases. The reader should assume that no sign before the β represents a positive sign. An example of this would be that as manager education decreases, authoritarianism increases.

Finally, the stepwise linear regression analysis model was selected for data analysis for much of the 1979 study. Nie et al. (1975) indicate that the stepwise procedure is indicated:

> . . . . when a researcher wishes to isolate a subset of available predictor variables that will yield an optimal prediction equation which has as few terms as possible. . . . The variable that explains the greatest amount of variance in the independent variable will enter first; the variable that explains the greatest amount of variance in conjunction with the first will enter second and so on. In other words, the variable that explains the greatest amount of variance unexplained by the variables already in the equation enters the equation at each step. (p. 345)

Findings

From the 1979 study, some descriptive statistics are now presented to aid in data interpretation. The mean alienation score for the resident A group was 44.68; for the B group it was 49.25. Both of these means were considerably higher than the mean of 36.6, reported by Dean (1961) and Robinson and Shaver (1973), who reported group means of 32.65 and 34.36, respectively. However, all of these authors were reporting alienation means for normal populations. Also reporting group means from the Dean Alienation Scale, Teeter (1972) found the mean for 41 former psychiatric inpatients to be 38.5. However, her sample was not limited exclusively to those with schizophrenic diagnoses, as was the 1979 study. Thus, Teeter's findings and the findings from the 1979 study indicate that former psychiatric inpatients and current psychiatric inpatients appear to be more alienated than normals. Moreover, the A group's scoring 4 points lower on alienation than the B group gives some support to the claim that being out of the hospital for a long period of time mitigates against alienation. Furthermore, it should also be noted that the B group consistently had higher mean scores on the alienation components of (1) normlessness (2) powerlessness, and (3) social isolation than the A group.

Manager authoritarianism scores ranged from − 89 to + 138 (maximum score possible). The mean score on authoritarianism was 12.69, considerably higher than group means of 4.19 and 4.39, as reported by Robinson and Shaver (1973). In the following four tables, data from the 1977 study are presented. Table 4–3 is now presented to show the mean differences between the A and B_2 resident groups on alienation and its components.

Data from Table 4–3 indicate a statistically significant difference on alienation between the two groups. That is, the group which had been in the adult foster home program for a prolonged period of time scored lower. Also of interest from Table 3 is the finding of a $p = .070$ for normlessness. If a one-tailed test had been used, this finding would also have been statistically significant. Table 4–4 is now shown to show differences between the A and C resident groups on alienation and its components.

From Table 4–4 a statistically significant difference can be observed between the two groups on the alienation component of social isolation. Table 4–5 is now presented to show that managers with more education scored lower on authoritarianism than those with less education.

Data from Table 4–5 indicate that managers with more education scored lower on authoritarianism, while those with less education scored higher. This finding is consistent with the observations of Christie and Jahoda (1954) to the effect that people with authoritarian personality traits differ with respect to their educational levels of attainment. Table 4–6 is now given to show the association between manager authoritarianism and religion.

Table 4–3. Differences in Alienation and Alienation Component Scores Between A and B₂ Groups

Category	Powerlessness	Normlessness	Social Isolation	Alienation
A	Mean = 18.5 S.D. = 7.3	10.9 4.7	14.7 5.5	44.6 14.5
B₂	Mean = 20.7 S.D. = 5.9	13.2 4.3	16.5 5.9	53.1 15.4
(Two Tail)	t = -1.28 P = .206	-1.87 .070	-1.14 .261	-2.09 .045

Decision: Alienation statistically significant.

Table 4-4. Differences in Alienation and Alienation Component Scores Between A and C Groups

Category	Powerlessness	Normlessness	Social Isolation	Alienation
A	Mean = 18.5 S.D. = 7.3	10.9 4.7	14.7 5.5	44.6 14.5
C	Mean = 18.9 S.D. = 5.0	11.3 4.1	17.7 4.8	47.7 10.9
t =	-0.29	-0.35	-2.49	-1.05
(Two-tail) P =	.774	.729	.015	.298

Decision: Social Isolation statistically significant.

**Table 4–5.   Association Between Manager Authoritarian-
ism and Education**

	Authoritarianism		
Education	High	Low	Totals
Some College	4	13	17
High School Grad.	11	15	26
Less than H.S. Grad.	16	6	22

x^2 = 9.808   d.f. = 2   Two-Tail   P = .0074

Decision: Statistically significant.

**Table 4–6.   Association Between Manager Authoritarian-
ism and Religion**

	Authoritarianism		
Religion	High	Low	Totals
Catholic	18	14	32
Protestent	13	10	23
Other	0	10	10

x^2 = 10.775   ·d.f. = 2   Two-Tail   P = .0046

Decision: Statistically significant.

Noteworthy from Table 4–6 is that managers in the "Other" religious category scored uniformly low on authoritarianism. This finding is consistent with that of Gregory (1957) who reported that authoritarians are more religiously orthodox than nonauthoritarians.

Of the 10 managers in the "Other" category, 7 reported no religion, 2 were Jewish, and 1 reported unconventional religious beliefs.

Not reported in tabular form from the 1977 study was the finding ($p = .0675$) of an association between manager authoritarianism and ethnicity. The English-Scotch-German group was about evenly divided on authoritarianism. However, the Italian group scored high on authoritarianism; over twice as high as they scored low. Those categorized as "Other" scored low on authoritarianism by a ratio of over 2:1. A plausible explanation for some of these findings is that many of the Italian group were from the "old country" and they were not as well educated as the "Other" group. Also some members of the "Other" group did not identify their ethnicity with a foreign country because their families had been in the United States for many generations, or else they did not know the country of their ethnic origin.

Another finding of interest from the 1977 study was the association between manager authoritarianism and marital status ($p = .088$). That is, 64% of the married group scored low on authoritarianism while 36% of the unmarrieds scored low. Table 4–7 is now presented to show regression analysis from the 1979 study for the A group of residents.

Only the first 7 of 24 variables entering into the regression analysis are shown in Table 4–7. Variables 1–7 explain 38% of the variance. Variables 8–24 (not shown in Table 7) explain 24% of the variance for a total of explained variance of 51% in the analysis. Interesting is that being legally competent explains 9% of the variance and the negative β denotes that alienation is a decreasing function of being legally competent. However, a positive β indicates that alienation is an increasing function of being Italian. Table 4–8 is now presented in abridged form to show the first seven steps in a 33-variable multiple regression analysis for the B group on alienation from the 1979 study.

From the seven variables listed in Table 4–8, it can be observed that 32% of the variance is explained by these variables. Variables 8–33 (not shown in the table) explain 19% of the variance for a total of explained variance of 51%. Moderate impairment explains 11% of the variance and the negative β indicates that alienation is a decreasing function of being moderately impaired. Table 4–9 is now presented in abridged form to show the regression analysis of manager authoritarianism and selected independent variables.

Table 4-7. Stepwise Linear Regression of A-Group Resident Variables on Alienation

Step Number	Variable Entered	Multiple r	r^2	Beta	Increase in r^2
1	Legal status: Competent	.2961	.0877	-.2961	.0877
2	Ethnicity: Italian	.3978	.1583	.2662	.0706
3	Financial status	.4716	.2224	-.2578	.0641
4	Education: 10-11 years	.5157	.2659	-.2106	.0435
5	Ethnicity: French	.5491	.3015	.1968	.0356
6	Marital status: Married	.5762	.3311	.1781	.0296
7	Ethnicity: Czech.	.6171	.3808	-.2570	.0497

Table 4–8. Stepwise Linear Regression of B-Group Resident Variables on Alienation

Step Number	Variable Entered	Multiple r	r^2	Beta	Increase in r^2
1	Impairment: Moderate	.3361	.1130	-.3361	.1130
2	Education: Advanced degree	.4385	.1923	.2842	.0793
3	Hospitalization: 7-10 yrs	.4769	.2275	.1878	.0352
4	Impairment: Mild	.5073	.2574	-.1987	.0299
5	Religion: Protestant	.5293	.2801	.1537	.0227
6	Diagnosis: Simple Schizo	.5478	.3000	.1441	.0200
7	Ethnicity: Czech.	.5646	.3187	.1472	.0187

Table 4-9. Stepwise Linear Regression of Manager Demographic Variables on Authoritarianism

Step Number	Variable Entered	Multiple r	r^2	Beta	Increase in r^2
1	Religion: None	.4206	.1769	-.4206	.1769
2	Age: 50 - 54	.4860	.2366	-.2444	.0597
3	Age: 30 - 34	.5557	.3088	-.2704	.0722
4	Ethnicity: Italian	.6111	.3745	.2575	.0657
5	Religion: Protestant	.6812	.4640	.3739	.0895
6	Marital status: Widow	.7168	.5138	.2317	.0498
7	Age: 25 - 29	.7363	.5421	-.1721	.0283

From steps 1–7, shown in Table 4–9, it can be observed that 54% of the variance is explained by these seven variables. Steps 8–22 (not shown) account for 8% of the explained variance for a total of 62% of explained variance. Explaining 18% of the variance is the variable of having no religion, and the negative β indicates that authoritarianism is a decreasing function of having no religion. A positive β indicates that authoritarianism is an increasing function of being Italian.

Tabular presentations are not being made for the nine attitudinal categories of manager authoritarianism. On five of the nine categories, the variable of no religion entered first in multiple regression analysis and all had negative β. The variable entering first on anti-intraception was being Italian. This explained 9% of the variance and the β was positive. With a positive β, being widowed, explained 8% of the variance on superstition and stereotypy. Being married explained 5% of the variance, with a negative β on destructive-cynicism. Having between 1–3 years of college explained 12% of the variance on projectivity and the β was negative.

CONCLUSIONS

Conclusions are made with caution due to the lack of empirical validation of the Dean scale, possible sampling error with the manager sample, and the collapsing of many nominal categories into smaller numbers to expedite data analysis. However, it does appear that the theoretical concepts of alienation and authoritarianism are reasonably well operationalized by the Dean and California F Scales, respectively. Moreover, these scales would appear to have relevancy for clinical use in adult foster homes and possibly with psychiatric inpatients, especially the Dean scale. However, the finding of no statistically significant differences between long-term adult foster home residents and hospitalized psychiatric patients on the alienation components of powerlessness and normlessness presents interesting questions. One plausible explanation could be that these feelings are so deeply ingrained in the damaged self-concepts of people with schizophrenia that they are not amenable to the socialization process which presumably occurs in adult foster care. Furthermore, the statistically significant differences on social isolation between long-term adult foster home residents and psychiatric inpatients could be an indication that schizophrenic people are amenable to the socialization process of adult foster care, or possibly merely by being out of a hospital environment. The finding of higher mean scores on resident alienation and manager authoritarianism, than those reported in the literature for "normals," presents interesting questions. However, this study and the findings of Teeter (1972), who also used the Dean scale, support the contention that psychiatric patients are more alienated than normals. Moreover, Fromm (1955) conceived "schizophrenia and alienation as complementary" (p. 207). Thus, it may be that people with histories of psychiatric hospitalization, especially people with schizophrenia, are more alienated than normals.

The sample of managers being higher on authoritarianism than normals reported in the literature presents interesting questions. One of these is, do more authoritarian types of people gravitate to becoming managers? If so, does this have a deleterious influence on residents, especially people with schizophrenia? Sullivan interpersonal theorists would probably answer this question in the affirmative. However, observations by some have been made toward the possibility that an authoritarian approach may be needed with certain types of people, i.e., people with paranoid types of personalities and people who are themselves authoritarians (McCoin, 1977; Tessler & Polansky, 1974). Moreover, the high alienation and authorianarism scores of managers and residents would seem to support the contention by Whorley (1978) that both residents and managers are rather dependent groups, especially elderly managers, and that they may be helping to sustain each other in the community through a symbiotic relationship. That is, both groups could be considered socially marginal.

Having a college education and being religiously unorthodox appear to be powerful predictors for indicating low authoritarianism. While there are strong indications that Italian ethnicity is associated with high authoritarianism, this finding can probably be explained by their being less well educated than other groups. Nevertheless, more research is needed in this area, not to mention numerous other areas in this chapter.

Chapter 5

GENERAL REVIEW OF CURRENT
PROGRAMS

In mid-1979 identical letters were mailed to all of the state licensing agencies. Letters were also sent to the District of Columbia, Puerto Rico, and the VA. Information was requested from all agencies regarding licensing policy on adult foster homes, the number of homes and residents, and a categorical listing of residents who were (1) former psychiatric inpatients, (2) mentally retarded, (3) elderly. In subsequent usage, the data from this survey will be termed the mid-1979 survey.

Again in December 1979, additional data were requested by mailing letters to the 50 state offices of (1) mental health, (2) mental retardation, (3) aging. Also the same offices in the District of Columbia and Puerto Rico were written. The letters sent to each division were identical for each division. In one-third of the states the offices of mental health and mental retardation were listed jointly. All states had offices for the aging listed separately. In this survey information was again requested on the number of homes and residents in each state. That is, each office of mental health was expected to supply data pertaining to homes and residents categorized as former psychiatric inpatients, and the offices on mental retardation and elderly were asked to do likewise. However, with some exceptions, most agencies tended to indicate that separating residents by categories was difficult, or the statistics were not available. Thus, it would appear that most adult foster homes serve a variety of categories, including the three under consideration.

A total of 157 letters were sent out in the two original surveys. For clarification purposes, about 50 follow-up letters and 25 telephone calls were made. Most of the telephone calls emanated from the agencies and most of the follow-up letters emanated from me. The only state from which no communication transpired was Missouri. Most states responded to only one to two of the three original inquiries. Also, a few leads were not followed up, ostensibly because they were received after the closing date for data collection.

The information obtained from the surveys tended to confirm the observations of many authors from Chapter 2. That is, in the United States the adult foster home program is not unlike a huge projective-type ink blot. Even among professionals, the program means different things to different people. For example, in some states one agency official was not aware of the existence of the program, while another official in the same state reported one or more. Thus, data from some states tended to be contradictory and difficult to interpret, leaving the possibility open for misinterpretation. Nevertheless, the states and data were categorized as best that could be determined with the information supplied. Since the majority of states have some regulation of what appears to be an adult foster home program or its equivalent, it appears that the "adopted child" of the social work profession is surpassing its adopted parent in gaining official state regulation. By way of comparison, only about one-half of the states license/certify social workers. In the hierarchy of regulation, licensure is considered at the apex, while certification is somewhere down in the hierarchy.

The first assessment in this chapter is of states with licensed programs, followed by certified programs, programs with mixed regulatory packages (e.g., some sections licensed/certified and some not), states with no apparent official program, and states in which the status of the program could not be determined from present data. In each section, the states are presented alphabetically. Generally, the criteria for categorizing programs as adult foster home programs are that they be privately owned and managed and that they not be too large, e.g., not over 20 residents. Generally, brief reference is made to programs which seemed borderline as to meeting the above criteria. References for this chapter differ somewhat from previous chapters because frequent use is made of personal communications from state officials and unpublished materials from states. In the latter instance, the state is listed first as the author, followed in the text by a short title. The reader should look for these in the reference section by states, followed by departments and full titles.

To aid the reader in obtaining an overview of the states with regulatory practices and those in which official regulatory practices are questionable, Table 5–1 is shown. Following Table 5–1 is further elaboration on data from the table.

LICENSED PROGRAMS

The State Division of Social Services is required by state statute to license adult foster homes in Alaska (Monroe, 1979). Scott (1979) indicates that California's Department of Social Services licenses "Small Family Homes—Adult." Scott does not consider California's other residential facilities as analogous to adult foster homes.

In Connecticut the Department of Mental Health licenses "Community Care Homes" for former psychiatric inpatients and the Department of Mental Retardation licenses homes for its population (Walker, 1979). It appears that these homes are analogous to adult foster homes.

Roy (1979) reports that Delaware's Department of Health and Social Services licenses "Rest" or "Family Care" homes for three or fewer residents and "Residential Homes" for four or more. However, it is doubtful if the latter category could be considered as analogous to adult foster homes as the manager must be a "Licensed Administrator."

Kentucky's Bureau of Health Services licenses "Family Care Homes" for two to three residents (Kentucky, 1977, p. 1).

The Michigan Department of Social Services licenses three categories of "Adult Foster Care Facilities," but the one corresponding to adult foster homes is "Family Homes" for one to six residents (Michigan, 1977, p. 1).

In Montana the state Social Services Bureau has final licensure authority for "Adult Foster Family Care Homes" for one to three residents (Montana, 1976, p. 1).

The New Mexico Health and Social Services department licenses

Table 5–1. State Regulation of Adult Foster Home Programs

Licensed N = 12	Certified N = 6	Mixed N = 17	No Official Programs N = 9	Undetermined N = 9
Alaska	Iowa	Colorado	Arizona	Alabama
California	Nebraska	Florida	Arkansas	D.C.*
Connecticut	Nevada	Georgia	Idaho	Hawaii
Delaware	New Hampshire	Maine	Indiana	Illinois
Kentucky	New York	Maryland	Kansas	Louisiana
Michigan	Pennsylvania	Minnesota	Massachusetts	Missouri
Montana		New Jersey	Mississippi	North Dakota
North Carolina		Oregon	Oklahoma	Puerto Rico*
New Mexico		Rhode Island	Wyoming	Texas
Ohio		South Dakota		
South Carolina		Utah		
Tennessee		Vermont		
		Veterans Admin.*		
		Virginia		
		Washington		
		West Virginia		
		Wisconsin		

*Non-States

"Adult Residential Shelter Care Homes" for 3–15 residents (New Mexico, n.d., p. 1).

The North Carolina Division of Facility Services, Department of Human Resources, licenses "Family Care Homes" for two to five residents (North Carolina, 1977a, p.1). The same agency also licenses "Homes for the Aged and Infirm" for 6 or more residents but the large size of many of these (often over 20 residents) and the fact that some are managed by corporations precludes them from inclusion as adult foster homes (North Carolina, 1977b, pp. 3–5). Also the same facility licenses "Group Homes for Developmentally Disabled Adults" for two to nine residents. However, managers are hired by nonprofit boards to live in and manage these homes (North Carolina, 1978, pp. 9–10). Thus, these homes would not qualify as adult foster homes by the criteria used in this book, namely that the homes must be privately owned and managed by the owners.

In Ohio, licensure of adult foster care facilities by the Department of Public Welfare began in January 1980. The category that seems most analogous to adult foster homes is "adult family homes" for up to five residents (Ohio, n.d.). The Ohio Division of Mental Health/Mental Retardation is responsible for the licensure of four types of residential facilities (Ohio, 1979a, pp. 2–4). Of these four types, the type "B" facility seems most analogous to adult foster homes as it serves up to five residents and is a family type home. Cashaw (1979) reports that the facility operators, apparently in all four types of facilities, have the option of keeping either children, adolescents, or adults. "Family Homes" for the developmentally disabled are licensed for up to eight residents (Ohio, 1979b, p. 2). Though licensure of adult foster care facilities in Ohio is relatively new, that state seems to be making substantial progress in this area.

Garrett (1979) indicates that the South Carolina Department of Mental Health is mandated to license "Community Care Homes." These average eight residents per home and appear analogous to adult foster homes.

Tennessee (Headrick, 1980) reports that state's licensure act went into effect in 1979. That state's Department of Mental Health/Retardation licenses adult foster care facilities (Watson, 1979). Moreover, the state also licenses "Residential Homes for the Aged" for up to 15 residents (Tennessee, n.d., p. 1).

In summary, it can be observed that licensing authority varies considerably between the states with licensed programs. Now, let us turn our attention to the certified adult foster home programs.

CERTIFIED PROGRAMS

In Iowa the Department of Social Services certifies "Family Life Homes" for up to two residents (Turner, 1979). The certifying agency for Nebraska's "Adult Foster Home" program is the Department of Public Welfare and the capacity is for up to four residents (Nebraska, n.d., p. 2). Nevada's State Welfare Division certifies "Adult Family Care Homes" for one to three residents (Fish, 1980).

The New Hampshire Division of Welfare certifies "Family Shared Homes" for up to three residents. Moreover, the state is considering sharing certification responsibility with the Public Health Department (Richards, 1979).

In New York, the Department of Mental Hygiene certifies "Family Care Homes" for up to 10 residents (New York, 1977, p. 1). Furthermore, Sherman and Newman (1977) indicate that New York sponsors a second adult foster home program under the state Board of Social Welfare/Department of Social Services with the title "Foster Family Care for Adults" (p. 515). Homes keeping only one resident are not certified by the state, but homes serving two to four residents are certified by the State Department of Social Services (Hammer, 1980). Moreover, Hammer indicates that the one-resident homes are called "One-Guest Foster Care Homes" and the homes for two to four residents are termed "Family Type Home for Adults."

Pennsylvania's Department of Welfare certifies "Domiciary Care Homes" for one to three residents (Kinsinger, 1979).

As in states with licensed programs, states with certified programs vary considerably as to the certifying authority. Now, let us turn our attention to those states which appear to have an admixture of regulations for adult foster homes.

MIXED REGULATION

McCurdy (1980) reports that in Colorado, "The Certification of Participation is the final document of approval. The state issues no licenses or certificates." Thus, it appears that Colorado has a semiformalized regulatory system for its adult foster homes.

According to Palmer (1979), Florida's Department of Health and Rehabilitative Services is statutorily required to license "Congregate Care Facilities" for four or more residents. However, that agency only "approves" adult foster homes (Palmer, 1979). Moreover, Palmer reports that the Developmental Services Division certifies homes for the mentally retarded. However, another reference indicates homes for the mentally retarded are licensed for up to three residents (Florida, n.d., Chapter 10–F, p. 16).

Issuing "permits," Georgia's counties are the final authority for regulating "Personal Care Homes" (Clifford, 1980). Clifford considers permit as synonymous with license. Maine has an "Adult Foster Home" program for up to two residents; these are not licensed. However, "Boarding Homes" for three to six residents are licensed (Fuller, 1979). Folkemer (1979) reports that Maryland has " . . . no statewide foster care program . . . local Departments of Social Service in some subdivisions operate adult foster care programs." It is not clear whether the departments of social services actually operate the homes or whether they supervise and approve them. Also the status of this approval is undetermined.

Lindren (1980) reports that Minnesota currently does not license adult foster homes. However, the counties are presently responsible for "regulating and controlling" them. Work, however, is in progress, according to Lindren, under Department of Public Welfare Rule 51 which will license and set program standards at the state level under the authority of the State Department of Public Welfare.

In New Jersey the "Sheltered Care Boarding Homes" program could probably be considered analogous to adult foster homes. Contingent upon local regulations, some of these are licensed and some are not. However, it is anticipated that New Jersey will institute a uniform licensure procedure in the near future (Borland, 1980). Also, Kott (1979) reports that it was expected that the Division of Mental Retardation would license the homes under its jurisdiction in the near future.

Oregon's Department of Human Resources certifies homes for up to five residents (Oregon, Administrative Rules, Chapter 461, 1979, p. 137) and the same organization licenses homes for six or more residents (Oregon, Administrative Rules, Chapter 410, p. 5).

Regulating "Community Residences" in Rhode Island is the responsibility of the Department of Mental Health/Mental Retardation. However, licensure in Rhode Island appears to be unique in that the homes are regulated by "problem" area, i.e., alcohol or drug abuse, mental illness, or mental retardation. Most of these programs are certified (Cate, 1979). However, another source indicates that the state does not have statutory responsibility for facilities specifically designated for the mentally disabled and mentally retarded (DiCenso, 1979).

South Dakota has an "Adult Foster Home" program. Each home must be "approved" by the Department of Social Services and can keep up to four residents (South Dakota, Chapter 67:42:02, n.d., pp. 1–2). Utah's Adult Foster Homes are "licensed and approved" through local district offices of the Department of Social Services (Nelsen, 1979). However, Long (1979) indicates that Utah has ". . . no statutory requirements for the licensure of residential facilities for adults." Furthermore, Long reports that "certificates" are issued to "approved" homes.

Surles (1980) reports that Vermont's Department of Mental Health licenses homes for three or more adults, but homes for two or less are not licensed. In Vermont both categories are called "Community Care Homes." The VA does not have licensing authority with its adult foster home program. However, the VA does use homes licensed by states when such is required by the state (Engquist, 1979). In Virginia, the Department of Welfare licenses "Homes for Adults" which keep four or more residents but does not license those with fewer residents (Abell, 1979).

Zinnikas (1979) reports that Washington's 37 county service offices, State Department of Health and Social Services, licenses adult foster homes. Another reference is to two categories of homes, i.e., homes for "Developmentally Disabled Adults" and "Adults in Need of Protection" (Washington, 1978, p. 1). West Virginia's Department of Health licenses "Personal Care Homes" which keep over six residents and are predominantly for the elderly (Bays, 1979). However, the program most similar to adult foster homes, called "Adult Family Care Homes," are not licensed in West Virginia; these can house up to three residents (Ginsberg, 1979).

Albright (1978) reports that Wisconsin was developing a licensing procedure. However, Lizon (1979) indicates that Wisconsin has no statutory requirements for licensing adult foster homes. However, the counties' Departments of Social Services certify homes serving up to two residents.

In summary, the states listed in this section do indeed appear to have an admixture of programs, some certified or licensed and some not. In general, it appears that the states in this section do not have as uniform a regulatory procedure as those mentioned earlier. We will now switch to those states which were determined to not have a formalized adult foster home program.

No Official Programs

Gersten (1980) reports that Arizona does not have an adult foster home program which can be identified specifically as serving the mentally disabled. However, the state does have 56 "Supervisory Care Homes," licensed by the State Department of Health Services. Due to the size of these homes (average over 30 residents), they could not be considered analogous to adult foster homes by the criteria established so far. Moore (1979) reports, however, that the majority of residents in these homes are elderly and mentally disabled. Miller (1979) indicates that Arkansas is assessing its "Boarding Home" situation and expects to become involved in licensure or certification by 1981. Miller does indicate that the state does license group homes for the mentally retarded.

Idaho does not have licensure laws for adult foster homes (Fowler, 1979). Moreover, it would appear that the state does not have an adult foster home program that can be identified as such. Likewise, Indiana has no licensure law or identifiable program (Heighway, 1979). Also, according to Morrissey (1979), Kansas does not license adult foster homes but plans to begin such a program in the 1980s.

Lawry (1979) reports that Massachusetts has no general procedure for licensing adult foster homes. Sanna (1980) confirms this. Some pilot and exploratory work, however, is apparently proceeding. Of interest is the class-action suit of 1976. The suit was instituted on behalf of present and future patients of Northampton State Hospital. The suit charged that the patients' rights were being violated because they were being deprived of the "least restrictive" type of care (Massachusetts, 1976 p. 3).

The community residential facilities for developmentally disabled adults in Mississippi would not appear to be analogous to adult foster homes; that is, because they are group homes and supervised apartment living situations (Larsen, 1980). Hartwick (1979) reports that Oklahoma licenses 59 "Room and Board" homes containing a total of 1,296 beds. Thus, it would appear that the average number of residents per home would rule this program out as not meeting the criteria of adult foster homes.

Kellow (1979) states that Wyoming does not license adult foster homes. Moreover, a review of that state's *Medical Facilities Directory* does not reveal any homes resembling adult foster homes. However, apparently the state has an unofficial program, as Noë (1979) indicates that Wyoming uses adult foster homes as transitional facilities in some instances.

In summary, because the states in this section have no official, discernible adult foster home programs does not mean that they do not exist in unofficial or semiofficial form. Finally, let us turn our attention to the states in which the status of adult foster home programs are undetermined.

UNDETERMINED

Vaughn (1979) reports that Alabama has 60 adult foster homes with 264 residents who are mentally disabled. However, the status of licensure is undetermined. The District of Columbia has licensed "Health Care Facilities" (Kemp, 1979). Moreover, Barquin (1979) indicates that the District of Columbia has 14 licensed homes for a "mixed group," apparently the mentally disabled, mentally retarded, and elderly. However, the exact status of the adult foster home program is undetermined due to a dearth of information.

Hawaii has an adult foster home program for former psychiatric inpatients, i.e., 475 homes with 2,153 beds (Inouye, 1979). Schuler and Kamakawiwoole (1979) indicate that the Office of Aging supervises 244 adult foster homes with 988 beds. The status of licensure in both instances is undetermined.

Rose (1980) reports that Illinois is just beginning an adult foster home program. For the mentally and developmentally disabled, that state had only one home and one resident as of January 1980.

Steinhauer (1978) reports that Illinois had a small adult foster care program in the state; these appear to be unlicensed.

From Sewell's (1980) observations, it would appear that Louisiana does not have an official adult foster care program. However, Fuller (1980) records that the Pinecrest State School for the Mentally Retarded has had what appears to resemble an adult foster home program since 1974. Moreover, Fuller indicates that the program has recently become a permanent part of the Office of Mental Retardation. The status of licensure, however, is undetermined.

The absence of data from Missouri prohibits any conclusions about adult foster care in that state. Hartze (1980) reports that North Dakota's adult foster homes are "controlled by the county Social Service Boards." However, whether this includes licensure is unclear.

Jiménez-Colon (1979) reports that in Puerto Rico the Department of Social Services is mandated to provide adult foster home services. However, another reference refers only to regulations for licensing facilities for the aged, including institutions (Puerto Rico, 1979, p. 1). The status of other possible adult foster homes in Puerto Rico is, therefore, undetermined.

The interpretation of information from Texas likewise led to a determination to categorize that state's adult foster home program as undetermined. Bernstein (1979) reports that the Department of Human Resources licenses adult foster homes keeping up to three residents. However, Orton (1979) indicates that "Foster Family Homes" are certified by the Department of Human Resources. However, Orton further indicated that there is no state statute regulating "adult family homes" which are only authorized to keep up to three residents. Finally, Orton reported that several state agencies "regulate" the various types of other residential facilities. Thus, it appears that Texas has a conglomeration of facilities for the three groups under study, e.g., Donnelson (1979) indicates that the State Health Department licenses "Personal Care Homes," following a complaint, for keeping up to 15 residents. Based upon contradictory information, therefore, Texas' adult foster home program was included in the undetermined category.

This concludes this section of Chapter 5. The last part of the chapter gives the number of homes and residents and categories according to disability, as reported by the states.

REGIONAL STATISTICS

As previously mentioned, the mid-1979 and December 1979 surveys requested data from all of the states, the District of Columbia, and Puerto Rico. Data were also requested from the Veterans Administration Central Office in Washington, D.C. on the VA's overall foster home program in the United States. In the December 1979 survey, the number of homes in each state was requested. Also, the number of residents in each state was requested by category, i.e., mentally disabled, mentally retarded, and elderly. The state agencies were also asked to provide other information, most of which will be provided in Chapters 7–10.

The letters going to the states were form letters, i.e., they were focused rather generally and used the term "adult foster homes." The use of this generic term largely left the interpretation of the term open to the respondent. However, since there was considerable variation in responses, the final interpretation of the data rests with me. As Morrissey (1967) found, collecting and analyzing data from the states is no mean task, due essentially to the fact that there is no uniform definition on adult foster care. Thus, statistics are frequently subsumed under other categories, e.g., community care facilities. Also, organizations for standardizing statistics are practically nil on the national level and in the states. Steinhauer (1978) succinctly delineates part of the problem when she states:

> . . . adult foster care is an existing national occurrence . . . [but] it presents the paradox of being relatively invisible. There is at present no way to document the incidence or prevalence of foster care. . . . Many informal structures have evolved without a systematic program design . . . almost all states have some informal or formal arrangement. . . . The tracking for accountability purposes required of other services is not demanded and hence, no count of individual utilization has been recorded. (pp. 5–6)

The preceding observations notwithstanding, data will be summarized and presented as reported by the states. Readers should bear in mind that numerous states which provided data for the first part of this chapter did not provide data for this section and vice versa. Moreover, reports from some states frankly acknowledged that the data were not

available, or were in the process of being collected. A few states referred me to districts or counties, but these were generally not requested
due to the nature of the surveys, which were designed to secure
statewide data from centralized state offices. Readers, therefore,
should keep these considerations in mind. That is, there are countless
variables involved. Finally, the data reported in this section is just
that—reported data. However, these data should be fairly representative of adult foster home programs in the United States, in my opinion.

For this section, the states will be categorized by region, depending
to some extent on the number of states providing requested data.
Another variable involved in this decision was to assist the readers in
conceptualizing how different regions responded to the surveys and
the variation of programs between regions. The largest number of
states reporting data were from the East. Therefore, data are reported
separately from the Northeast and Southeast. The second largest number of states reporting data were from the West and the smallest
number reporting data were from the Midwest. The categorization of
states by regions is more for convenience in reporting data, but generally tries to follow established geographical boundaries. Therefore, no
deliberate attempt has been made to slight the regional pride of any
state. With the above considerations in mind, we will now proceed to
report data from the Northeast.

Northeast

Connecticut (Walker, 1979) reports that the state has 135 facilities,
primarily for the aged. These facilities include two categories. One of
these, homes for the aged, appears to be beyond the scope of this book.
"Community Care Homes" is the other category which seems analogous to adult foster homes. There appear to be two categories of these,
one for the mentally disabled and one for the mentally retarded.
Stevens (1980), moreover, reports that the state has 74 homes and 163
residents living in homes under the auspices of the Department of
Mental Retardation.

Fuller (1979) indicates that Maine has three categories of homes
for adults. The category "Adult Foster Homes" is for up to two residents and "Boarding Homes" is for over six residents. By the definitions of this book, many of the latter would not qualify as adult foster
homes as many appear to have over 20 residents and the capacity of the

largest is 88. Both categories of homes have the mentally disabled and aged.

Massachusetts (Lawry, 1979) communicates that there are approximately 30 residents in adult foster care and the majority of these were over age 60. According to Proctor (1979), New Hampshire has 10 homes serving the mentally disabled and mentally retarded. About 100 of the residents are former psychiatric inpatients and about 16 are classified as mentally retarded.

Statistics reported from New Jersey indicate that the state has over 750 "Boarding Home" facilities, serving about 1,900 residents with histories of emotional problems (Borland, 1980). Furthermore, Borland estimates that the state has up to 1500 boarding homes with as many as 3,700 "former mental health clients." Zdanowicz (1980) writes that New Jersey's Division of Mental Retardation has established 233 "family care homes" which serve 634 mentally retarded adults.

Kaplan (1979) delineates that New York State's Office of Mental Health has certified 960 "family care homes" for 3,085 residents. Half of these are estimated to be over 65. Furthermore, Hammer (1980) estimates that New York's State Department of Social Services had certified about 963 "family type" homes for two to four residents with a total capacity for 2,908. Moreover, there are an additional 614 "one-guest family care homes." Hammer, furthermore, indicates that the majority of the homes under the jurisdiction of the State Department of Social Services are located in New York City.

Data from Rhode Island indicate that the state is responsible for providing residential facilities for the mentally and developmentally disabled (Cate, 1979). Another source indicates that Rhode Island has 16 group homes, or "Community Residences," serving a total of 158 mentally retarded residents (Zanella, 1980). By their size, these homes would seem to fit the category of adult foster homes, but this cannot be stated as fact.

Surles (1980) describes Vermont's program which has 155 licensed "Community Care Homes." These keep over two residents each, but the maximum capacity is undetermined. Thus, it is possible that some are too large to be categorized as adult foster homes. Homes for less than two residents are not licensed. In the 155 licensed homes, there are an estimated 600 former psychiatric inpatients.

This concludes the section on adult foster home programs as reported from the Northeast. Readers will, no doubt, notice that the data tend to vary from state to state. Of particular interest is the fact that the state with the oldest established program in the United States, Massachusetts, now has a very small semiofficial program. We will now shift our attention to data as reported by the states in the Southeast.

Southeast

Alabama (Vaughn, 1979) communicates that the state has 60 adult foster homes for the mentally ill for a total of 264 residents. Cain (1980) reports that Delaware has 350 homes which are open to the aged and these homes have 210 residents. Barquin (1979) states that the District of Columbia has 400 adult foster homes, only 14 of which are licensed for "mixed groups," of which a large percentage appear to be elderly. The average size of homes corresponding to adult foster homes would be for four to six residents. Furthermore, the District of Columbia is establishing a Central Referral Bureau to assist in monitoring the program, home finding, and home placement (Steinhauer, 1978). Thus, it appears that the District of Columbia is an innovator for the country in establishing such a bureau. It seems that more such practices are needed by the states and nationally to help standardize communication, record keeping, and reporting.

The state of Florida (Palmer, 1979) indicates that the state has an adult foster home program for three or fewer residents per home. Most of the residents appear to be former psychiatric inpatients. Clifford (1979) explains that Georgia has approximately 200 adult foster homes for about 375 residents who are former psychiatric inpatients. Clifford also states that Georgia has about 80 homes for the mentally retarded with a total of 193 residents.

Folkemer (1979) states that five of Maryland's counties had a total of 297 in adult foster care in 1978. Of these, 116 were "non-aged" and 181 were over 65. The remaining counties do not appear to have programs.

From North Carolina, Parker and Pettee (1979) report that the state has 896 "foster care facilities" serving about 13,089 residents. Of this number, approximately 35% are reported as mentally retarded. However, by the delimitations established for this book, not all of these would qualify as adult foster homes. North Carolina's "Family Care Homes," however, would seem to qualify as such. Pettee (1979) indicates that the state has 626 residents in family care homes (licensed for two to five residents). These homes appear to have a mixture of mentally disabled and elderly. A recent survey, as reported by Pettee, indicates that there are 118 residents in "Group Homes for the Developmentally Disabled" (for two to nine residents). Finally, the data reported from the homes for the developmentally disabled were obtained from only 38% of this type of home in the state. The group of foster care facilities in North Carolina with the largest resident population are "Homes for the Aged and Infirm." These homes serve six or more residents. Since the maximum capacity for these homes is unknown, they were ruled out as being analogous to adult foster homes.

Garrett (1979) states that South Carolina has 109 "Adult Residential Care Facilities" with a bed capacity of 2,468. Due to the average capacity of these homes, it appears that they must be ruled out as being analogous to adult foster homes. However, South Carolina's 53 "Community Care Homes" would seem to qualify; these have a bed capacity for 448. Moreover, Garrett presents an approximation of the numbers of residents in both programs as: (1) former psychiatric inpatients, 928; (2) mentally retarded, 25; (3) elderly, 1,138. Elsewhere (Hall, 1979) reports that South Carolina has 70 "Community Care Homes" serving 800 former psychiatric inpatients. Thus, it would appear that most, if not all, of South Carolina's mentally retarded and elderly residents are not served by traditional adult foster homes.

Data from the VA are being reported in the Southeast section for convenience only, the primary reason being that the central office is located in Washington, D.C. However, the data reported are national in scope. Engquist (1979) communicates that recent surveys indicate the VA has 12,000–15,000 residents in adult foster homes. Of these, 94% have primary diagnoses of psychoses. However, 81% of these had primary diagnoses of functional psychoses, primarily schizophrenia. Engquist, moreover, reports the mean age of 57, and that 95–98% of the veterans in adult foster homes are estimated to be male. The VA is placing greater emphasis on adult foster care, including its use for general medical and surgical patients.

From West Virginia, data indicate that the state has licensed 27 "Personal Care Homes" for 705 residents. Again, the average number of residents in each home would seem to preclude this category as being analogous to adult foster homes. However, the state's 600 "Adult Family Homes" would seem to qualify. These may keep up to three residents per home and the reported total number of residents in these homes is given as 1,040 (Bays, 1979). Ginsberg (1979) reports that these homes are not licensed and that statewide statistics are being compiled on data such as that requested by my surveys.

This concludes the section on the Southeast. In this region of the country, there appears to be a trend toward having large residential-type facilities, many of which could not be considered as analogous to adult foster homes. Now, let us switch our attention to programs as reported from the Midwest.

Midwest

In all of the regions of the United States categorized in this book, the Midwest provided the greatest paucity of statistics. The states reporting statistics from that region will now be discussed.

Steinhauer (1978) indicates that Illinois has an adult foster care program but that the state has no uniform licensure regulations. Furthermore, Steinhauer states that in 1978 there were 340 residents in Illinois. In the Chicago area there were 113 residents in 90 homes with the majority being in the 60–90-year age range. Furthermore, Steinhauer indicates that the Department of Public Health is responsible for setting minimum standards for these homes. The syndicated columnist, Jack Anderson, reports (1978) that "psychiatric ghettos" are being created in Chicago as a consequence of the "purge" of psychiatric patients in that area. He indicates most of them are placed in "boarding homes" with little supervision. Rose (1980) states that the Illinois Department of Mental Health and Developmental Disabilities is just getting started in adult foster care, having but one resident and one home.

Iowa (Turner, 1979) communicates that the state has 91 residents in 77 certified "Family Life Homes," the program having begun there in 1976. Turner estimates that 40% of the residents are mentally retarded, 10% are mentally ill, and 50% are over age 65.

Zuckerberg (1980) indicates that Michigan has over 3,000 adult foster care facilities with "mixed" populations. Michigan, however, has three categories of adult foster care facilities under the umbrella term of "Adult Foster Care Facilities." Two of these categories would appear to be analogous to adult foster homes; these are: (1) "family homes" for up to 6 residents, (2) "group homes" for 6–20 residents. The third category, "congregate facilities" are for over 20 residents and, thus, beyond the scope of this book (Michigan, 1977, pp. 1–2). Steinhauer

(1978) reports that Michigan has one of the largest programs for residents for age 60, having about 6,000 placements. It should be noted, however, that a large percentage of these probably reside in "Homes for the Aged" which, on the average, are considered too large to be considered as adult foster homes.

Minnesota (Lindren, 1980) reports that the state has about 330 adult foster homes with about 660 residents. Presently, 13 counties in Minnesota have adult foster home programs. Diagnostically, these residents seem to be mixed groups.

Wisconsin (Lizon, 1979) reports that the county departments of social services had 859 adults in foster care in 1978 and that 121 of these were over 65. The age range was given as 46 to over 75. Furthermore, Lizon reports that 575 other adults were in foster care in 1978, apparently under the auspices of the Division of Mental Health and Developmental Disabilities of the State Department of Health and Social Services. In the latter category, 103 were mentally retarded and 11 residents were identified as 65 or older.

This now concludes the statistics, as reported from six states in the Midwest. From the information provided, as well as the sparse responses, it would appear that the Midwest is lagging behind the rest of the country in implementing adult foster care programs.

West

Eleven states from the West responded to the two surveys, providing some data which will now be presented. California (Harmon, 1980) reports that state has approximately 1,884 small homes, apparently all serving the three categories under consideration. Colorado (McCurdy, 1979) reports the state has 33 licensed adult foster homes for 139 residents. Of these residents, 118 are described as "disabled" and 21 are over age 60 (McCurdy, 1980).

Hawaii (Inouye, 1979) states that the State Department of Health is responsible for about 475 adult-foster-care-type homes with 2153 bed spaces. Approximately 1,040 former psychiatric inpatients reside in them. Schuler and Kamakawiwoole (1979) indicate that Hawaii has 244 residents and 988 beds under the jurisdiction of the Office on Aging. These are called "family care homes" which keep up to four residents. The majority of these residents are over age 60. There is another category under the Office of Aging, "residential homes," but the average size of them precludes their consideration as adult foster homes. Schuler and Kamakawiwoole further indicate that about 50% of the residents in both of these categories are former psychiatric inpatients; about 30–40 of the residents came to the homes from other hospitals or nursing homes, and about 10% came from their own homes. Furthermore, they report that the primary diagnoses of most of the elderly are: (1) hypertension, (2) cardiac problems, (3) chronic brain syndromes, (4) schizophrenia, (5) diabetes, (6) general arteriosclerosis, and (7) cerebrovascular accidents.

Sekora (1980) reports that Montana's Department of Social and Rehabilitation Services has 150 "Adult Foster Care Homes." In these homes are approximately 70 former psychiatric inpatients, 83 mentally retarded, and 105 elderly (Sekora, 1979). Bratka (1980) reports that Nebraska has 138 adult foster homes serving elderly and disabled adults. Nevada (Fish, 1980) reports that the state has two types of facilities which can be categorized as adult foster homes. One of these is "adult family care homes" for one to three residents. Of these, there are 10 homes certified for 27 beds. Occupying the beds were seven elderly, and further categorical data were not given. The other category of homes in Nevada is "adult group care facilities" for four or more residents, but their average size is too large for their inclusion as adult foster homes.

Garcia (1979) indicates that New Mexico has eight "boarding homes" in the Las Vegas area serving postpsychiatric inpatients. Oregon (Treleaven, 1980) reports that that state has 24 residential care facilities for 6 or more mentally ill, 105 homes for the aged serving about 240 residents, and 76 adult foster homes, serving from 1–5 residents, for a state total of about 200 residents. South Dakota reportedly has 401 residents in adult foster care, including 255 aged, 145 "disabled," and 1 blind (Schmit, 1979). Nelsen (1979) states that Utah's Department of Social Services is responsible for 51 adult foster homes. Further, Nelsen reports that 17 of the residents are elderly, 1 blind, 1 mentally retarded, and 1 alcohol related. The remainder are presumably former psychiatric inpatients.

Zinnikas (1979) indicates that Washington's Department of Health and Social Services is responsible for 181 licensed "adult foster homes" with a total of 267 residents. Of these residents, 177 are described as disabled, 66 as elderly, 19 as "General Assistance Unemployable," and 5 blind. Stern (1980) reports that Washington has 170 developmentally disabled residents living in 211 homes specifically for this category.

In concluding the section on the West, it appears that this section of the country is making progress in the implementation of adult foster home programs.

Conclusions

Writing this chapter has been a humbling experience in many ways. Perhaps the most difficult task has been what statistics to include under the term adult foster homes and which to exclude. No doubt, my categorization leaves room for refinement. While brief elaboration was made on some programs which seemed borderline as to whether they could be considered adult foster homes by the definition delineated in this book, some other borderline ones were possibly discarded. Generally, an effort was made to delimit the term adult foster homes to privately owned and operated homes serving up to 20 residents. However, many programs with homes serving over six were not discussed because they appeared to be corporations, or to be directly controlled by agencies, e.g., by boards. In some instances, agencies seem to hire employees for these types of homes. One gets the impression that many of these types of homes are group homes for the mentally retarded/developmentally disabled. However, it is obvious that many of these categories do reside in traditional adult foster homes and so do the elderly. However, with the elderly, there appears to be a growing trend toward using more large homes for the aged. By their huge size, on the average, they would not qualify as adult foster homes. The status of the so-called *welfare hotels* and *boarding homes* needs much more research. It seems quite feasible that, in many instances, these categories are inadequately supervised, licensed, and controlled. Moreover, the probability exists that many residents of such facilities are incorrectly reported as being residents of adult foster homes. For example, it seems feasible that some of the data reported in the past, including Morrissey (1967), included such data. At that time Morrissey reported Illinois had 2,016 residents in adult foster care in 1963. By 1978, however, Illinois was reported to have only 340 residents in adult foster homes (Steinhauer). On the other hand, the VA appears to have grown in the number of placement of 4,499 in 1964 (Morrissey) to

12,000–15,000 in 1979 (Engquist). Overall, when compared to the published literature in the field, it appears that the adult foster home program has grown considerably in the United States in the past decade. Privately, however, some line social workers and first-line supervisors are pessimistic about adult foster homes, feeling they are on their way out in favor of larger nonfamily-type homes. The conclusions from this chapter are that such is not the case. However, we must not lose sight of the fact that the survival rate for small private enterprises is small indeed. However, I remain optimistic that the adult foster home will continue to survive, as it has for several hundred years. The proliferation of licensure/certification in many state programs in the past decade would seem to indicate that the program is coming of age, at least, in the United States.

SIX CASE EXAMPLES

Six managers and residents from Kent County, Michigan, were interviewed for the purpose of giving more qualitative substance to this book. The largest city in Kent County is Grand Rapids, with a population of 186,000; the county's population was given as 430,000 (Grand Rapids Chamber of Commerce, 1980). Furniture manufacture is the primary industry in the area. However, there are numerous other types of industries and there are several institutions of higher education. The area is commonly known as former President Ford's home territory. An acquaintance of mine refers to the area as "The Bible Belt of the North." Ethnically, people of Dutch descent predominate, but most other ethnic groups are also represented.

Michigan has had an adult foster home program since 1942 and licensure since 1972. However, licensure was apparently not fully implemented until around 1975. Based upon these and other criteria, e.g., strong administrative leadership from both the state and Kent County Department of Social Service, it appears that Kent County's adult foster home program would have to be ranked high nationally. However, Sheerin and Sheerin (1977, p. 82) question the theoretical base upon which Michigan's program rests; that is, the concept of "normalization" which the authors charge lacks a sound empirical scientific base. The literature from a few other states also indicates that they also use the concept of normalization. However, I am inclined to agree with Sheerin and Sheerin's criticisms of the use of the concept in adult foster care, essentially since the field has a nationwide reputation of being custodially focused rather than rehabilitation oriented. Nevertheless, the concept certainly warrants further research.

Preliminary to doing the data collection for this chapter, permission to conduct the study was obtained from the State and Kent County Departments of Social Service. To work out the details, several conferences were held with the supervisor, Adult Community Placement Services in Kent County. Overall, the program is controlled by the Kent County Department of Social Services, including most of the ongoing case management services. In the future, however, it is expected that the community mental health agencies will assume more direct responsibility for their residents in placement, as one such agency now does for the developmentally disabled/mentally retarded (Thiele, 1980). Generally, these agencies contract for all of the beds in a particular home as also does the Veterans Administration, which provides its own social services. Thiele (1979) indicates that about 40% of the county's adult foster care population consists of the mentally ill, 40% mentally retarded, and 20% elderly or physically disabled. Stahl (1979) reports that the state has about 3,500 adult foster care facilities for about 18,000 residents and that Kent County has about 152 homes for 950 residents. Of these, about 250 are either private residents or others who do not want social services (Thiele, 1980). It should be noted that the state has some homes with over 20 residents; these are not considered adult foster homes for purposes of this study. Statewide, there are about 2,220 "family"-type homes (for up to six residents) for a total of 8,497 beds. Also, there are about 794 "group" homes for 9,488 beds (Statewide Home Care Association, Inc., *Newsletter*, 1979, p. 10). Thus, the average number of residents in these group homes would appear to be 10.7. Both family and group homes will be utilized in this chapter.

Selecting respondents for this study was left with the Kent County Department of Social Services. However, it was requested that respondents be reasonably representative of the county's manager and resident populations, and that the three disability categories be represented, approximately a quota sample of each category in proportion to their actual percentages. Moreover, it was requested that all respondents be mentally and physically capable of participating, as ascertained by the departmental staff, and that the line social worker explain the project and obtain written informed consent. All of these procedures were accomplished by the department, except that in two cases I obtained the written informed consent. The supervisor of the program furnished names, addresses, and telephone numbers of all respondents and, subsequent to interviewing them, I arranged appointments by telephone. All data collection was performed in March and April 1980. One resident reported that she had a guardian and his written informed consent was later obtained. Other than the information necessary to contact residents, no other information on respondents was requested or obtained from the agency. Standardized interviewing schedules were used but most of the questions were open-ended and spontaneous remarks were usually recorded and many of them are utilized in this chapter.

A standardized "Agreement to Participate in Research" form was utilized with all respondents. On the form, respondents were assured that their names would not be used in the book and that the information furnished would be held in confidence, except that it would be published in a forthcoming book. For confidentiality and organizational purposes, the letters A–F are utilized in the following case examples. For example, manager A was the first manager interviewed and resident A was the resident in that home, while manager and resident F were the last ones interviewed. In no case does either of the above letters correspond to either the first letter of the first or last names of any respondents. The following information is assumed to be reliable. For this reason and for brevity, the material will often be reported as factual, notwithstanding the risks this entails and that social workers usually eschew such practices. Some responses were so similar that they will not be reported in the following cases, e.g., the managers all thought that most of them become managers out of a concern for others and for financial gain. Also for the sake of brevity, Social Security, Supplemental Security Income, and the Veterans Administration will be referred to respectively as SS, SSI, and VA.

MANAGER A

This is a 66-year-old, female, Caucasian, married manager of Irish and French descent whose religion is Roman Catholic and she considers herself religious. Prior to becoming a manager 17 years ago, she was a foster parent for children and a licensed practical nurse in a nursing home. For hobbies, she enjoys card playing, dancing, and picnicking. Legally blind and with a heart condition, her husband lives in the home but appears to take a passive role in its management. They have three children and two foster children, ranging from ages 29–46. One daughter and her children live in the A home.

Located in a rural setting, the home has eight rooms and two baths. Upon entering the home, I encountered a hostile dog with which I had to deal on my own. Once inside, however, this and the other five well-groomed dogs were quite friendly. The manager does not accept residents who dislike dogs. Inside, the home is comfortably furnished, especially the well-cushioned chairs. One bathroom is equipped with bars for infirm residents. To wash the elderly female residents' hair, the manager seats them on a stool in the tub. Parenthetically, she complained that she would prefer male residents "so I wouldn't have so much hair to wash and men are not as picky." She prefers keeping the elderly or mentally ill for fear that her grandchildren would "pick on" mentally retarded residents.

The A home is licensed for six residents but had only four assigned and three present, all of whom appeared to be over age 60. Briefly, I spoke with all three who seemed in good spirits. All live in a large room, which is well furnished, including a large color TV. The manager brings the meals to them on trays because she thinks they prefer eating by themselves. However, she frequently takes them shopping and consults with them about menus. No curfew is imposed as long as they are with relatives or friends. The manager screens the latter thoroughly. The residents have complete household freedom.

Manager A complained about the licensing regulations and referred to a large door she had to install for easy egress of infirm residents in emergencies. She became interested in being a manager because her father lived with them for 30 years and "had a mental breakdown the last 4 years of his life." The part she likes best about being a manager is being able to be with her husband; the part she dislikes most is finding part-time help. Also, she does not feel the $410.60 per month per resident is adequate.

As to her relationship with the social worker, she offered no complaints. The social worker is female and "is the first social worker who ever gave me her home telephone number." The social worker visits weekly and sometimes takes residents home with her for meals.

She believes the social worker has a college degree and appreciates the worker's sharing the residents' problems with her. However, she thinks that supervisory personnel should become familiar with the homes and managers. The manager was complimentary of community support services for residents, both formal and informal.

Basically, I would categorize this as a custodially oriented home, due primarily to the advancing ages of manager and residents. The manager appeared to be sincerely concerned about the residents' health and welfare. She appears to be in good health and to possess average intelligence.

RESIDENT A

Resident A is female, Caucasian, age 88, widowed, and of German, Scotch, English, and native American ancestry. Her parents were born in Canada. She is a member of the Reformed Church of Jesus Christ and considers herself religious. Although she is quite literate, she completed only the eighth grade. Often mistaken as a retired professional person, she attributes this to the fact that "I've read a great deal." She stated she has a daughter, age 56, a granddaughter, and great-granddaughter. A son is now deceased.

Having lived in the A home for 7 months, the resident likes it much better than the nursing home from which she came. In the A home she has more freedom and her relatives and friends visit more often than when she was in the nursing home. The most difficult problem she has experienced in the A home has been "learning to get along with my roommates." Like manager A, she was quite complimentary of her social worker for "she is a good conversationalist and cares for me as a person." She said manager A encourages residents to vote, visit friends and relatives, and to have them visit residents. Her biggest complaint was that income from SS and SSI is inadequate.

For her age, this resident is remarkably alert, intelligent, has excellent hearing, and seemed in good mental health. Although ambulating slowly, she does so on her own. Her eyesight is failing but she hopes to ameliorate this with new glasses and to resume reading and crocheting. When asked if there were anything else she wanted to say she commented, "I like to encourage those around me" and politely disagreed with me when I commented on this quality being a mark of leadership.

Without benefit of her background history, I think this lady has lived a productive life and that her problems are primarily those of the aging process with its concomitant physical and social problems.

MANAGER B

This is a 30-year-old, Caucasian female, married, Roman Catholic, who considers herself religious. Her ethnicity is Spanish and Scotch; her husband is Czechoslovakian and Polish. They are childless. Manager B has brunette hair and is physically attractive, despite being slightly overweight. She graduated from high school and her brother is an optometrist; her intelligence is estimated to be in the bright normal range.

Manager B and her husband have two adjacent adult foster homes. In the interview, we focused on the home where resident B lives. This home is licensed for 12 residents. Presently, it is filled, having 11 mentally ill residents and 1 alcoholic resident, age 52. All residents in the B home are male, and the ones with histories of mental illness are all in their 20s and 30s. Her husband has an associate degree in business administration and previously worked in nursing home administration. Apparently, they became disillusioned with nursing homes, the elderly, or both, and decided to shift their efforts toward younger residents. Manager B enjoys working with people but finds the job restricting, not to mention being physically and emotionally draining. Moreover, she believes managers are inadequately compensated for their services.

As for the assigned social worker, the manager believes she has a college degree. The worker is female, black, and visits the home one to two times weekly. Some of the residents question the worker about her race, but she handles the questions professionally and relates well to both residents and manager. Sometimes the social worker eats with the residents in the home and sometimes the residents invite her out to eat. Manager B thinks managers need more in-service training and complained because community activity programs for residents have been curtailed recently. Also, she thinks local zoning requirements are too restrictive. Once she and her husband were denied licensure of another home in another part of the city, ostensibly because they refused to build a 6-foot high fence around the house and to plant trees close together, near the fence, so as to hide residents from public view.

Manager B encourages residents to visit friends and relatives but there is little interaction between residents and neighbors because the latter "are afraid" of the former.

Due primarily to this manager's "young" orientation, I would categorize this home as being a transitional rather than a custodial home. Thus, the B home could be considered atypical since the literature review from Chapter 2 generally categorizes adult foster homes as custodially focused.

RESIDENT B

Resident B is a 22-year-old, single, male, Caucasian whose religion is Christian Reform, although he denies being religious. His father's parents are from the Netherlands; the ethnicity of his mother is unknown as she was reared in an orphanage. That he completed only the ninth grade notwithstanding, he appears to have normal to bright normal intelligence and aspires to complete the high school equivalency examination. When informed that the researcher has a high school equivalency certificate and later earned a Ph.D. degree, he seemed positively impressed. Requesting the publisher's address, he plans to buy a copy of this book.

This resident has been in and out of institutions since age 16. He has been in the B home for 3 years, with part of this time being with previous managers who lost their license; he compared them quite unfavorably with present managers. Compared to living with parents or institutional living, he much prefers an adult foster home because it allows more freedom. Another positive experience he has had in the home was learning that he likes mentally retarded people. In trying to help them, he feels better about himself. Although he has a valid drivers license, he does not own a motor vehicle.

Resident B is employed as a custodian in a local hospital where his net pay is $260 every 2 weeks. Soon, he plans to move to an independent living environment, ostensibly for more privacy. However, by being employed and living independently, he expects to lose about one-half of his SSI income. Like manager B, this resident is quite complimentary of the social worker and she supports him in his aspirations for independent living.

Although he grew up in this city, he has lost contact with former friends but visits parents twice monthly. He thinks these homes serve a very useful purpose for people leaving institutions because adult foster homes "keep them from having to live in dumpy apartments."

Resident B is of average height and moderately obese. His finger nails are short, apparently bitten. His affect is appropriate and he dislikes the term *mentally ill,* preferring the term *emotionally disturbed* instead. For his emotional disturbance he takes medication. Tentatively, a diagnostic impression of schizoaffective schizophrenia is proffered. The prognosis for independent living would appear to be reasonably good, provided that he continues to receive professional supportive services and chemotherapy for some time.

MANAGERS C

This was the only instance in which a husband-wife manager team was interviewed for this study. In the joint interview, some competitiveness between them was observed. Mrs. C seemed somewhat more self-confident, possibly partially attributable to her being better educated and a few years Mr. C's senior. She is aged 27 and has a college degree in special education; he is 24 and a high school graduate. Both are Caucasian, Roman Catholic, and childless. Her ancestry is Dutch and his is basically English and Irish, but he also claims some German, French, and native American heritage. Mrs. C enjoys piano playing, skiing, and bicycling, while Mr. C participates in boxing, tennis, and racquet ball. She was born fourth of seven siblings; he was the last of seven. Both were reared in an urban setting.

The C home is about 65 years old and appears to be in a middle- to lower middle-class neighborhood, located adjacent to a public park and close to several other adult foster homes. The managers succeeded in persuading zoning officials to let them open the home 5 months previously by successfully utilizing the argument that they were restoring an historical landmark. Indeed, several improvements have been made and are still in progress. The home is licensed for six but currently they have only four male residents. Of these, they categorized two as mentally retarded and one each as mentally ill and elderly. The managers are preparing a room with a large water bed for two female residents. The home has nine rooms and three baths. There are two residents per room. The managers' bedroom is off limits for residents.

They expressed no preference as to disability category because "they are all neat people."

Managers C shop with residents and plan to take them on vacation this summer. Admitting that managing is confining, they consider the benefits greater. Both learned a great deal about managing from Mr. C's older sister who has had considerable experience in managing an adult foster home.

The social worker, a male, visits the home one to two times monthly. They think that he does not give them adequate background information on residents and that he is insufficiently assertive about linking residents with community activity programs. Also, they were critical of the "licensing people" about being overly concerned with the physical environment and insufficiently concerned with residents and managers as people. The managers encourage residents to participate in community recreational facilities, e.g., bowling, movies, swimming, and fishing. They said the residents have little contact with neighbors except for the C's immediate friends and relatives.

In summary, Mr. and Mrs. C appear to have normal to bright normal intelligence. They are a handsome couple who seem genuinely concerned about the health and welfare of their residents. They have a well-groomed dog. Tentatively, I would categorize this home as custodially oriented, due primarily to the type of residents they have. However, if desired, this could probably become a transitional home.

Resident C

Resident C is a 63-year-old, single, Caucasian, male with grayish balding hair who is about 5 feet 10 inches tall and slightly overweight. Managers C categorized resident C as "mildly retarded." The American Psychiatric Association (1968) categorized the IQ range for mild mental retardation as between 52–67. Resident C prints his signature and his first and last names run together in the process. He recognized George Washington's likeness on a dollar bill and the value of the bill. Also, he recognized the value of coins, but managers indicated that he has difficulty in counting money.

This resident is quite affectionate, greeting me with a partial embrace, shaking hands left-handed, and acting as if he had known me for many years. For example, he called me by my first name and acted as if he had known someone else like me in the past and that he was confusing the two of us. Resident C said he was in the "state home" for 64 years but managers reported he was in a state hospital for 40 years. Resident C had several photographs and wanted one of my identification cards with a photograph on it. However, he agreed to let me mail him a photograph, which was subsequently done.

Indicating that his religion is Lutheran, resident C could give only limited family background information, except that his father was a railroad engineer and left him a gold railroad pocket watch; this he proudly displayed. Resident C has a toy electric train in his room, pictures of old steam engines on the walls, and a book with photographs of old trains. He takes considerable pride in his toy train set.

While I was interviewing managers C, resident C would sometimes briefly interrupt as if he did not like to be excluded from conversation. Drying dishes nearby, he was quite noisy in the process. Managers attributed this to resident's being hearing-impaired which they attributed to having wax in his ears. The managers expressed some disgust, claiming the resident's physician refused to remove the wax because of resident's mental retardation. Thus, part of the communication problems experienced with this resident could have been attributable to his hearing impairment. He did have difficulty comprehending structured questions but was quite talkative when allowed to be spontaneous. Verbally, his enunciation left something to be desired in terms of quality.

In summary, resident C is an affectionate, likable, moderately physically attractive man, who exhibited problems in interpersonal communications, due to apparent mental retardation and hearing problems. However, he seemed happy, was complimentary of managers C, and he enjoys interacting with people. Besides helping in the kitchen, he also enjoys yard work.

MANAGER D

This manager is female, Caucasian, recently divorced, age 47, a high school graduate, and a member of the United Holiness Church who considers herself religious. By the halting manner in which she answered the last question, she may have had some reservations or qualifications but she did not elaborate. She is about 5 feet 9 inches tall, moderately thin, has graying blackish hair, is physically attractive, and appeared to have average intelligence. Her husband's leaving her and the subsequent divorce appeared to still be troubling her. However, there was one indication that their marital problems had been long-standing. For example, 5 years previously she took in-service training to be a manager but postponed becoming one until after her husband's departure.

Mrs. D was born "in the middle" of four female siblings and was "rowdy" as a child. Her ethnicity is Irish and German. She had three sons ranging in age from 16–25. The youngest one comes home on weekends from a boarding school. She has at least one grandchild, a toddler, for whom she was caring upon my arrival.

This manager had been in business as a manager for only 5 months. The home is of contemporary design, located in a middle-class neighborhood and on the outskirts of an urban area. Of the six homes visited, this home was the most attractive. Licensed for five residents, the home had only one during my visit but she was expecting another 32-year-old female resident. As to the three categories, she would prefer keeping the mentally retarded but did not elaborate. The home has eight rooms, covered patio, spacious back lawn, and two and one-half baths. The primary room for four residents was converted from a garage. It is ground-level and a permanent part of the house. Another private room for one resident is upstairs. The manager and resident(s) dine together and manager seeks input from resident(s) on menu selection. The manager's desire to have an electronic device, which would warn her when a door is opened from the inside, could be indicative of overprotectiveness. She rationalized this need on the grounds that her aged mother-in-law walked away from an adult foster home last winter and froze to death.

Manager D finds the job to be confining and to frequently test her patience. For example, dealing with her current resident requires considerable tact because the resident gets upset if she talks too long on the telephone and becomes suspicious when manager is talking with someone else when they are outside of resident's hearing range. On the positive side, manager D said the job keeps her physically and mentally occupied. She wants a copy of this book.

As to the manager's relationship with the social worker, she would like more input from the social worker in terms of "her wisdom." Moreover, she believes the social worker has "some college" but the worker does not give her adequate information about community resources for residents. As a person, she likes the social worker "because she is warm and makes me feel comfortable." Mrs. D was critical of the licensing department "because it is too strict on some things and too lenient on others." For example, she was required to remove a piece of decorative plastic from a door frame and its removal stripped away some of the paint.

In summary, I would consider this as a custodial home, due primarily to the type of residents she apparently prefers. However, manager D seems capable of a more in-depth relationship with the social worker and may have the potential for becoming a transitionally oriented manager, if desired. Having gone through a recent divorce, she will undoubtedly have lingering emotional scars for some time to come.

RESIDENT D

Resident D is female, Caucasian, age 51, single, a member of the Christian Reform Church, and considers herself religious. Her ethnicity is Dutch and she completed the sixth grade. She had one daughter, given up for adoption in infancy, who would now be an adult. Resident D had plans to marry the child's father but they "fell through." Resident has a twin sister and a brother; both are considered mildly mentally retarded. Her sister visits her but her brother does not.

Throughout the interview she appeared rather guarded, so much so that consideration was given to the possibility that she may be mildly mentally retarded. The medication she takes, Prolixin (Fluphenazine hydrocloride) and Cogentin (Benztropine mesylate), point toward a diagnosis of schizophrenia, however, possibly paranoid type. Support to that impression is given by her being guarded and her apparent distrustfulness of others.

Resident D enjoys working with puzzles and other games, e.g., checkers. She was in a state hospital for many years and her income is from SSI which could indicate a poor work history. She considers her weekly spending allowance of $10 as inadequate. In the community she participates in sheltered work activities. She is of average height and slightly overweight. Resident is a plain-appearing person, both in dress and overall demeanor, appearing rather typical of many long-term hospitalized people with schizophrenia whom I have known. At this point, I would consider the prognosis for a more independent life style for her to be guarded.

MANAGER E

Overseeing and managing seven adult foster homes, this manager does not live in any of them. Nevertheless, a decision was made to interview him because of his request to be included in the sample and also to provide variety to the managers selected. The live-in manager, a woman in her 20s, was caring for a small child. She requested to be interviewed jointly with resident E. When informed that I desired to interview residents individually and that I would interview her jointly with owner E, if agreeable with him, she made no further request to be interviewed.

Owner-manager E is male, Caucasian, married, age 34, and has two female children aged 2 and 6. He has an M.A. degree in black history and previously taught history and government on secondary and college levels. A member of the Dutch Reform Church, he considers himself "very religious." His father, a retired minister, is of Dutch descent and his mother is of French Huguenot ancestry. Manager E has one sister, 11 years his senior. Besides being active in the church, he is a member of the local Christian School Board, the Republican Party, and the Statewide Home Care Association (an organization of adult foster home managers). Moreover, he is on call around the clock by use of an electronic beeper. His being continually on call sometimes irritates his wife but the children handle it very well. For hobbies, he enjoys playing with his children and tennis.

The home in question is in an urban neighborhood which is considered to be low middle class. Manager E categorized the neighborhood as "transient." Appearing to be 40–60 years old, the home is neat and well maintained but plainly furnished. Also, the inside paint and furniture are conservative in appearance. The home is licensed for 12 residents and has 12 rooms. Presently, it is full. Ten of the residents are considered mentally ill. Of these, six are male and four are female. Additionally, there is one mentally retarded female and one elderly male. The manager's preference is the mentally ill. He attributes his primary motivation for being a manager as that he enjoys working with people. The part he dislikes most about being a manager is having to settle disputes between residents. One of his seven homes has predominantly military veterans, whom he considers more pugnacious than other residents. With SS and VA benefits, some service-connected veterans receive around $1,000 monthly. He thinks they could afford to pay more than the standard monthly rate, established by the state at $410.60. Moreover, he added that SS recipients receive $52 monthly in spending money, while SSI recipients only receive $31 monthly. Manager E reported that the state requires that managers dispense medication. This policy sometimes conflicts with that of the VA which encourages veterans to be on self-medication whenever possible. About one-half of all residents manage their own money.

Manager E said the social worker only visits the home every 2–3 months, but that he visits her office about twice weekly. As a person, he likes the social worker but would like more input from her in terms of helping to link residents with community programs, claiming that this process often takes 6 months with mentally ill residents. Also he dislikes the fact that he cannot make direct referrals for community programs. Excluding the home which keeps veterans, where the VA social worker makes regular visits, some of his homes go as long as 5 months without a social worker visit. Furthermore, the manager thinks the city needs more programs for the mentally ill and that the Department of Social Services needs a more liberal policy about granting general assistance.

Manager E is of average to medium build, approaching 6 feet tall, and appeared to have bright normal to higher intelligence. On community resources, he is extremely knowledgeable and he appeared to be sincerely interested in residents' health and welfare.

Resident E

This is a 33-year-old, "almost 34," female, single, Caucasian, Roman Catholic, who does not consider herself very religious. Looking considerably younger than her stated age, she has red hair, wears expensive-looking, gold-rimmed glasses, slacks, blouse, and sweater. About 5 feet 1 inch tall, she did not appear to be overweight and was neat, physically attractive, and well groomed. She has not been married but had a daughter about 2 years ago who was subsequently adopted.

Resident E completed the ninth grade. Parenthetically, the manager said resident E is considered mildly mentally retarded, but he thinks her IQ would fall in a slightly higher range. It is possible that her good appearance and social habits are somewhat misleading. Affectively, she seemed appropriate but did appear somewhat naive and suggestible, e.g., not mentioning tiredness of the interview until I mentioned this possibility. After this, she complained considerably of tiredness. Several times she requested, and received, reassurance that her name would not be used in the book.

This resident had been in the E home for 2 months. She was in another adult foster home for about 2 years, and a group home, apparently for the mentally retarded, for sometime, plus two satellite housing living situations for awhile. Her chief complaint about manager E was that "He buys the cheapest food he can find, including Hamburger Helper." She expressed empathy for the live-in managers because they are a struggling young couple, under considerable stress, and she thinks their frustrations may sometimes be displaced onto residents.

As for her own family, resident E said she is of Irish-Dutch descent and has a married sister with three sons. She does not get along with her family "because I am the black sheep of the family; they don't understand me." For hobbies, she likes dancing, jogging, swimming, and socializing. Her income is from SS and SSI and she considers her $52 monthly spending money inadequate. Regarding the social worker, her complaints were similar to the manager's, i.e., inadequate home visiting and inadequate guidance with her personal problems. She considers her social worker to have a high school education. Resident E's goal is independent living but she doubts this is feasible "because I have been blackballed by too many of the agencies, they don't like my background." She participates in sheltered work activities at Goodwill Industries where she assembles items on a piecework basis.

In summary, resident E was spontaneous, verbal, and rather well socialized. Yet, she does have difficulty conceptualizing, especially in a structured interview situation. She is rather uninhibited in some ways, including criticizing the manager. Her IQ would probably fall within the borderline to mild mentally retarded category. At this time, I would not consider her prospects good for independent living.

Manager F

This is a female, married, black, manager of average height who appears slightly overweight. Her age is 58 and she is a member of the Baptist church where her husband is the minister; she considers herself "quite religious." In apparent reference to herself, she used the terms "missionary" and "evangelizing" several times. She had five sons and two daughters ranging in age from 20–40, but one son had died recently in a fire accident at age 36. One son, about age 20, answers the telephone much of the time and appears to do a great deal of the on-site managing, apparently because manager E works in a local garment industry as a "set-up machine operator."

Mrs. F was born in Mississippi but was reared in Chicago. She completed cosmotology school and operated her own shop for 3 years, after which she completed 3 years of college. Having written one book, she has another one in progress. Her interest in helping the elderly and disabled can be traced to age 7. At that time, her paternal grandmother was elderly and lost a leg. When a neighborhood boy told her grandmother that she should do everyone a favor by dying, Mrs. F felt deeply hurt.

Having opened the first adult foster home in another city in this state, the manager now has 17 years experience in this area. She enjoys the work and eats with the residents. The home is licensed for three but the home had only one resident when I was there. The manager's sociological views on the adverse influences of institutionalization were quite contemporary. For example, she believes that adult foster homes should be used more frequently to prevent psychiatric hospitalization. Also, she thinks that institutionalization contributes to homosexuality.

The house has six rooms and a washroom but the number of baths was not obtained. It is located in a middle- to low middle-class urban area, only a few blocks from home C, previously described. There was no number on the outside of the house, which was painted gray with red window frames. The inside was neat and clean, although plainly furnished. The manager desires to purchase the adjacent house for 6 residents and another home for 12–20 residents. She considers the $431 monthly she receives for the resident to be inadequate. Also she considers the $31 monthly which the resident receives to be inadequate. For the one resident, she spends about $2.01 per day on food purchases.

Manager F likes her social worker, a female, but would like for her to visit more frequently than she does, approximately once monthly. The worker visits more frequently upon request but has not given the manager her home telephone number. The manager enjoys attending the weekly "provider" meetings because these provide them with an outlet for their frustrations and expose them to different views. (In Michigan, the term *provider* is analogous to the term *manager*, as used in this book.) For a hobby, the manager enjoys "teaching the young and old the Bible and the word of God."

In summary, manager F appears to be in the bright normal intellectual range. Her religiosity may be culturally influenced or it could also serve partially as a rationale for her deep concern for humanity. Presently, this home appears to be more custodially focused but would appear to have some potential for becoming a transitional one, if desired.

RESIDENT F

This resident is female, Caucasian, single, age 56, and a Methodist who graduated from high school in 1975. Her father was of Irish and German descent and her mother was of Irish, German, Swedish, and Norwegian ancestry. Her mother died at age 25 when resident was 6 weeks old; her father died at age 74 of diabetes and cancer. One sister died at age 42 of cancer and one sister still survives, but resident has not seen her for 20 years. The resident has a 30-year-old divorced daughter; they see or telephone each other occasionally.

As a child, resident F had rickets. She was an inpatient in a state hospital for 6 months, 2 years, and 5 years, respectively. Resident worked in a factory for 25 years and in a laundry for several years. She has been in the F home for 2 years and likes it "all right" except that her "$1 spending money every day" is inadequate. Her income is from SS and SSI.

Since age 33, resident has had diabetes. Daily, she injects herself in the thigh with insulin. For her emotional problems, she takes Mellaril (thioridazine) and an unknown white pill. Without them, she said, "I'd be sick at my stomach and vomit and they help me to sleep." Based upon the history, given by resident, her moderately flat affect, and her slight tendency to rock while sitting, I would proffer a diagnostic suggestion of chronic undifferentiated schizophrenia. Resident is of average size and build, moderately physically attractive, and relates reasonably well in an interpersonal situation. She has more contact with more residents from other adult foster homes than the other residents interviewed. In the community, she is quite involved in therapeutic social activities. Her intelligence would seem to be within the average range and she feels generally positive about the social worker. As for the manager, the resident thinks that "she should get at least $500 a month for keeping me because I have special problems."

Summary

Due to several variables, caution must be exercised about generalizing from these findings. Some of these are small sample size, unknown procedures in sample selection, and the qualitative-exploratory nature of this study. Nevertheless, some patterns emerged which need further inquiry. The median ages of managers and residents are slightly lower than those mentioned in the literature. The fact that, of managers under age 40, two of the three were childless is interesting. Also interesting is that two managers, in their 50s and 60s, had a grown adult child in the home. Thus, the question of the nesting syndrome arises. Also interesting is that there was some variation reported in manager income for keeping residents. With one resident, there was a slight discrepancy in resident's spending money, as reported by manager and resident.

Some comparisons with other states seems indicated so as to compare the income managers receive in Michigan with these states. As a couple of managers in this survey reported, in Michigan managers normally receive $410.60 per resident, per month, or about $13.50 daily per resident. Nelsen (1979) reported that Utah's managers receive $6.50 per day, per resident, from SSI funds plus a "service fee" of unknown amount. Folkemer (1979) indicated that Maryland's managers receive $343 monthly for "general services" and $690 monthly for "special services." Colorado (McCurdy, 1979) reported that state's adult foster care program provides services to "Old Age Pension recipients 60 years of age and over" and no reference was made to SSI. However, these funds could be from SSI as McCurdy indicated that managers receive a supplement from state and local funds. For comparative purposes, Oregon (Treleaven, 1980) reports that the state's "group care home" facilities receive $213 monthly per resident "plus base funding." Moreover, the managers receive a salary of $12,800 annually. Other employees receive $3.10 per hour plus fringe benefits. Due to the managers' being salaried, therefore, these homes would not be considered analogous to adult foster homes.

Switching back to adult foster homes now, we find that apparently the federally administered programs of SS and SSI are often supplemented by other funds, including those from state and sometimes local sources, and apparently some special fundings under some other programs.

The managers in this sample appear to be better educated than those reported in the literature. The high religiosity of managers in this sample could be reflective of the "Bible Belt of the North" culture. Tests on these managers for authoritarianism might help to answer the lingering question as to whether managers, who are high on religiosity and low on education, are also high on authoritarianism (McCoin, 1977, 1979).

All three female residents, with apparently mentally ill/mentally retarded diagnoses, having conceived out-of-wedlock children posit questions for further inquiry. Also needing further inquiry is the possible therapeutic benefits of having dogs or other domestic animals in the homes. Could these animals serve residents with a nonthreatening outlet for some of their blocked affectual needs?

In this sample, there appears to be inconsistency in visiting patterns to the homes by social workers, not to mention giving managers their home telephone numbers. In my experience as a social worker with an adult foster home program, we were required to give managers our home telephone numbers so as to be on call in emergencies.

Finally, based upon my experience as a social worker with an adult foster home program and considerable research in this area, it appears that Kent County's adult foster home program would rank high nationally in terms of physical care provided for residents. Also, it appears that Michigan ranks high nationally in terms of licensure and financial remuneration provided for managers. However, there does appear to be room for improvement in social service delivery and possibly community resources in Kent County. More research is needed locally and nationally on the effects of environmental factors in the homes, including managers' personalities, and community attitudes toward residents, and how these variables impact on residents.

Chapter 7

RELEVANCY

Most of the material utilized in this chapter was obtained from the later 1979 survey, previously described in Chapter 5. Briefly, form letters were sent to the 50 state departments of (1) mental health, (2) mental retardation, and (3) elderly, and the same offices were also written in the District of Columbia and Puerto Rico. The agency heads were simply asked their opinion on the relevancy of adult foster care for the population served by that agency. A total of 21 states responded to the question of relevancy. Of these responses, 13 were from the East. Except for Tennessee, all of the other states in this category were Eastern seaboard states. For purposes of this chapter, all other states responding to the survey were considered Western, with only eight such states responding. Before the results of this survey are discussed further, however, brief references will be made to literature which is considered appropriate to the question of relevancy.

From the 1960s there can be little doubt that the rights movements accelerated the movement of many of the three categories under consideration, from institution to community. The right to treatment or discharge for civilly committed psychiatric patients, who were not considered dangerous to themselves or others, is one example (Brierland & Lemmon, 1977). Thus, the rights movements of the 1960s helped precipitate court cases on behalf of the three categories under consideration. This, in turn, influenced statutory law and administrative action toward the direction of the least restrictive form of care and treatment for the three categories under study. Moreover, Schrader and Elms (1972) indicate that isolating patients in custodial institutions deprives them of their right to interact with friends and relatives in their own communities. Cupaiuolo (1979) indicates that available research data indicate that community-based treatment is more effective than institutionalization. Whorley (1978) reports that the goals of community-based care for the mentally ill are twofold. That is, to help the patient move back into the mainstream of society, if possible. If not, the goal is to provide an "optimal" environment in the community, as opposed to an institution (p. 9). The principle upon which adult foster care is based is analogous to the legal principle of "least drastic means" (Miller, 1977, p. 278). Miller further explains that this principle provides a reasonable rationale for moving mental patients into adult foster homes where they can be encouraged to assume nonpatient roles. This same principle would also seem to be relevant for the institutionalized mentally retarded and elderly. However, Miller indicates that the least drastic means principle rests largely on the faith that the more normal the environment, the better. Also Miller indicates that the social work profession has long espoused this principle and that the courts are increasingly doing so. An example of the latter would be the class-action suit in Massachusetts to deinstitutionalize the mentally ill and mentally retarded (Massachusetts, "U.S. District Court, Civil Action #76-4423-F," p. 3). By inference, the concept of normalization, previously discussed in Chapter 3, would also appear to be a motivating principle behind the class-action suit in Massachusetts. Thus, the principles of least drastic means and normalization would seem to be analogous and to have some relevancy for adult foster care for the three categories under consideration.

From the authors cited so far in this chapter, considerable authoritative support can be mustered for adult foster care as a relevant means for facilitating deinstitutionalization. Now, let us proceed to explicate the information obtained from the late 1979 survey on the relevancy of adult foster care, as viewed by state administrative officials. Data from the East will be discussed first, followed by that from the West. In both instances the data are presented alphabetically by state.

EAST

Connecticut (Stevens, 1980) reports that adult foster care is relevant for mentally retarded adults, ostensibly because it has enabled numerous residents to remain outside institutions for up to 15 years. Cain (1980) indicates that adult foster care in Delaware is considered to be a viable alternative, as opposed to institutionalization, for the elderly because it enables them to "abandon" the "loneliness" of institutional living.

Kimber (1980) states that Florida's Developmental Services Program administrator and staff consider community placement for the mentally retarded to be preferable to institutional care. As a rationale, Kimber refers to recent court decisions and legislative acts. Georgia (Clifford, 1979) considers adult foster care to be relevant for the mentally ill/mentally retarded, provided that they are not seriously disabled and that they are desirous of community living. However, Clifford adds that the level of residents' integration into the community is contingent upon the managers' expertise.

Representing the mentally ill/developmentally disabled in New Hampshire, Proctor (1980) considers adult foster care to be " . . . a viable alternative to institutional care as long as the homes are rehabilitative in nature." Proctor also indicates that adult foster care would be more relevant if managers were better trained and paid so that standards could be raised so as to be more rehabilitation oriented, as opposed to custodially focused.

Commenting on behalf of the mentally ill in New Jersey, Borland (1980) thinks that the atmosphere of small adult foster homes provides a greater potential for interpersonal interaction than do larger homes or institutions. Zdanowicz (1980), representing the mentally retarded in New Jersey, considers adult foster homes to be an " . . . essential link in a continuum of alternate living arrangements."

North Carolina (Parker & Pettee, 1979) considers adult foster care relevant for the mentally retarded. However, they emphasize the use of small homes " . . . coupled with appropriate day activities and support services" to be " . . . the most viable alternative to institutions." Following the normalization principle for the mentally retarded, Pennsylvania officials consider adult foster care to be a positive alternative to institutionalization. That is, the normalization principle demands that mentally retarded citizens enjoy " . . . maximum integration . . . into

[the] societal mainstream" (Pennsylvania, Office of Mental Retardation, 1978, p. 1).

Addressing himself generally to the relevancy of adult foster homes for the mentally retarded in Rhode Island, Zanella (1980) considers the homes as providing suitable alternative to living in large public institutions. Representing the aging in South Carolina, Denny (1980) considers adult foster homes to be "invaluable for those who cannot maintain independent living." Hall (1979) feels "very positive" about the relevancy of adult foster homes for the mentally ill in South Carolina. Headrick (1980) also considers them to be relevant for the mentally ill in Tennessee because mental illness and long-term institutionalization have largely depleted their emotional and financial resources so as to preclude independent living.

A Vermont publication reports that recent federal court rulings in favor of the "least restrictive" form of care and treatment for the mentally ill make adult foster home placement more relevant. That is, the least restrictive principle indicates that inpatient hospitalization is to be avoided whenever possible because a hospital environment restricts the individual's decision-making abilities (Vermont, State Association for Mental Health, Inc., 1976, p. 1).

Payne (1980), reporting for the mentally retarded in Virginia, thinks that adult foster care is relevant to assist in deinstitutionalization because the residents are in a better position to learn "practice living skills" in the community.

This concludes the section on the relevancy of adult foster care for the Eastern states. Interesting is the fact that nine state officials (or publications) answered the question as to the relevancy of adult foster care for the mentally retarded, while only six answered the same question for the mentally ill; only two officials answered the question for the elderly. The responses, or lack of them, could be indicative of ambivalence toward the relevancy of adult foster care for the elderly. Since the relevancy of adult foster care is fairly well established for the mentally ill, the relatively large number of responses on behalf of the mentally retarded could indicate that adult foster care for this population is gaining wide acceptance. However, further research is needed in this area.

West

Harmon (1980) indicates that California considers the placement of the mentally retarded in "small family homes" to be relevant because this arrangement affords residents greater opportunities to partake of community activity programs than when they were institutionalized. Also, Harmon thinks that community activity programs are better tailored to meet individual needs. Thus, adult foster home placement, coupled with individualized community activity programs, are viewed as helpful for mentally retarded residents in California. That is, in helping them to become integrated into the community.

According to Schuler and Kamakawiwoole (1979), Hawaii considers adult foster homes to be relevant for the elderly because some residents have been successfully placed in them for 12–15 years. Moreover, they consider the "normalizing" atmosphere of the homes to be reinforcing of residents' self-esteem and feelings of independence, which they consider extremely important for the elderly.

Illinois (Rose, 1980) reports that adult foster care, for the developmentally disabled, is considered relevant for those residents who need minimal supervision. Reporting for the mentally ill, Lindren (1980) indicates that Minnesota considers adult foster homes relevant for this group because they are "cost effective alternatives" to institutionalization. However, Lindren considers them relevant only if the managers are adequately trained and supervised. Moreover she adds, sufficient community programs are also necessary for adult foster care to be successful.

Iwan (1979) discloses that Nebraska considers adult foster homes relevant for the mentally ill, provided that the managers can be trained to be "empathetic" in meeting the needs of residents. Also, Iwan considers adult foster homes to be a viable alternative to hotels and board and care homes because the former are better regulated, thereby tending to reduce the number of abuses. Furthermore, Nebraska considers adult foster home placement to be relevant for the three categories of disabled adults being considered in this book because the special needs of these groups can only be met outside of institutions, preferably with families (Nebraska, State Department of Public Welfare, n.d.). More specifically, Nebraska considers adult foster care as less restrictive than hospitalization and nursing home care. Bratka (1980) considers adult foster care to be relevant, for the three disability categories under consideration in this book, and in Nebraska, provided that managers can be helped to develop empathy for residents.

Fish (1980) states that Nevada considers adult foster homes relevant for preventing premature admissions to nursing homes for the elderly. Also Fish thinks that adult foster homes provide the elderly with more privacy and independence than they would receive in long-term care facilities, e.g., nursing homes.

Reporting for the aging in one county in North Dakota, Kane and Sanders (1980) consider adult foster care to be relevant for the aged because the "family home" atmosphere, provided by them, is necessary for people who have usually been accustomed to long periods of independent living. Moreover, they believe that adult foster care affords residents with better opportunities to develop community "roots" with friends, relatives, and community resources than does institutional living.

Nelsen (1979), representing Utah's elderly, believes that adult foster care is beneficial for both clients and taxpayers. For example, in Utah, nursing home care costs about $40 daily, while adult foster care costs only about $6.50 daily. Besides saving money, Nelsen believes residents' self-esteem is enhanced in adult foster homes because they come to understand that people care about them, thus helping to preserve their sense of dignity and self-worth as human beings.

This concludes the section on the relevancy of adult foster care, as reported by the Western states. The number of responses was the greatest for the elderly, with five state agencies responding. Next, three agencies responded for the mentally retarded/developmentally disabled, and only two responded for the mentally ill. Some states responded for more than one disability category. What the responses, or lack of them, means in terms of the relevancy of adult foster care is difficult to discern. However, one plausible possibility is that Western states rely more heavily on adult foster care for the elderly than for other categories. The relative paucity of responses from Western states on the question of relevancy also posits interesting questions. Again, it can be easily assumed that adult foster home programs are better developed in the East than in the West. However, much more research is needed in this area.

CONCLUSIONS

Responses from officials of the 21 states responding to the question of relevancy for adult foster care indicate that generally the program is considered relevant for the three disability categories under consideration. That is, adult foster care is considered relevant for meeting the needs of certain mentally ill, mentally retarded, and elderly populations, provided that they are not too disabled. Of the total of 27 responses from 21 states, 8 represented the mentally ill, 12 represented the mentally retarded/developmentally disabled, and 7 represented the elderly. The meanings of these data are difficult to interpret. However, one possibility is that more states consider adult foster care to be more relevant for the mentally retarded than for the other categories. This is, nevertheless, a risky interpretation due to the self-selecting nature of the respondents' replies to the question on relevancy.

That several state officials consider adult foster care relevant, only if certain conditions are met, posits some interesting questions. The need of managers to impart empathy to residents was mentioned several times. Moreover, it was assumed that empathy for residents could be learned by managers, apparently from social workers. Also mentioned was the cost saving element involved in adult foster care. Frequently mentioned was that the family atmosphere of adult foster homes and their community base, including therapeutic programs, fostered individuality and self-esteem. Both of these values are intrinsic to the social work profession, if not most or all of the human service professions.

Based upon the opinions of several state officials, the idea emerges rather clearly that adult foster care is viewed as having a reasonably well-established place on a continuum between institutional care on one end and completely independent living on the other. Some state officials obviously regard nursing home care as analogous to institutionalization. Consequently, they consider adult foster care as less restrictive and more normalizing than institutional care. Numerous court cases and statutory laws have, no doubt, made adult foster care more relevant in the past 15 years. There is an old saying that, "You can't legislate morality." However, if being in adult foster care is more moral than institutional care, I would take exception to the above quotation. There are numerous indications, from the literature and state officials, that adult foster care is indeed more humane than long-term institutional care.

Chapter 8

SUCCESSES

Before elaborating on the responses from various officials on the successfulness of adult foster care, a literature search was conducted to help explain some of its successes and philosophical rationale. As Murphy, Engelsman, and Tcheng-Laroche (1976) explained, the effectiveness of adult foster home placement for residents is difficult to assess. One reason for this is that frequently the most chronic patients with the poorest prognoses are the prime candidates. Another problem in measuring effectiveness is that there are few readily available instruments for such measurements. However, Willetts (1978) claims that behavior modification techniques can be taught to managers and cited five of eight residents whose behavior had significantly improved as a consequence. Of those showing improvement, four were elderly and one was middle-aged and had a schizophrenic diagnosis. Hall and Bradley (1975) challenge the belief that long-term psychiatric patients are not very amenable to supportive services, actually finding them more so than short-term patients in a social demonstration project.

Murphy et al. (1976) found significant symptom reduction in former psychiatric inpatients who had been in adult foster homes for 18 months. This was comparable to a control group of inpatients.

Thus, this finding has serious economic implications in that adult foster care is considerably less expensive than hospitalization. Professional humanitarians, however, aschew such instrumental practices as putting monetary value on the care and treatment of human beings. Instead, they rely more on the intrinsic value of people simply because they are human (Soyer, 1976).

In the philosophical foundations of social work practice, society has a responsibility to help its citizens attain their maximum level of self-realization. Among other things, this includes the right to social responsibility through active participation in a democratic society (National Association of Social Workers, 1977). This publication also emphasizes that, "The individual is the primary concern of this society" (p. 344). The preceding are some of the basic philosophical concepts of social work practice, commonly known as the value base for social work. Social work is admittedly a value-based profession; more elaboration on this follows.

As Levy (1976) indicates, social work is largely based on moral obligations, or intrinsic values, which the profession requires even " . . . though they may not be demonstrably more proficient than alternative choices" (p. 109). Elsewhere, Levy (1979) differentiates between general and professional values and ethics. Generally, values are "preferences" which people hold about others; these preferences are held in "affective regard." These preferences can be either positive or negative and they "may affect others" (p. 1). Like values, ethics are also preferences, held in affective regard, but additionally they connote partiality toward a particular course of action and they " . . . must affect others" (p. 1). The preceding are more general explanations of values and ethics. Levy (1979) believes that professional values and ethics " . . . tend to converge" (p. 2). Moreover, he believes that, unlike the general public, professionals are expected to take action on their values and ethics, e.g., by their peers and the society which sanctions them. In 1960 the National Association of Social Workers implemented a Code of Ethics, which was revised in 1979 (National Association of Social Workers, 1980). Members of that association are required to subscribe to that code. Thus, the social work profession is officially committed to take action on what it believes to be the most humane course of action in the amelioration of social ills, or to foster human self-determination. However, as Boettcher and Vander Schie (1975) indicate, prolonged hospitalization helps produce patient dependence on the hospital and weakens their motivation to leave. Thus, becoming institutionalized is not believed to be in the best interest of client self-determination.

Another fundamental value to which social work has had a long-standing commitment is that of strengthening family life. Moreover, President Carter's similar commitment is evidenced by his announcement of a White House Conference on Families (National Association of Social Workers, 1979). Aptekar (1965) indicates that adult foster care rests upon many culturally accepted values, the most important of which is that the contributions of family life far outweigh those of institutional living. For various reasons, however, candidates for adult foster homes often cannot return to their own families to live. Thus, an alternate form of family living is often the outcome, i.e., surrogate family living, more commonly known as adult foster home living. The presumed positive value of a family-type atmosphere is the primary rationale for adult foster homes. As Pilsecker (1978) indicates, many people seem to gravitate to social work because of the value system it espouses. Moreover, he thinks that we are "merchants of morality," that we cannot avoid being judgmental, and that we should uphold our values (p. 55).

As mentioned earlier in this book, society's values are somewhat dependent on what is fashionable, or new. Brown, Windle, and Stewart (1959) reported that community placement was becoming fashionable for the mentally retarded because human service professionals believed it fostered ego development. Wohlford (1968) indicated essentially that adult foster care increased the sense of dignity in the elderly and that the emergence of an adult foster home program in a welfare department helped to " . . . draw the staff together" (p. 226). Morrissey (1967) believes that adult foster home living permits residents to benefit from the numerous values associated with family living, e.g., one-to-one relationships and integration into the community. Finally, McCoin (1977) found that residents who had been in adult foster homes for up to 15 years scored significantly lower on measures of alienation and social isolation than patients who were just entering them from a psychiatric hospital.

By now, the basic rationale for adult foster care should be fairly well understood, albeit this rationale is somewhat moralistic and idealistic. With these observations in mind, we will now proceed to expound on the responses from officials dealing with adult foster home programs; they were simply asked to briefly explain successes they had experienced with adult foster care. The apparent paucity of empirical validation and sufficient quantification can often be observed. Many responses are descriptive and value laden. The following material was obtained from the late 1979 nationwide survey, previously described in Chapters 5 and 7. Except in New York City and one county in North Dakota, all of the following information was obtained from state officials who are involved in administering adult foster home programs. For reporting purposes, responses are categorized into those emanating from the East and West. From the East, 14 useful responses from 12 states and 1 city were included; from the West, 10 useful responses from 9 states and 1 county were included. All of the included Eastern states are from the Atlantic seaboard with the exception of Alabama and Tennessee. In each instance, the states will be discussed alphabetically.

EAST

Alabama (Vaughn, 1979), representing the mentally ill, reported that, "The return rate [to hospitals] for persons placed in the foster care program has been significantly lower than the overall return rate." Thus, for the mentally ill in Alabama, adult foster care is viewed as an asset in the deinstitutionalization process, more so than other forms of community placements. Reporting for the mentally retarded in Connecticut, Stevens (1980) gave some examples of residents' having successfully been in adult foster homes for up to 15 years. Moreover, many of these work in sheltered workshops and some have become competitively employed in the community. Also representing the mentally retarded in Connecticut, Avis (1980) cites numerous examples of residents' having successfully made the transition from large training schools to adult foster homes.

Representing the aged in Delaware, Cain (1980) gave a case example of a disturbed, frightened woman whose symptoms abated in an adult foster home. Another example was given where an adult foster home was successfully utilized for temporary emergency care. Clifford (1979), writing for the mentally ill/mentally retarded in Georgia, indicated that the state had been successful with both groups in adult foster homes, provided that they had been hospitalized for relatively long periods and that they came from rural areas. The former finding is consistent with that of Cunningham, Botwinik, Dolson, and Weickert (1959) to the effect that residents with longer periods of hospitalization are more likely to remain in adult foster care.

Responding for the mentally ill/developmentally disabled in New Hampshire, Proctor (1979) listed two case examples of two female residents who successfully adjusted in adult foster homes. One developed affective ties to the managers and even baby-sat for them. The other's agitation and explosive temper abated as she tried hard to please the managers. Zdanowicz (1980), representing the mentally retarded in New Jersey, reported a high degree of "client satisfaction" from adult foster home residents and that some "graduate" to group homes or to independent apartments where they often live with another mentally retarded adult.

The New York City Human Resources Administration maintains a Division of Foster Homes for Adults which has about 800 homes and 950 residents (Bogen, 1980). About two-thirds of these are former psychiatric inpatients. Most of them successfully adjust to adult foster homes and participate in community activities. Independent living is encouraged whenever possible and some do successfully make that move. Parker and Pettee (1979), responding for the mentally retarded in North Carolina, state that adult foster care is a " . . . primary resource . . . in the deinstitutionalization process."

Zanella (1980), reporting for the mentally retarded in Rhode Island, noted that about 60 residents have successfully used adult foster homes as a bridge to help them move into semi-independent apartments. Also, Zanella stated that residents often report being happier in smaller foster homes. Notwithstanding initial community resistance to the homes, the homes gradually become fully integrated into the communities, according to Zanella. Responding for the mentally ill in South Carolina, Hall (1979) noted that a limited number of residents had become competitively employed and some were even supporting dependents.

Reporting for the mentally ill in East Tennessee, Headrick (1980) indicated that patients with 25–50 years of hospitalization had been successfully placed in adult foster homes. Some used these homes to "prove" their worth so that they were able to move back with their own families. Another advantage reported was that medication dosages were frequently reduced after placement in the homes. Also, residents have been afforded the opportunity to "relearn community skills" and to be more independent. Virginia (Payne, 1980) noted that the press had been successfully utilized in helping to get zoning ordinances modified so that more homes could be established for the mentally ill/mentally retarded. Finally, Surles (1980) indicated that Vermont's experiences with the mentally ill in adult foster care had been "almost totally positive."

This concludes the reports from the East on reported successful experiences with adult foster care in 12 states and New York City. Some states reported for more than one category, so there were a total of 17 categorical responses. Of these, the mentally ill/mentally retarded were evenly divided with eight responses each. Only one response was for the elderly. The meaning of these responses, or lack of them, is difficult to interpret. However, it does seem safe to conclude that adult foster homes are regarded in a rather positive light by officials in the East charged with helping administer the programs. Now, let us turn our attention to the West.

WEST

California (Harmon, 1980) reported that for the mentally retarded in adult foster homes:

> . . . residents are afforded the conveniences of "family living" and complete integration into the community. . . . They attend sheltered workshops, adult education classes, and other activity programs. . . . After [they] have made adequate progress, they are referred to Vocational Rehabilitation for screening and subsequent placement in the competitive job market.

Schuler and Kamakawiwoole (1979) claim that some aged residents in Hawaii improved in adult foster homes to the point that they moved back with relatives or into licensed boarding homes. Representing the mentally ill in Hawaii, Inouye (1979) commented, "Generally we are very pleased with the number and kind of homes made available for psychiatric inpatients."

Reporting for the mentally retarded in Louisiana, Sewell (1980) stated that several residents had married and some were competitively employed. Others have completed training programs which are expected to assist these residents in finding jobs. Sewell thinks the program should be expanded and he has found the program to be " . . . a very rewarding service system." Representing the mentally ill in Minnesota, Lindren (1980) was supportive of small adult foster homes because the one-to-one relationships they afforded residents are more supportive, more like normal life experiences than they have in large homes or institutions. Also in adult foster homes Lindren believes residents have enhanced opportunities to complete work for their GED high school diplomas, possibly attend college, and obtain full-time employment.

Responding for the mentally ill in Nebraska, Iwan (1979) stated, "Overall, we feel our program has been successful; the number of adult foster homes is on the increase." A publication from Nebraska lists six personal characteristics of managers, considered essential for successful adult foster home management. Paraphrased these are: (1) ability to help residents reach personal goals; (2) concern for needs and feelings of residents; (3) a comprehension that residents have strengths and weaknesses like other humans; (4) a positive value system about all people; (5) secure, stable home life; and (6) willingness to work with social agency staff and community organizations (Nebraska, n.d., p. 5).

Acting for the elderly in Nevada, Fish (1980) stated: "This level of care has been an excellent means of preventing early admissions to nursing homes. Residents are afforded more privacy and independence than they would have in a long-term care facility."

Admitting that success in adult foster home placement has not been systematically evaluated for the mentally ill, in New Mexico, Garcia (1979) believes that adult foster care can be very effective under certain conditions. Namely, Garcia believes that clear lines of communication must be maintained between managers, state hospital officials, and community mental health agencies.

Representing Stutsman County, North Dakota's mentally ill, Kane and Sanders (1980) consider adult foster care as a viable alternative to nursing home placement for elderly psychiatric patients. Also, they noted that adult foster home residents, requiring rehospitalization, are rehospitalized for shorter periods than other former psychiatric inpatients in the community.

Finally, Nelsen (1979), representing the elderly in Utah, claims a high degree of client satisfaction with the adult foster care program. Moreover, Nelsen cites two case examples where the residents' "dignity has been restored," i.e., they are active at senior citizen centers, take pride in their personal appearance, and question why they were ever institutionalized in the first place.

This concludes the reports from the West on reported successful experiences with adult foster homes in nine Western states plus one county in North Dakota. A total of 11 categorical responses were received. Of these, five represented the mentally ill, two represented the mentally retarded, and four represented the elderly. By the officials responding from the West, it appears that they generally regard adult foster care as successful, e.g., in such areas as deinstitutionalization, prevention of early admissions to nursing homes, helping to enhance residents' sense of dignity, and helping to reintegrate them into the community.

Conclusions

Responses from officials in 21 states, 1 city, and 1 county on their reports of successful experiences with adult foster care generally indicate that the program is considered successful for several purposes. Some of these are to: (1) assist in the deinstitutionalization process; (2) prevent early nursing home admissions; (3) assist in reestablishing positive affective ties with own families; (4) help to reestablish a stronger feeling of self-worth and self-determination; (5) aid in advancing oneself educationally, vocationally, and socially; (6) saving money for taxpayers; and (7) symptom reduction.

Altogether there were 13 categorical responses for the mentally ill, 10 for the mentally retarded, and 5 for the elderly. The meaning of these data is difficult to interpret. However, a tentative indication is that, by the large number of officials reporting for the mentally ill/ mentally retarded, successes with these categories could be more numerous than with the elderly. Why more officials, representing the aged, did not respond to this question, however, must be considered unknown at this time. Certainly, more research into the successfulness of adult foster care for all three categories is sorely needed.

Chapter 9

FAILURES

The late President Lyndon Johnson once reportedly stated, "It's not hard to do the right thing; it's hard to know what's the right thing to do." In the case of adult foster care, it is both hard to know what is the right thing to do and how to do it. As previously mentioned, social work has a strong value base. However, Gordon (1965) reminds us that social work is also knowledge based. Moreover, he believes there can be an alignment between the profession's use of both concepts in the cause of humanity. By analogy, value could denote what we should do about adult foster care and knowledge, and how we should go about it. This, however, oversimplifies the problem.

Page (1977) reported a strong relationship between the academically developed values of social work and the theory of economic competition. Furthermore, he views values as difficult to justify scientifically and exhorted social workers to develop greater expertise in economic theory, apparently considering it more scientific than social work theory. In an apparent rejoinder to the Page article, Aigner and Simons (1977), referring to microeconomic theory, consider that theory antithetical to social work values, due to its emphasis on competition and reward rather than need. In other words, there is inherent conflict between the social work values of the intrinsic dignity and worth of humans and the instrumental values of competitive economics. In the United States there is a group of radical social workers who are anticapitalistic and pro-socialistic. Galper (1975) is probably their leading proponent; he blames the Protestant ethic and capitalism as being responsible for many of the ills of the mental health and social service systems. Lichtenberg (1976) is another radical social worker who charges these systems with being value laden from capitalistic and political influences. Knickmeyer (1972), another radical social worker, believes that social workers have been placed in the "dirty" role of implementing dehumanizing policies of social control when we should be focusing more on social change (p. 64). Change implies conflict, a term which is largely alien to many social workers trained in the psychoanalytic model and being products of a capitalistic society.

Then Heraud (1970) considers that economic capitalism has strongly influenced the form of the family. For example, the industrial revolution helped to break down the extended family and to favor the more mobile nuclear family. The term *family,* however, is hard to define as Schneiderman (1979) indicates. Part of the problem seems to be that Americans value individualism at the expense of the family; social work is no exception. So there is little surprise in the many value conflicts in and between social work, economics, the family, individuals, and society. Barbardo (1979) states, "Abundant evidence exists that the family probably inflicts as much pain as it provides pleasure and threatens its members as much as it supports them" (p. 455). Other authors indicate that families have territorial boundaries, which they guard against outsiders (Anderson & Carter, 1978). They also note that families are agents of social control and socialization. One then might question why some families take strangers into their homes, e.g., adult foster home families. One possibility is to fill the empty nest. Another possibility is that the managers have had experience with "augmented families" (Anderson & Carter, p. 111). Basically, this entails the incorporation of unrelated members into families. Although the authors attribute this practice more to black families, it could be more of an outgrowth of economic deprivation. For example, many managers have informed me that their primary motivation for becoming managers was a combination of financial need and altruism.

It is well known that the mental health system discourages the extended family and encourages the nuclear one. In addition to the radical social workers, there are other critics of the mental health model, derived from the medical model which connotes illness. Szasz (1961) claims that psychiatrists do not treat mental illness (which he considers a myth) but instead help people with their social, personal, and ethical problems. Plant (1970) considers mental health to be a scientifically unsound concept, essentially because of its moralism. Scheff (1966) and Solomon (1975) consider the mental health system to be basically insane. Social workers have been heavily influenced by the medical disease model which Osmond (1970) defends as "... one of the greatest of human inventions" (p. 275). The reader must admit, however, that the contemporary mental health and social service systems share some commonalities with private enterprise, which has historically not been the most supportive population of the downtrodden.

Switching now to the area of mental retardation we find that, like its treatment of adult foster care, social work is a late comer. Horejsi (1979) stated that between 1956–1965 the *Social Work* journal devoted only 1.4% of its space to mental retardation. Likewise, Nooe (1975) admonished social workers for not taking more action on their behalf. Skarnulis (1974) noted that legally the mentally retarded are considered noncitizens, ostensibly because they are legally considered "eternal children" (p. 57) which leaves their parents with nearly absolute power over them. This has often included the power to withhold the giving of informed consent for much-needed surgery for them, thus jeopardizing their very right to exist (Brierland & Lemmon, 1977). These authors also indicate that 23 states maintain sterilization statutes for the mentally retarded who are being released to communities from institutions.

Turning our attention now to the problems of the dependent elderly, we find several indications of their neglect. One example is that Brierland and Lemmon devote only one chapter to the ageds' legal problems; yet they devote four chapters to juvenile courts and six chapters to family problems. From the news media and some employees from the Kent County, Michigan Department of Social Services, I learned that parent abuse, by adult children, is becoming a discernible social problem. Kaufman (1980) thinks that social policy makers need to provide far more incentives for traditional family support for dependent-aged relatives.

Killian (1970) found that transferring elderly psychiatric patients to other hospitals, or community-based residential facilities, caused a higher death rate among them than among the control group, which was not moved. Wood (1978) and Berger and Piliavin (1976) cited scientific studies indicating that elderly clients, receiving casework services, had a higher mortality rate than those who did not receive these intensive services. These studies have led some to believe that casework services may be dangerous to the health of the elderly. Assuming that the elderly can and do benefit from some mental health and social services, they are often relegated to low positions on the priority list. Again, it would seem that the law of the economic market-place is functioning "efficiently" with the aged, i.e., in terms of social control. As we shall see later, one way to keep down the costs of care for the dependent elderly is to keep them in adult foster homes.

Finally, we turn our attention to some of the negative aspects of adult foster care, as gleaned from the literature. Buxbaum (1973) questioned the wisdom of the Joint Commission on Mental Illness and Health report of 1961 on its claim that psychiatric hospitalization was to be avoided whenever possible. Moreover, he doubts if a mental patient's simply remaining in the community is a valid indicator of mental health and that such inferences may be setting a dangerous trend. Segal (1979) claims that " . . . few attempts have been made to elaborate on the social policies of community care and deinstitutiona-lization" (p. 521). Moreover, he is critical of the widespread practice of transferring mental patients to the community without an adequate network of supportive services.

Willetts (1978) reported that behavioral modification techniques, designed for a target group of managers, were unsuccessful in chang-ing the managers' negative attitudes toward residents. Murphy, Pen-nee, and Luchins (1972) found that often managers have double standards for themselves and residents, e.g., separate eating facilities. Also they noted that many residents did not seem to be really accepted into the households and communities. Murphy, Engelsmann, and Tcheng-Laroche (1976) found that, after 18 months in adult foster homes, residents manifested virtually no improvement in social func-tioning. Sherman and Newman (1979) interviewed managers from two major state-sponsored programs in New York dealing with the elderly, and reported that two-thirds of them stated the sponsoring agency had provided no training for them, or even printed material.

Zweben (1977) claims that numerous professionals, politicians, and news media people have expressed serious reservations about the use of adult foster care facilities as an alternative to institutionalization. Moreover, he cites several examples of alleged resident abuse in the New York City area. Apparently representing the Philadelphia area, McCrary and Keiden (1978) refer to psychiatric patients as the "ideal victims" who are often transferred to the community with little preparation or follow-up services. They report having known of residents being sold from one "boarding home" to another at a cost of $100 per person. Thus, at least in the cases of some mental patients, it would seem that slavery has been resurrected. McCrary and Keiden also indicate that no less than 11 federal agencies are involved in implementing community-based residential care for the mentally handicapped and plead for a more unified national policy in this area. Inferring more neglect than abuse of psychiatric patients in the community in the Chicago area, Anderson (1978) thinks the mental hospitals are being "purged" and "psychiatric ghettos" formed as a consequence.

In conclusion, some of the criticisms of mental health, social work, and the monied interests of our society have been examined in relation to the three groups under consideration in this book. Also, some of the philosophical issues of the three groups have also been examined, not to mention some of the problems of adult foster care. While these issues have been discussed philosophically, they are nevertheless believed to contribute to the failures experienced with adult foster care. The following sections of this chapter are concerned with reports from various officials from the United States who are responsible for the implementation of adult foster care programs. As usual, we will begin with reports from the East, followed by the West; both will be discussed in alphabetical order. The data were collected as previously described in Chapters 5, 7, and 8. Officials were simply asked to report negative experiences, including failures, that they had experienced with adult foster care.

EAST

From the East, 12 states and 2 large cities responded to the question of negative experiences they have had with adult foster care.

There were a total of 16 responses representing 17 categorical references. Of the latter, seven represented the mentally ill, six the mentally
retarded, and four the aged.

Representing the mentally ill in Alabama, Vaughn (1979) reported that zoning laws had created the most problems for the adult
foster home program. Parenthetically, Cupaiuolo (1979) found community resistance to the placement of psychiatric patients in communities in lower New York State to be most often expressed through
zoning laws. Also he found the higher socioeconomic status of the
communities, the greater the resistance.

Stevens (1980), responding for the mentally retarded in Connecticut, indicates that some residents had to be rehospitalized or imprisoned. Moreover, she adds, "Some of the more serious events have
included car theft, breaking and entering, assault, disorderly conduct
and . . . the inability to adjust to the family setting." From Stevens'
reply, one can infer that the failures were primarily caused by these
residents' maladaptive behavior patterns. Responding also for the
mentally retarded in Connecticut, Avis (1980) believes the greatest
problem is providing adequate supervision, in terms of quality and
quantity, for carefully selected managers. Answering for the elderly in
Connecticut, Walker (1979) believes that many residents in adult foster
homes need more services, i.e., " . . . stimulation and recreational
activities to promote their well-being and to get them back into the
mainstream of society. In many instances they are a forgotten group."

Delaware (Cain, 1980) states that some failures result from a
"mismatch" between managers and residents. Another problem is the
naiveté of some managers who are not cognizant of the potential
problems which can be expected in caring for the aged. Some residents' excessive smoking and drinking causes problems for some managers. Here, Cain seems to infer some of the blame for the failures on
the managers. Reporting for Washington, D.C., Barquin (1979) indicate that locating managers for adult foster homes for the aged was a
problem. For example, in many instances, former domestics have
rented homes which are being used to house the elderly. From Chapter
5, it should be mentioned that the status of licensure there is undetermined.

From Georgia, representing the mentally ill/retarded, Clifford
(1979) claims some problems are experienced because some managers
encourage unnecessary dependence from residents. Also, some mana-

gers impede treatment goals and some terminate due to insufficient income from managing.

Proctor (1980), representing the mentally ill in New Hampshire, relates that most failures in adult foster care are due to residents' inability to relate socially to others. More specifically she states:

> Often residents will set themselves up to be rejected by families. Many residents are uncomfortable in the closeness that a family setting provides; they much prefer institutional living. In others, a real problem has developed when former state hospital residents' having made an investment in a family are then put in a position of feeling rejected because the family decided to move, sell their house, or discontinue serving as a family care provider. . . . [One] provider arbitrarily closed her home [and the female resident] had to return to the state hospital. . . . In many foster homes it is difficult for a younger person to adjust . . . because the provider is too controlling. . . . In many instances the provider has had no experience with mentally ill persons. Therefore, when a crisis . . . develops the provider immediately wants the individual returned to the state hospital.

Commenting for the mentally retarded in New Jersey, Zdanowicz (1980) states, "We anticipate more clients will be placed in group homes and supervised apartments . . . and we will have less reliance on the Family Care Program." Furthermore, Zdanowicz believes that the mentally retarded can more easily integrate into the routine of unlicensed homes but admits this can lead to overprotection of residents. However, he believes the licensed homes are more efficient and impersonal. A few instances of client abuse and misuse of residents' personal property were reported, but he did not specify whether these managers were licensed or unlicensed. Zdanowicz also states that the physical structure is only marginally adequate in 10% of the homes and the majority of managers come from the lower middle class.

Representing the mentally retarded in North Carolina, Parker and Petter (1979) consider zoning laws to be the most detrimental to the program. Another problem is a paucity of supportive community activities. From New York City, Bogen (1980) states the largest cause of failures there is the inability of the mentally ill to adjust to the family life of the homes.

Writing for the mentally retarded in Rhode Island, Zanella (1980) inferred that the most severe problem had been the defeat of the state's plan to establish large homes for 15 residents. That plan was successfully opposed by the Rhode Island Association for Mentally Retarded Citizens. Denny (1980), responding for the aged in South Carolina, indicates that he could not respond to the question of failures because no statistics on this were kept at the state level. Parenthetically, one gets the impression that such is probably the case with perhaps many departments in other states. However, Hall (1979), representing the mentally ill in South Carolina, states, "Some negative experiences result in their [residents] elopement with the drastic results of being in trouble with society."

Reporting for the mentally ill in East Tennessee, Headrick (1980) states some residents cannot make the adjustment to family life and have to be rehospitalized, usually after creating turmoil in the home and community. Surles (1980), communicating for the mentally ill in Vermont, indicates that there has been some client abuse (including misuse of their funds), and lack of physical and emotional supports from managers. Responding for the developmentally disabled in Virginia, Payne (1980) gives zoning ordinances as causing the most problems for the program there.

This concludes the section on reports from the East. Among the most frequently mentioned problems for adult foster care are (1) residents' inability to adjust (especially psychiatric residents), (2) restrictive zoning ordinances, (3) residents' "acting out", and (4) manager abuse of residents. In many instances, the data were descriptive and qualitative. The possibility must be considered that few statistics are kept in many state-level departments. More research in this area in sorely needed. The reader may want to refer to Chapter 5 to see that some reports, used in this current chapter, were from states where the status of official regulation is either mixed or undetermined. Now, let us focus our attention on reports from the West.

West

From the West there were 11 states and 2 counties responding to the question of negative experiences, including failures. Totally, there were 14 responses. Since a few states reported for more than 1 category, there were a total of 17 categorical responses. Of these, six each represented the elderly and mentally ill and five represented the mentally retarded/developmentally disabled.

Representing the mentally retarded in California, Harmon (1980) states that most failures are caused by residents' "acting out" which occasionally precipitates admissions to state hospitals because of managers' inability to handle them. McCurdy (1979), representing the elderly in Colorado, states their biggest problem is moving institutionalized patients from nursing homes to adult foster homes. Another problem is that the counties must pay 20% of the costs for adult foster care while they pay none of the costs of nursing home care.

Schuler and Kamakawiwoole (1979), representing the aging in Hawaii, indicate that the primary way of handling residents, who have adjustment problems in one home, is to transfer them to another home. In my own experience with adult foster care, I have also seen this practice used considerably. For the mentally ill in Hawaii, Inouye (1979) indicates that specifics are not readily available, but he listed some general complaints from former residents and concerned others which are:

1. Food habits peculiar to various ethnic groups due to Hawaii's multiethnic setting
2. Insufficient activities within the home to keep patients consistently occupied
3. Occasional disturbed and unmanageable behavior manifested by patients requiring extrusion from the home
4. Complaints from home operators of insufficient care payments in light of rising inflation and cost of living

Reporting for the mentally retarded in Louisiana, Sewell (1980) indicates one problem is locating suitable homes and finding replacements for those that close. Some residents have difficulty adjusting to the homes. Occasionally, there are some reports of alleged resident abuse and one resident became pregnant.

Studying problems of Adult Protective Services in Kalamazoo County, Michigan, Wink-Basing (1980) reports that some residents in adult foster care facilities have been found to be in need of protective services. Moreover, she adds, "The nature of the client's endangerment tends to be neglect and financial exploitation, although there are some cases of physical or sexual abuse by AFC operators."

Responding for the mentally ill/retarded in Minnesota, Lindren (1980) states some of the problems experienced there are finding adequately qualified managers and the tendency for them to "burn out" early, due to the frustrations of working with the mentally ill. Furthermore, she thinks that working with the mentally retarded requires less training for managers. As for specifics on failures experienced with the mentally ill, these are paraphrased from Lindren as (1) rehospitalization of one resident, (2) residents taking advantage of managers or vice versa, (3) suicidal attempts for residents, (4) one resident's mistaken belief that the manager would provide psychotherapy.

For the mentally ill in Nebraska, Iwan (1979) indicates that most of their failures are caused by the managers' not having adequate training in mental illness, crisis intervention, and behavior modification. Other problems are managers' need for more free time and the need for more community support services. Writing for the elderly in Nevada, Fish (1980) notes that the demand for family-type homes are down, apparently in favor of larger facilities. (For the elderly there are some indications that this trend may be fairly widespread in the United States.)

New Mexico (Garcia, 1979) indicates that a problem in working with the mentally ill is that closer coordination is needed between the Mental Health Bureau and the State Licensing Division. Writing for Stutsman County, North Dakota, Kane and Sanders (1980) state that a problem with the aging in adult foster care is they have difficulties in adjusting to the homes and they often have inadequate funds to pay for their care. The latter necessitates county supplementation of their SSI funds. An additional problem is coordinating the efforts of the funding sources. Finally, there have been some personality conflicts between managers and residents.

Communicating for the mentally ill in Texas, Donnelson (1979) indicates that a problem there is that managers in privately owned homes tend to financially exploit residents by offering them few or no therapeutic programs except "smoking and watching TV." Representing the elderly in Utah, Nelsen (1979) reports difficulties in finding "quality" homes and social agencies prioritize adult foster care too low on their work lists. Finally, responding for Washington, Stern (1980) states that a problem there is the negative attitudes of some managers toward mentally retarded residents, e.g., treating them like children and trying to take over total control of them.

From the West, zoning ordinances did not appear to be a serious problem, as they seem to be in the East. Also, a frequently mentioned problem in the West was residents' difficulty in adjusting to family life. From the West, two reports of possible resident abuse by managers were given. Also two other reports inferred that possibility. One of these indicated a mutual exploitation of each other by managers and residents. Managers' getting time away, lack of training for them, and "burn out" were also mentioned. Financial problems were mentioned from the standpoint of one county and at least one manager and resident. Mentioned several times was the dearth of community support programs and difficulties in locating suitable homes. In concluding this section, the plea is again postulated for the need for more research in the area of failures and problems in adult foster care. The reader may want to refer back to Chapter 5 in order to see that some reports, used in this current chapter, were from states wherein the status of official regulation is undetermined or mixed.

QUESTIONS AND CONCLUSIONS

In concluding this chapter, the author is struck with a barrage of questions and impressions about adult foster care and several related issues. Nevertheless, I will attempt to maintain as much objectivity as possible.

Given that the primary responsibility for direct implementation of adult foster care has been delegated to social work, one is struck by the paucity of identified social workers responding to the nationwide survey. From that survey, 31 responses were used in this chapter. Of these, only five could clearly be identified as from social workers. While it is true that the inquiries were all directed at state agency heads, responsibility for replies were sometimes delegated to assistants or occasionally to line workers. Why, then, did so few respondents identify themselves as social workers? One possibility is that a large proportion of those responding were actually social workers by education and credentials. If so, why did they not identify themselves as such? If they are not social workers, who are they? The possibility exists that many of them possess a diffuse array of qualifications from being professional human service workers, to having business administration degrees, to being political appointees with varying educational and experience backgrounds. If the latter assumption is valid, are they better qualified to administer adult foster home programs than social workers? On this question, I will not hazard a guess except to say it posits food for the social work value and knowledge mills.

A central question is the relevancy of the family as a model for adult foster home care, especially in light of the many contemporary problems of the family. Is it realistic to expect surrogate families to take in disabled strangers, nurture them, and, hopefully, to try to help socialize many of them at minimal cost to taxpayers? To me, this is a tall order indeed, given that many managers are relatively poorly educated and come from the lower middle class. Such a practice probably fits in with the spirit of economic capitalism, but how do social workers and other human services professionals reconcile this with humanistic values?

The radical social workers and other authors have a valid point in questioning the status quo orientation of the mental health and social service delivery systems, which many of them accuse of being too closely allied with monied interests. Should we as social workers switch our energies more toward an orientation of "change," with society and its institutions as the targets (Glassner & Freedman, 1979, p. 247)? Perhaps a realistic beginning would be to take a multicausal approach to the problems of the mental health and social service systems. That is, integrate the scientifically validated concepts of many diverse schools, from many disciplines, so as to, hopefully, produce a synergistic effect on these systems.

The lack of a uniform social policy at the national level is obvious, i.e., a policy to deal consistently with the problems of adult foster care. Among existing national policies there is too much overlapping, duplication, and loopholes. Intentionally or unintentionally, these loopholes would seem to be weighed in favor of the more organized money interests with political power, e.g., the medical and nursing home professions. It seems that in many cases residents, managers, counties, and states must take up the financial slack created by the vacuum of insufficient funds from SSI. A uniform national policy on adult foster care would exert more pressure on states, counties, and communities to provide a better network of community support services for adult foster care.

The difficulties of many adult foster home residents, especially those with schizophrenia, to adjust to family life has been previously discussed in Chapter 3. While many schizophrenic people do not require prolonged hospitalization or adult foster care, many do. More research into the relationship problems, which many residents of all categories experience, is sorely needed. Perhaps it is unrealistic to expect all, or most, of the three categories of disabled people to adjust in foster homes. Is it such a failure if some must continue to be hospitalized?

As for the plight of the mentally retarded, it seems that often legally and socially they are relegated to positions even behind second-class citizens, i.e., to "noncitizen" positions. If the social work profession has treated adult foster care as an unwanted stepchild, it has treated the mentally retarded no better at best. While we have focused more attention on the problems of the dependent elderly in the past 15–20 years, there is still much to be done. For example, it is now commonplace to read or hear about "battered" children and wives. However, little has surfaced in the literature about elderly parents who are abused and neglected by their children. Moreover, as some data in this chapter indicate, agencies are receiving some complaints about abuse and neglect from adult foster home managers toward residents. These reports certainly warrant follow-up studies and in-depth research.

As for the managers, it would seem that more effective screening devices could be used in their selection. For example, they could be required to take personality tests and case histories could be obtained on them. Such a practice could help improve the quality of managers. However, given the relatively low rates of financial compensation they receive, it would be difficult to be this selective. Given the present situation, it would seem that better initial and continuing training programs would help them do a better job, not to mention effective, ongoing casework services. More attention needs to be given to the problem of inadequate recreational activities and the apparent relatively high burn out rate for managers. In the homes more structured activites, designed to stimulate more interaction between managers and residents, are sorely needed. The problem of resident acting out needs further study. Perhaps this behavior from residents is, in part, caused by their frustrations with existing mental health and social service systems. Yet, too often, they or the managers are blamed for this behavior.

Finally, some simple arithmetic shows that responses to the question of problems with adult foster care were proportionally more numerous from the East. Does this mean that these officials are more aware of problems, more concerned about the residents, or simply more critical than those from the West? Does the relative paucity of responses from the West mean apathy or what? Needless to say, I have advanced more questions in this section than answers. Much more research is needed to answer these lingering questions. Finally, does this rather negative chapter indicate that I am a revolutionary who believes the mental health, social services, and adult foster programs should be abolished and something new created in their stead? No, I believe that sufficient reform can come from within, but this will require much dedication, intelligence, introspection, and action from human service professionals, especially social workers.

Chapter 10

PROSPECTS FOR THE FUTURE

Writings, especially in recent years, have undoubtedly stimulated more interest and understanding of adult foster care. This and other factors have contributed to its growth. During this growth, however, more influential critics have emerged; also more research has evolved. Aptekar (1965) pinpointed the fundamental problem in adult foster care as the lack of interpretation. Moreover, it seems that Morrissey (1967) helped to partially solve this problem. However, many mis-understandings still exist. Such publications as Segal (1979a, 1979b) seemed to help in comprehending the problems of community-based residential care for former psychiatric inpatients. In the latter publica-tion Segal exhorts us that, unless we continue to support these services, families and communities may again reject the mentally ill. Thus, the mentally ill may again become so isolated as to resemble those rescued by Dorothea Dix over 100 years ago. Spence (1978) recommends the development of a "universal philosophy" for those institutionalized populations needing community care services, even going so far as to suggest that institutions may be needed more by professionals than clients (p. 512). Other authors chastise professionals over not adequately recognizing adult foster care, the "Cinderella" of the mental health field, and making wider use of its potentialities (Shrader & Elms, 1972, p. 9).

In a more positive vein, Zweben (1977) sounded a positive note for adult foster care for the mentally disabled when his research findings contradicted the findings of some authors to the effect that the adult foster home concept is analogous to merely moving "chronic care" psychiatric wards into the community (p. 147). Herrick (1972) was also optimistic for adult foster care because of its ties with community psychiatry and the community mental health movement. Another author claimed that adult foster care, for former psychiatric inpatients, " . . . has been successfully tried as an alternative to hospitalization" (Miller, 1977, p. 275). As indicated in Chapters 8 and 9, however, defining and measuring success in adult foster care is difficult. One of these problems is the apparent conflict between the values of social work and economics. Yet, O'Connor, Justice, and Warren (1970) do not appear to find such conflict, arguing that residential community placement of aged mentally retarded adults meets the requirements of being both humane and economical. Moreover, Linn and Caffey (1977) believe that adult foster homes are an appropriate, but underutilized, resource for many of the hospitalized elderly. Other authors suggest the intensification of casework efforts between elderly residents and the managers of the homes in order to stimulate more interaction between them (Sherman & Newman, 1979).

Finally, Brook, Cortes, March, and Sundberg-Stirling (1976), studying adult foster care as an alternative to hospitalization for acutely disturbed people in Denver, found this approach to be quite relevant in terms of safety and treatment effectiveness. Such a procedure would, however, require rather extensive professional services in the community. Following this concept, it would appear that adult foster care can be rehabilitative in nature.

Let us now switch our attention to the results of the late 1979 survey (previously discussed) in which administrative officials from throughout the country were asked their opinion on future prospects for adult foster care. They were asked to give their opinions on prospects both locally and nationally. As usual, the responses were separated into those from the East and West. All states are discussed alphabetically.

EAST

From Alabama, Vaughn (1979) seems to think the status quo will prevail in the state for adult foster care for the mentally ill. Nationwide, he thinks it " . . . will never achieve acceptance on [a large] scale." Representing the aged in Delaware, Cain (1980) thinks that adult foster care will " . . . continue to be a strong, viable option as long as safeguards against mismanagement are in place as they are now." Nationally, Cain seems pessimistic due to lax or nonexistent regulatory standards and other inadequate safeguards against client abuse. As a minimum, she believes that managers should be certified before being authorized to take in residents.

Clifford (1979) believes that adult foster homes for the mentally ill/retarded in Georgia will remain about the same in number for the present. However, in the future, he envisions an expansion of group homes and independent living facilities, thus implying a future decline in adult foster homes as defined in this book. From Maine, Fuller (1979) implies that the adult foster home program for the elderly there will probably maintain its present course. Many of their residents have been in mental hospitals. She considers the largest problem there to be inadequate funding for community support programs.

New Hampshire (Proctor, 1980) reports that there is considerable interest there in:

> . . . developing specialized foster home settings for the mentally ill and integrating . . . [them] into a community support and case management system that will adequately meet the needs of mentally ill persons placed in such settings.

Furthermore, Proctor indicates that a special demonstration project is being planned to demonstrate the effectiveness of adult foster homes as a viable alternative to institutionalization, provided that adequate community support programs are available. Nationally, Proctor essentially believes that the family care concept is in difficulty because managers are not given adequate support and community programs are inadequate. Moreover, Proctor emphasizes that the Housing and Urban Development's Demonstration Program favors developing group homes. Apparently these would be operated by non-owners and, thus, would not be considered as adult foster homes. Finally, Proctor thinks that funding sources are inadequate for adult foster care and that the National Institute of Mental Health should provide more leadership in linking its recently developed "community support systems model" with the family care concept.

For the mentally ill in New York, Bogen (1980) considers prospects as "promising" for adult foster care. Nationwide, he envisions a strong need for expansion as, "They are a vital link in the process of resocialization of the formerly mentally ill and thus reintegrating them back into the community." Representing the mentally retarded in North Carolina, Parker and Pettee (1979) consider that both statewide and nationally, "Prospects are excellent if resources . . . and community education . . . can be forthcoming." By resources, they mean local, state, and federal; by education, they apparently mean efforts designed to educate the public about adult foster care and the problems and needs of the mentally retarded.

Zanella (1980), responding for the mentally retarded in Rhode Island, states:

> In the future . . . we will see much larger numbers of group homes . . . for the mentally retarded. Our State Plan for Mental Retardation Services calls for the establishment of many more such facilities in the next few years.

By his strong emphasis on the development of group homes, therefore, it would seem that the prognosis for traditional adult foster care in Rhode Island is not good for the mentally retarded.

Writing for the aged in South Carolina, Denny (1980) depicts adult foster homes as " . . . invaluable for those who are no longer able to maintain independent living." (This reason and preventing or postponing nursing home placement appear to be two major reasons for adult foster homes for the aged.) Nationwide, Denny forsees, "Slow development, due to the small amount allowed to be charged to income-eligible residents." He gives this as $300 (maximum) for board and services. The interpretation of these data is difficult as it is not clear as to whether he is including a state supplement to SSI. The above financial problems notwithstanding, Denny thinks that the increasing aging population will create more need for adult foster homes for them. For the mentally ill in South Carolina, Hall (1979) apparently considers prospects good for the expansion of adult foster care for this population.

Reporting for one region in Tennessee, Headrick (1980) appears optimistic about the future of adult foster care there and in the state for the mentally ill. She thinks the new licensure law will help improve the quality of care " . . . both physically and programmatically." However, she adds that SSI income for residents is not state supplemented. Thus, they only receive $208.20 monthly and a minimum of $25 goes to the resident. (For comparison with a state giving a generous supplement see Chapter 6, e.g., where Michigan managers receive about $410 monthly and residents receive about $31.) Finally, Headrick believes that licensure will provide some impetus for the state legislature in Tennessee to provide a supplement.

A Vermont publication (1976) implies optimism with the statewide system of Community Mental Health Centers there which were instituted in 1976. These centers often eliminate the need for state hospitalization, but only two of the four centers provided day treatment services for outpatients at that time. The same publication connoted enthusiasm with the state's boarding home system and indicated that their residents and managers were serviced by professionals from these centers. While such a practice would seem to mitigate against the stigma often associated with receiving outpatient services from state hospital staffs, Perlmutter and Silverman (1972) criticize such community mental health centers as being too large, bureaucratic, and too much under the control of large hospitals. Thus, outpatients from these centers may also become stigmatized. It seems nearly axiomatic that stigma comes to be associated with anything using the term mental.

Reporting for the mentally retarded in Virginia, Payne (1980) thinks that the community is the most logical place for them and thinks that adult foster homes are a viable and economic means to this end.

This concludes this section on reports from the East relating to future prospects for adult foster care. Responses were received from 11 states and 1 city. Categorically, six responses represented the mentally ill, four the mentally retarded, and three represented the elderly. Overall, these reports must be considered mixed as to future prospects. However, generally they seem to be tilted in favor of adult foster homes for the mentally ill and aged. For the mentally retarded, there appears to be a definite trend away from adult foster care and toward group homes. As for prospects for adult foster care nationally, I would categorize a slight majority as being negative or positive with reservations. I agree with the critics of the federal government (exclusive of the VA) over not providing more leadership in adult foster care. Also, it seems to me that national leaders should take another look at SSI because in some states managers and residents receive no supplement, while they do in others. Such a system, it seems to me, provides many people involved in adult foster care with grossly inadequate incomes. Now, let us switch our attention to responses from the West.

West

Although Arizona does not have an official adult foster home program, Gersten (1980) indicates that prospects are good for the development of one for the mentally ill there. He thinks that sentiment in favor of them is growing. Gersten also states, "We . . . have a community support system contract with the National Institute of Mental Health that is assisting in the design and implementation of a system of residential opportunities . . . for this population." He also adds that the state plans to explore possibilities for an adult foster home program . . . utilizing qualified low-income families as foster parents." Finally, Gersten believes that nationwide prospects are good because of the increasing emphasis on community care by the federal and state governments.

For California's mentally retarded, Harmon (1980) thinks that prospects for "small family homes" are excellent as the state continues to process " . . . numerous new applications." Reporting for Colorado's elderly, McCurdy (1979) thinks prospects for adult foster homes are "fairly bright" as SSI supplements are state funded. Nationally, he thinks prospects are also good because of the volume of inquiries received from other states. However, he sees " . . . the definite lack of Federal leadership and involvement and this could prove to be a definite disadvantage."

Reporting for Hawaii's aging, Schuler and Kamakawiwoole (1979) seem to be optimistic for the adult foster home program there. That state is short on "ethnic-type" homes, e.g., for Japanese and Caucasians. The anticipated increase in the aging population there is also expected to be a boon for adult foster care. However, a problem for managers is that their income does not keep pace with the inflationary spiral. Finally, they comment:

> Present payments for Welfare recipients are funded by state funds. If Medicare funding can be obtained, no doubt there would be more persons serviced in care homes. The gap most in need are those persons who do not meet Welfare criteria but who are nevertheless in the very low income range.

From the last quotation, they apparently mean state supplementation to SSI when they refer to welfare. By Medicare funding, I assume that they mean that all residents should receive Medicare, as opposed to Medicaid benefits. Writing for Hawaii's mentally ill, Inouye (1979) thinks more homes will be needed, especially as the population ages. Apparently he feels the same way about adult foster care nationally.

Responding for the fledgling adult foster home program for the developmentally disabled in Illinois, Rose (1980) implicitly seems optimistic. There, they became interested in adult foster care when some of the children in licensed foster homes became adults, thus necessitating different licensing and funding systems. For the mentally ill/retarded in Minnesota, Lindren (1980) thinks that the anticipated implementation of statewide licensure will be an impetus for adult foster homes there. Lindren also thinks that the heavy volume of correspondence she has with other states indicates strong national interest and probable future commitment.

Iwan (1979), reporting for the mentally ill in Nebraska, thinks additional homes are needed in that state and nationally. Apparently meaning statewide and nationally, she thinks residents are all too frequently placed in nursing homes in lieu of adult foster homes. Also, she adds that increasingly more cases of abuse are being reported in "food and board" homes and hotels in the state. Apparently such facilities are uncertified in Nebraska. Finally, Iwan thinks that more manager training in empathy is needed. For New Mexico's mentally ill, Garcia (1979) reports:

> The future prospects for continuation and expansion of foster homes in this State should be aggressively pursued. This concept of care may be extremely beneficial and most important cost effective in the delivery of mental health services.

Garcia also thinks that more coordination and cooperation is needed between local, state, and federal officials. Responding for the elderly in Stutsman County, North Dakota, Kane and Sanders (1980) think that prospects for adult foster care there are good, if the state assumes responsibility for supplementation of SSI and passes protective services laws for the residents. They believe that adult foster care programs will likely grow in the United States because the concept blends well with the community psychiatry concept.

From Utah, Nelsen (1979) thinks that the future of adult foster homes for adults for the elderly " . . . is looking brighter every day." As for the nationwide outlook Nelsen states:

> . . . Looks good! I have had many states inquire about our program. I'm led to believe, because of this sort of inquiry, that States are taking a serious look at Adult Foster Care as an alternative to nursing homes and institutionalization. Many states have excellent programs in operation today.

Finally, a Washington publication (1979) states "The base rate for Adult Family Home care has been increased to $278.20 per month for all clients" (p. 1). This apparently means that the state supplements SSI payments.

This concludes the section on responses from the West about the prognosis for adult foster care there and nationally. A total of 10 states and 1 county responded to the question. Categorically responding were six for the mentally ill, four for the mentally retarded, and five for the elderly. Collectively, the responses were tilted considerably in favor of the program in the reporting states, including ones who are developing programs, and nationally. As previously mentioned, adult foster care does not seem as well developed in the West; however, reports from there were generally more optimistic than those from the East. However, some observations from the West and East were similar. That is, both are concerned about potential resident abuse, concern about cost effectiveness, concern from some states about lack of state supplementation, the growing aging population, and lack of federal leadership. The proliferous correspondence between several reporting Western states and other states is encouraging, indicative of the vitality that is needed to help any system develop.

Conclusions

The literature on adult foster care has expanded rapidly in the past 15 years. It is believed that this has helped adult foster care to grow by stimulating interest, comprehension, and research. Although many of these publications have been in social work journals, other professional human service journals are also increasing the number of articles on the subject of adult foster care. Although there are many critics on the lack of federal leadership, the Department of Housing and Urban Development appears to be becoming involved in the development of group homes for the mentally retarded, possibly to the detriment of traditional adult foster homes. At least in Arizona, the National Institute of Mental Health (NIMH) is involved in helping to develop community-based residential facilities for the mentally ill. Such services notwithstanding, others continue to be quite critical of NIMH over not providing more leadership. The problem of state supplementation for SSI recipients seems to be in the process of slow remedy. However, the inequity of manager and resident income from state to state and region to region is obvious. Why should a manager in Tennessee receive half as much income as a manager in Michigan?

Considerable agreement exists that the need will exist for more adult foster homes as the population ages. That time is now. Also, there is considerable concern about apparent actual and potential abuse of adult foster home residents. The time appears ripe for state legislatures to tackle this problem. Presently, the development of adult protective services seems to be undeveloped in many states.

In conclusion, it appears that developmentally, adult foster care could be depicted as being middle-aged in the East. It may be near the middle-age crisis and needs to work at self-renewal. In the West, adult foster care seem analogous to an adolescent with considerable hope and optimism. I agree with the critics who state that more federal leadership is needed in adult foster care. If the federal government will not or cannot generate this leadership, then perhaps it is time for "the tail to wag the dog," figuratively speaking. That is, for the communities, counties, and states to provide the leadership. Overall, however, it appears that the state of health and prognosis for adult foster care in the United States is reasonably good.

Chapter 11

SUMMARY

BACKGROUND AND DEFINITIONS

This book begins with a brief historical account of how humanity has dealt with the problems of the mentally ill, mentally retarded, and dependent elderly. With particular reference to mental illness, theories on its causality have ranged from the "bile" theory of Hippocrates to the "demon" theory of the Middle Ages to the organic disease concept of the late nineteenth century. More recently, the theoretical thinking has swung from single cause to multiple causation. This applies not only to mental illness but also to mental retardation and the problems of the dependent aged. For example, the mentally ill can have intrapsychic, interpersonal, and social problems. While the aged and mentally retarded can also have these problems, they are more likely to also have physical problems.

For a variety of reasons, the three groups under study in this book do not or cannot live with relatives. Therefore, alternate living arrangements must be made. Traditionally, this was handled in the colonial United States by such measures as auctioning the person off to the lowest bidder or his/her having to live in almshouses. Around the middle of the nineteenth century witnessed the beginning of the state hospital movement. Many of the three groups under consideration were warehoused in these. The Great Depression of the 1930s provided the impetus for less expensive forms of custodial care, of which the adult foster home movement was one. Beginning in the 1950s, the practice of utilizing large numbers of psychiatric drugs helped produce sufficient symptom reduction in many psychiatric patients so they could reenter the community. The rights movements, litigation actions, and legislative acts of the 1960s also helped to stimulate deinstitutionalization for all three groups under consideration. Additional federal and state legislation in the 1970s further accelerated the move from institution to community. No doubt, the implementation of the federally funded SSI plan helped in the move toward deinstitutionalization, as did also supplementation of that program by numerous states.

While obtaining precise statistics on the numbers of institutionalized people going back to communities is difficult to discern, sizable proportions of them went into adult foster homes. Nationwide, the population in United States mental hospitals declined by 44% from 1961–1979. Between 1950–1971 the hospitalized elderly declined by 56%. From 1950–1971 the number of mentally retarded in institutions declined by one-third.

The primary purpose of this book was to do a qualitative assessment of adult foster home programs in the United States with particular reference to managers and residents and the problems and rewards which confront them. Due to the magnitude of adult foster care in this country, however, a macrolevel approach was taken to this problem by contacting state administrative officials for answers. In addition to a thorough literature review, another purpose of this study was to formulate and test some theoretical propositions which were believed to be relevant to adult foster care. Hopefully, the latter will generate further research. Another purpose of this study was to help standardize the diverse terminology extant in the field. Thus, the slightly reformulated definition of adult foster homes is restated as those private homes, managed usually by the owner(s), which have been assessed and approved by a state licensing agency (or approved and supervised by a local facility much as a hospital, community mental health center, or department of social service) for the purpose of housing, feeding, and supervising the needs of certain categories of handicapped adults, not over 20 in number. The management of adult foster homes can be a full-time undertaking or a part-time job. Manager-income is usually derived from resident income, which is often in the form of SSI or SS disability checks.

The obvious influence of economics on adult foster care became manifest during the Great Depression of the 1930s. Most of the literature on the subject has been produced since then. While proliferous, it has tended to be contradictory, faddish, and not well based on social science and human behavior theories. Thus, replications of the studies have been difficult, if not impossible. However, this pattern has been changing in the past 15 years, especially among doctoral dissertations by social workers. For example, some of these have formulated hypotheses for further study. Evans (1976), for example, formulated several interesting hypotheses about managers which included demographic, social, and interpersonal predictors. These warrant further study and would seem to have practical utility in the complex problem of manager recruitment, selection, and retention. Zweben (1977) also formulated some interesting hypotheses regarding the motivation of managers to manage. Moreover, McCoin (1977), Whorley (1978), and Cupaiuolo (1979) tested hypotheses, respectively, on manager authoritarianism and resident alienation, social exchange patterns between managers and residents, and the characteristics of community resistance to adult foster homes. These studies used the most sophisticated research tools of the social sciences and are important contributions to the literature. Yet, except from University Microfilms, Ann Arbor, Michigan, they are unattainable. To confound the problem, many practicing social workers and administrators probably would be largely unable to make much practical use of them because of their research sophistication.

In the literature, references are found to adult foster care as being analogous to a bastard child, unwanted stepchild, Cinderella, or a mongrel. In the use of these terms, authors usually made actual or implicit criticisms of the mental health and social service systems. This leads to a quotation which I understand comes from Shakespeare which is, "Success has a thousand fathers; defeat is an orphan." Could it be that authors are being drawn to adult foster care more out of economic than humanitarian concerns? Perhaps the economic marketplace, coupled with humanitarian concerns, is turning a long-term loser into a winner! As indicated, however, the field has attracted some influential critics in this process. Some of these have indicated that transferring the mentally ill to adult foster homes is analogous to transferring chronic wards to the community.

While earlier literature refers to adult foster care as being rehabilitative, more recent publications have referred to it as more custodial in nature, albeit some still consider that it can be rehabilitative. However, most indications are that it is utilized primarily for custodial care.

Research in adult foster care for the mentally retarded has been far more neglected than for the mentally ill. However, Schrader and Elms (1972) devote a chapter to this topic. In terms of the mentally retardeds' having relationship problems (similar to many people with schizophrenia), the authors note that the mentally retarded will often " . . . progress far more quickly and easily in the home of strangers" (p. 112). Therefore, it seems that many mentally retarded people may share the emotional allergy syndrome with many schizophrenic people when it comes to relationship problems with close relatives. Morrissey (1967) notes that New York officially had an adult foster home program for the mentally retarded as early as 1931, or 4 years earlier than the one for adults. Yet, why have social workers and other human service professionals been so neglectful of the mentally retarded? The radical social worker would probably answer this question by saying that we got caught up in the laws of the marketplace where the mentally retarded have not been ranked very high. Especially in the Eastern United States, there seems to be a growing trend to place more mentally retarded adults in group homes with salaried managers. Thus, the question must be asked, are adult foster homes failing the mentally retarded, or are there perhaps additional variables operating?

Research on adult foster care for the aged has also been largely neglected until recent years. Once again, the question of the elderly's value in the economic market place comes to the fore. Possibly due in part to the rights movements of the 1960s, more attention has been focused on the problems of the dependent elderly in recent years. Besides social work journals, interest in the aged is being shown in various other human service journals. While the federal government has often been criticized in this book for not providing more leadership in adult foster care, it did provide federal grants toward getting welfare departments involved in adult foster care for the elderly and others in the late 1960s and early 1970s (Fenske & Roecker, 1971; Wohlford, 1968). Now, many departments of social service are involved in adult foster care, not just with the elderly but with other disability categories as well.

THEORY AND APPLICATION

Some theoretical concepts, considered relevant to the three groups under discussion, were discussed. These are (1) schizophrenia, (2) mental retardation, and (3) dependent elderly. Also discussed were some theoretical concepts, believed to be relevant for all three categories of residents under consideration. These are (1) social margin, (2) alienation, (3) nestling syndrome, and (4) family. Theoretical concepts considered relevant for managers were (1) nesting syndrome, (2) family, (3) authoritarianism, and (4) normalization. However, the latter concept would also be relevant for both managers and residents. The family would also be relevant for both groups. Now, each of the above concepts will be briefly discussed.

Generally, it is believed that a multicausal basis exists for the problems encountered by all three categories of residents under consideration. For example, schizophrenia may be caused by a combination of intrapsychic injuries, disturbed ability to relate on a mature interpersonal level, and possibly biochemical imbalances. All of these malfunctions, along with possible others, may combine to precipitate severe psychosocial malfunctioning, thus often necessitating the placement of such persons in institutions or adult foster homes.

While mental retardation has been traced to over 200 causes (American Medical Association, 1965), Schrader and Elms (1972) condense the major causal categories to three. These are (1) biological, (2) environmental, and (3) intermediate. By intermediate, they mean a combination of biological and environmental problems. Moreover, they indicate that about 90% of the mentally retarded have mild to borderline retardation. Many of these, with help, can lead relatively normal lives, but some do live in sheltered environments. Also many, who have moderate impairment, i.e., IQ ranges from 35–50 can function in sheltered settings.

Likewise, the causes of aging appear to be many. Disengagement theory holds essentially that the aging person gradually withdraws from life's traditional roles. Other theorists claim that activity and continued involvement with others slows down the aging process. The mutation theorists hold that the body gradually accumulates deleterious genes which cause a gradual deterioration of the human organism. Also societal expectations from the aged are believed to influence their self-concepts. That is, if society devalues them, they tend to devalue themselves. These are only some of the theories on aging. Of course, only a small proportion of the aged require custodial care. Indications are, however, that the number of aging people in adult foster care is increasing. Undoubtedly, economic factors also very strongly influence the care of the dependent elderly as it does the other categories of residents in this book.

The concept of social margin is believed to have practical utility for the three categories in this book. For example, all three categories tend to be stigmatized because they have largely failed in two basic societal areas. That is, they have failed to effectively compete in the marketplace and essentially have failed at maintaining effective relations with significant others in the community. Therefore, they tend to be viewed as low on social margin because their supply of debits overrides their supply of credits. Also tending to deplete their supply of credits is that their status as consumers is diminished. Thus, many are considered socially obsolete except for institutions or sheltered community placements. This tends to put them back into the role of consumers by way of receiving public funds, a large share of which is used for their own support.

An empirical research project was conducted, in a large adult foster home program, on resident alienation. Conducted with schizophrenic male veterans, the study results found that long-term adult foster home residents were less alienated than residents entering the program (see Table 4–3). Also, long-term residents were found to be less socially isolated than patients who were entering adult foster care (see Table 4–4). These findings pose interesting questions for schizophrenic and other resident groups in adult foster care. That is, does prolonged foster care contribute to diminished alienation and social isolation, or are there other variables also operating? Perhaps merely being out of institutions contributes to diminished alienation. The concept of alienation would seem to have practical utility, not only for further research, but also for clinical practice.

While highly theoretical, the nestling syndrome is believed to have practical utility for researchers. Notwithstanding the risks involved in studying what may be an instinctual part of humanity, such is nevertheless believed to be worthwhile. The ethic now in vogue in social science research seems to be to accentuate our humaneness and to deemphasize our animalness. Nevertheless, it seems that all humans do have a tendency to nestle, or at least to affiliate with others, possibly out of instinctual needs to survive. An institution which is conducive to nestling is the family, including possibly surrogate families such as those who manage adult foster homes. Since the family appears to be one of the primary institutions of our society, perhaps nestling with a substitute family is more socially palliative than the more total dependency that institutional living tends to foster. This line of reasoning may help to explain why the concept of normalization appears to be the most widely held rationale for adult foster care and as a goal-directing guide for same. That is, normalization appears to be utilized more by adult foster care programs than any other theoretical concept.

Switching now to managers, the nesting syndrome was considered to be a viable concept for middle-aged managers who may take in residents to compensate for children who have grown up and left home. Also the nesting and nestling syndromes are viewed as complementary, i.e., besides possibly having some instinctual basis, managers and residents living together may be utilitarian for both groups who are often low on social margin. Thus, the foster home may serve as a medium to help both to survive. The concept of the augmented family may be the most relevant family model for adult foster care. Basically, this means taking unrelated family members into the household. Much more research is needed on this model and its possible relevance for adult foster care. We apparently could learn much about this model from the study of augmented black families.

Another theoretical concept which was empirically tested was that of authoritarianism. Managers high on education were found to be low on authoritarianism (Table 4–5), and managers who were high on religiosity were high on authoritarianism (Table 4–6). Therefore, authoritarianism may be a valid concept to use in manager selection. If administrators are disinclined to use standardized tests, a fairly reliable estimate of the prospective manager's authoritarianism could be obtained from managers' religious convictions and educational achievements.

1979 Survey Results

Two nationwide surveys were conducted in 1979. In both surveys, letters were sent to the 50 state departments of (1) mental health, (2) mental retardation, and (3) elderly. The same offices were also written in Washington, D.C., and Puerto Rico. Also information was requested from the VA. The first survey was designed primarily to obtain information about regulation of adult foster homes; the second survey asked several questions, i.e., relevancy, successes, failures, and future expectations of adult foster care, both locally and nationally. The second survey also asked for the number of facilities and residents in adult foster care.

Analyzing information from the surveys was no mean task. Therefore, the possibility for misinterpretation exists. Nevertheless, considerable effort was made to ensure that information was included which pertained only to adult foster homes, as defined in this book.

Twelve states were determined to have licensed adult foster home programs, 6 certified programs, and 16 with mixed regulation, for a total of 34 states with some type of regulation. By way of comparison, only 22 states officially licensed or certified social workers as of the late 1970s (Wisconsin Chapter, National Association of Social Workers, approximately 1978). Therefore, it appears that regulation of adult foster care is proceeding faster than it is for the social work profession. As Schrader and Elms (1972) indicate, licensure for managers is an excellent means by which to gain official recognition.

Data from 7 Northeastern states and 1 city indicate a minimum of approximately 3,090 adult foster care facilities and 11,065 residents. Statistical manipulation of these data, however, are contraindicated due to the possibility of misinterpretation; and reporting states did not always report both categories of information.

From 8 Southeastern states and the District of Columbia, approximately 1,946 adult foster homes and 5,632 residents were counted. The same cautions should be exercised with these data, as previously mentioned. Data from 6 Midwestern states and 1 county gave a tentative count of 3,434 facilities and 20,494 residents. However nearly one-half of these were from Michigan. Analysis of reports from the 9 Western states tentatively accounted for 4195 homes and 12,267 residents.

Altogether a rough estimate from all the respondents gives a tentative figure of 12,665 adult foster homes and 49,458 residents. However, this represents only 30 states, the VA, 2 cities, part of a state, and 1 county. These figures should be parsimoniously considered when looking at adult foster care nationally. Moreover, they do not include the 1979 VA figures of 12,000–15,000 in adult foster care. These figures, added to the other reported figures would give approximately 61,000–64,000 in adult foster care, as defined in this book.

Even with these conservative figures, it is obvious that adult foster care has grown tremendously from the reported figure of 17,292 residents in 1963 (Morrissey, 1967). Morrissey's data were from 29 states and the District of Columbia. Moreover, a comparison of contemporary figures of VA residents in adult foster care (12,000–15,000) with the number of 4,499 for 1964, indicates close to a 300% increase. Overall in the United States, it appears that the number of residents in adult foster care has at least doubled in the past 15–20 years. However, this still leaves tens of thousands of people unaccounted for who are apparently in other types of community care residential facilities. Much more accountability and research is needed on their behalf.

From the question of relevancy of adult foster care, 27 responses from 21 states were received. Of the states responding, 13 were from the East and 8 from the West. Of the respondents, 12 represented the mentally retarded, 8 the mentally ill, and 7 the elderly. While most of the respondents thought adult foster care is relevant, several qualified this statement. For example, it is relevant if managers can be taught empathy, as a cost-saving measure for taxpayers, for deinstitutionalization and normalization, less restrictive than institutions, preventing nursing home placements, and helping residents become reintegrated into the community. Several respondents thought adult foster care is relevant if the means can be found to protect residents against abuse and exploitation. One respondent thought adult foster care is relevant for stimulating resident-manager interaction. One respondent, for the aging, thought the program is relevant for preventing or delaying institutionalization for the aged. Some respondents thought adult foster care is relevant for enhancing residents' self-esteem. Some positive values associated with family life were also mentioned. Also mentioned was that adult foster homes allow more privacy than hospitals. Finally, a literature review indicated that recent court decisions and legislation have combined to make this type of care more relevant, not to mention the rights movement of the 1960s.

On the question of successes, or positive experiences with adult foster care, a literature search uncovered some interesting philosophical issues. For example, the concept of the least restrictive form of care seems compatible with the social work values of supporting people's right to self-determination, to be treated with dignity and worth, and the rights of individuality. Also emphasized in the literature were the positive values of family and community living.

To the question of successes state officials have experienced with adult foster care, 12 states and 1 city responded from the East; from the West, 10 states and 1 county responded. Some of the more frequently mentioned reasons were helping residents remain in the community for up to 15 years, less recidivism than other forms of community care, advantages of community programs, opportunities to advance oneself socially, educationally, and vocationally, and delaying or preventing nursing home placements. Other indications of positive experiences included client satisfaction, symptom reduction, developing affective ties with managers and their families, and improving residents' sense of self-esteem. Overall, the respondents seemed quite positive about the program and several gave interesting case history material to substantiate their claims of success.

A literature review was conducted to find a philosophical base for failures, or negative experiences with adult foster care. Several authors found an apparent conflict between the economic rationale of free enterprise and the humanitarian values of social work. Some prevalent views of the radical social workers were discussed. Some of their criticisms of the mental health and social service delivery systems indicate that these systems are too much dominated by the Protestant ethic and capitalism. Therefore, they must inherently be opposed to the best interests of the poor and downtrodden. Also some of the negative viewpoints of the family were given, including its social control function and tendency to be territorial, i.e., to exclude strangers. Also considered was the deterioration of the extended family, long believed to be the primary model for adult foster care, and how this void can be filled. Apropos to this problem is that the passage of time makes manager inexperience with the extended family more paramount. Also considered was the need for a uniform national policy on community-based shelter care for the disabled, with special reference to adult foster care. For example, 11 federal agencies are now apparently involved in making such policy. Moreover, the states seem to emulate the federal government in this regard. For example, Cupaiuolo (1979) indicates that no less than nine agencies in New York State are involved in regulating, funding, administering, and operating community-based residential facilities. Thus, there appears to be too much overlapping and duplication of services on both the national and state levels.

Turning now to responses from state officials on the question of negative experiences with adult foster care, 12 states and 1 city responded from the East. From the West, 11 states and 1 county responded. Frequently cited as an obstacle in the East was restrictive zoning ordinances. Cupaiuolo (1979) reports that, generally, zoning codes will permit from two to five unrelated people to live together in a single family district. Homes for larger numbers of residents are often excluded from zones approved for single-family dwellings. Another frequently mentioned reason for failures was failure of the resident to adjust to a family setting; this sometimes included resident acting out, including creating disturbances in homes and communities. Also mentioned was that some managers tend to be too controlling or try to sabotage treatment plans. Manager inexperience, lack of empathy, and the tendency of some to exploit or possibly be abusive toward residents was also mentioned. A rather frequently mentioned problem was the lack of state supplementation of SSI funds and inadequate community support programs. Needless to say, answers to these thorny problems will only be found by diligent efforts from many sources.

On the question of prospects for the future of adult foster care, both statewide and nationally, responses were received from 11 states and 1 city in the East. From the West responses were received from 10 states and 1 county. From the East, future prospects for adult foster care were generally considered as mixed. Several respondents predicted a continuation of the status quo locally and indicated that the lack of federal leadership would hamper adult foster care nationally. In the East, there appears to be a growing movement toward group homes for the mentally retarded. Reports from the West were generally optimistic about the future of adult foster care, both statewide and nationally. Overall, it appears that future prospects for adult foster care in the United States are reasonably good. However, more federal leaderhip would appear to be a definite boon to the movement.

Chapter 12

CONCLUSIONS

GENERAL OBSERVATIONS

Although the treatment and custodial care philosophies for the mentally ill, mentally retarded, and dependent elderly have metamorphosed somewhat during recorded history, there is still disagreement about the effectiveness of modern methods in dealing with them. Science and technology have made phenomenal advances in numerous hardware areas such as communication and transportation. Yet it sometimes seems that science and technology may do more to harm the three groups under consideration in this book than it does to help them. Some social scientists believe that the planned obsolescence ethic, from the marriage of technology and the marketplace, adversely influences the care and treatment of the three categories of people under consideration in this book. That is, essentially they are carted off to social junkyards because they are no longer considered economically productive, not unlike rusting cars whose engines have lost their power. Nevertheless, modern society has some safeguards to prevent their destruction. So, in this respect, the analogy between people and cars ends. The three groups under consideration are not completely powerless as we shall see.

One of the human sciences which has helped the three groups is medical science. Pharmacological advances in the past three decades have helped in symptom reduction in the mentally ill, albeit often with undesirable side-effects such as lethargy and diminished reality-testing ability. Diagnostically, procedures for detecting mental retardation have improved to the extent that some mental retardation diagnoses can be made even before the person's birth. Proper diagnosis and treatment, soon after birth, sometimes prevents mental retardation. For most mentally retarded people, however, medical science has little to offer otherwise, except to treat the physical problems which many of them have. For the dependent elderly, medical science is continually finding ways to prolong their lives. This, however, is often at the expense of living economically deprived lives, fraught with physical and emotional pain and sometimes physical abuse.

While the software of the social scientists is more difficult to measure than the hardware of the hard scientists, in-roads into the amelioration of some of society's ills are being made by the former. One example is the adult foster home movement which began in Belgium around 600–700 A.D. Since then it has spread to numerous other countries, including the United States. Since its inception, the movement has been sustained by the Roman Catholic Church, the medical profession, and, more recently, numerous human science professionals and others have inherited responsibility for its implementation. However, primary responsibility for this now rests with social work.

Beginning in Massachusetts in the late 1800s, the adult foster home movement in the United States essentially lay dormant until the Great Depression of the 1930s gave it a renaissance and it has not yet stopped growing. No doubt, the development of psychiatric drugs in the 1950s, national executive and legislative leadership, and the rights movements of the 1960s also helped. The federal funding of SSI for the disabled and elderly of the 1970s also helped the adult foster care movement. Since the early 1960s the number of residents in adult foster homes seems to have doubled or possibly tripled. While the literature has proliferated since the 1930s, it has often not been soundly based upon social science and human behavior theories. Moreover, much of the research methodology used has been cumbersome, often making replication of studies difficult. Within the past 15 years, however, considerably more research sophistication in the literature has been observed, especially in social workers' doctoral dissertations. Other serious researchers of note have also made significant contributions. For example, Murphy, Engelsmann, and Tcheng-Laroche (1976) noted that the cost of adult foster care is about one-half to one-fifth that of hospitalization. The authors also indicated that in Canada one resident was in adult foster care for every six in mental hospitals. In the United States, the authors noted that the number was more like 1 in adult foster care to every 20 in psychiatric hospitals. However, my estimate is that the current figure in the United States is more like 7 in adult foster care for every 100 in psychiatric hospitals, and this is a conservative estimate which does not include the mentally retarded and elderly.

More research is needed for the theoretical concepts discussed. Particularly for residents the concepts of (1) schizophrenia, (2) mental retardation, (3) dependent elderly, (4) alienation, (5) nestling syndrome, (6) social margin, (7) family, and (8) normalization need more empirical testing by social scientists and human behavior researchers. For managers, the concepts of (1) nesting syndrome, (2) family, (3) authoritarianism, and (4) normalization need more empirical testing. Moreover, some of the above concepts appear to have had little, if any, empirical testing. Also needed are more rigorous research designs and statistical controls, but some recent doctoral dissertations have attempted to deal with these problems (McCoin, 1977; Whorley, 1978).

Notice that the concept of the family was included as needing further study for both residents and managers. Although the adult foster care concept uses the family as its model, this is rather poorly conceptualized in the literature. However, Evans (1976) dealt with the family in some depth. Evans seems to think that the typical manager comes from a rural background, characterized by large families where the emphasis is on openness and group cohesiveness rather than individuality. This seems somewhat antithetical to the ethic of individuality, espoused by social work. However, Evans' reasoning would tend to support the concept of the extended family or more probably the augmented family. However, Kaufman (1976) found that rural managers tended to be more repressive than urban ones, despite being better educated and being from a higher social class. It seems that being repressive would also tend to stifle individuality. Murphy, Pennee, and Luchins (1972) indicated that urban settings are preferable to rural settings because residents need the anonymity and support programs which are more likely to be provided in urban settings. This argument would appear to be realistic, especially for schizophrenic residents, who may be more threatened by an open-type family. Also favoring urban settings is the current gasoline problem which impedes travel from rural to urban areas for support programs.

Data analysis from the 1979 nationwide surveys indicated that at least 34 states have regulation of adult foster homes. From Chapter 11 we learned that there are probably a minimum of 61,000–64,000 residents in adult foster homes, as defined in this book. These data were obtained from 30 states, 2 large cities, East Tennessee, 1 county in North Dakota, and the VA. The respondents were asked to give the number of residents by category if possible. However, many respondents gave estimates, and I have done some extrapolations from the data received. Approximately 27,549 mentally ill residents were counted. For the mentally retarded the count was about 4,898; for the dependent elderly, my count was about 7,961. Parenthetically, the latter count did not include a figure of 7,000 elderly VA residents reportedly in VA adult foster homes in 1975 (Sherman & Newman, 1977). Assuming that the VA figures are essentially unchanged, this would place the figure of elderly in adult foster homes at nearly 15,000. Moreover, abut 21,638 additional residents were counted from my surveys. However, these could only be categorized as mixed. They appear to be a combination of the three categories under consideration in this book, plus a few physically handicapped, e.g., blind or being developmentally disabled other than being mentally retarded. Moreover, a few were listed simply as unemployable. These may or may not fit in with one or more of the three categories under consideration in this book. Altogether, the above figures tentatively account for 61,776 people in adult foster homes in the United States in 1979. This figure includes the VA figures that about 12,000–15,000 veterans were in VA adult foster homes in 1979.

Numerous officials responding to the survey seemed to equate family care with adult foster care. They tended to depict family care homes as having between 1–6 residents, while I am calling adult foster homes those which keep up to 20 residents and have tried to include these residents in the preceding counts. However, it is possible that some of these were not included in the statistics because of the tendency of officials to equate family care (1–6 residents) with adult foster care (1–20 residents). Thus, by my definition of adult foster home, the augmented family model would seem the most relevant family model to apply to adult foster care. Certainly, more conceptual refinement is needed here. If the augmented family model is the most relevant, much could be learned from those blacks and possibly others who have had experience with this model. However, assuming that this knowledge can (or will) be developed, the problem still exists of how to communicate this knowledge to managers. Perhaps the agencies could handle this by a combination of casework services and workshops, or possibly it could be better handled by formalized education. However, given the limited education of many managers, the latter suggestion may be of limited practical utility.

Due to the small sample size and questionable sampling procedures from the six case studies, generalizations from these data are risky. However, some interesting questions do arise suggesting further study. That one-third of the managers had a grown child in the home raises further questions about the nesting syndrome. Also, the data suggest a standardized agency rule about social workers visiting adult foster homes, e.g., at least monthly. Also from the data and past experience as a social worker in an adult foster home program, it seems that social workers should be required to give managers their home telephone numbers for emergency purposes. The fact that all three female residents, with apparent mentally ill/retarded diagnoses, had out-of-wedlock children which they gave up for adoption is interesting. The question arises: Did they become pregnant out of ignorance, vulnerability, unconscious or conscious desire, using sex in an effort to establish relationships or communication, a way to mitigate against loneliness, or an effort to assert their femininity? Possibly all of these and other variables were involved. Nevertheless, further study of single females and maternity among them, especially before they enter adult foster homes, is warranted. Are they denied the option of keeping these children, if desired, while the single woman from the general public is not? If the latter is the case, how do we reconcile this with the residents' right to self-determination?

From the 1979 survey, the general conclusion was that adult foster care is relevant and has a reasonably secure position on the continuum between institutional care and independent living. Generally, adult foster care was depicted as less restrictive and more normalizing than institutionalization. However, as previously mentioned, I have problems with the normalization concept. Murphy et al. (1976) found that hospitalized controls improved more on social functioning than adult foster home residents. Thus, they concluded that helping residents resume their previous level of social functioning (normalization) could better be accomplished by professional staffs, such as in hospitals. However, Murphy et al. (1976) found a significant reduction in symptoms among the adult foster care group when compared with the hospitalized controls. Could this be considered normalization? Murphy et al. did not think so. If the family is indeed the model for adult foster care, one must question why it may be failing in what is generally regarded as a family function, i.e., socialization, and apparently succeeding in another one, i.e., social control. Certainly, more research is needed to determine if this is indeed the case. At any rate, conceptual refinement is sorely needed on the family as a model for adult foster care. The same is also needed for normalization.

On the question of successes with adult foster care, respondents from the 1979 survey gave numerous rationales and some case examples of what they considered success. Some of the more salient ones were (1) helping residents to become deinstitutionalized, (2) providing residents opportunities to participate in the positive values of family and community living, (3) helping residents reestablish affective ties with their own families, (4) enhancing individuality and self-esteem, (5) symptom reduction, and (6) saving taxpayers' money. While many of these are generalizations and hard to measure, they do, nevertheless offer some good arguments in favor of adult foster care.

As a rationale for explaining some of the failures of adult foster care, some of the literature from the radical social workers and others was reviewed. Some of the shortcomings of the mental health and social service systems, which they depicted, do appear to be logically valid. For example, the downtrodden do appear to suffer from the Protestant ethic and capitalism. The lowest bidder mentality, from colonial times, of auctioning off unfortunate people has seemingly been recently resurrected in the form of Proposition 13. Therefore, logically it seems that more states and the federal government may follow suit. At any rate, the three groups under consideration in this book would seem to be among the first to suffer. For example, such austerity would likely result in stifling state supplements to SSI recipients, many of whom are adult foster home residents. Also, the nationwide trend toward declassifying social work positions appears to be a product of the Proposition 13 mentality; that is, properly trained social workers having to compete in the economic marketplace with people who have non-social work educations.

The lack of a unified national policy on shelter care living facilities for the three categories under consideration came across from numerous respondents from the 1979 survey and from the literature. To a lesser degree, the states seem to suffer from the same malady. From the respondents, other salient reasons given for failures in adult foster care were (1) administrators placing adult foster care too low on their priority lists (Proposition 13 mentality); (2) numerous residents' inability to adjust to a family setting, sometimes manifested by acting out; (3) manager burn out and lack of vacation time; (4) inadequate financial compensation for managers; (5) lack of community support programs; (6) the lack of (or inadequate) state supplementation of SSI; (7) potential or actual resident and manager abuse and exploitation; and (8) lack of federal leadership.

As for the future of adult foster care, respondents from the East tended to think that the status quo will prevail for the mentally ill. For the mentally retarded, there seems to be a growing trend away from adult foster homes to group homes. For the elderly, many are being sent to large homes for the aged and infirm, especially in the East and possibly the West also. Prospects for adult foster care nationally seemed to be less optimistic from Eastern respondents. Generally Western respondents, some with developing programs, were more optimistic about adult foster care locally and nationally than Eastern respondents.

RECOMMENDATIONS

Research

The findings of statistically significant associations between manager authoritarianism, education, and religion warrants further research, as also does the fact that managers from one setting were found to have considerably higher mean scores on authoritarianism than those of so-called normals, reported in the literature. Since the California F Scale is being criticized by some as being outdated, perhaps the "New F Scale" (Robinson & Shaver, 1973, p. 321) may be more relevant for measuring authoritarianism than the California F Scale. Also, the new scale is supposedly less ideological and more personality centered than the California scale. Thus, the new scale may give a more valid measure of authoritarianism as a personality trait. The concept of authoritarianism and its assessment would seem to have considerable potential for selecting those managers likely to be democratic, emphathetic, and emotionally secure.

With residents, the concept of alienation warrants further research. The finding that schizophrenic residents who had been in an adult foster care program for up to 15 years scored significantly lower on alienation than a group who was entering the program certainly warrants further research. Also, that the long-term adult foster home residents scored significantly lower on social isolation than a comparable group of patients warrants further research, as does the fact that the residents and control had mean alienation scores considerably higher than those reported in the literature for normals.

Numerous theoretical concepts were reported in Chapter 3 which appear to have had little, if any, empirical testing. These will not be repeated here but empirical testing of them is strongly recommended. Other concepts, which would seem to be relevant for adult foster care, needing more theory building and empirical testing efforts are: (1) the sick role; (2) medical, psychosocial, and other models of diagnosing and treating the three categories under consideration; (3) social change; (4) rescue fantasy; (5) chronic dependency; (6) blaming the victim; (7) planned obsolescence as it relates to humans; (8) motivation; (9) competition; (10) self-esteem; (11) loneliness; (12) empathy; and (13) comparisons of programs from capitalistic and socialistic countries.

The preceding concepts should be fairly self-explanatory, except perhaps for the rescue fantasy, competition, and loneliness. Therefore, brief elaboration on these will be presented. In psychiatric clinical settings the term *rescue fantasy* is often heard. Essentially, it means that some people seem to have fantasies of rescuing the troubled, sick, or misguided. An extreme example would be a religious missionary's zeal in going to primitive lands to enlighten heathens. For our purposes, more realistic examples would be social workers or managers who like challenges. For example, the three groups of residents under consideration would fit that bill. Perhaps people, working with the three groups under consideration, need missionary zeal or rescue fantasies. Moreover, there may be some association between the rescue fantasy and nestling/nesting syndromes.

As for competition, it seems that this concept could be considered relevant to Henry's (1963) assumptions (about the marketplace) on the necessity for consumption and creating desire for more of the same. An antecedent condition, however, would seem to be motivation and a competitive will. For the more motivated, competitive, productive, and consuming members of our society, marketplace support systems are programmed primarily to meet their needs, i.e., for those who produce and consume the most goods and services. Townley (1980) claims this is the 18–49-year-old age group. However, he is not considering the three disability groups under consideration in this book, albeit many of them are in the "over the hill" category in terms of age. Also, most of the three categories under study have to be excluded from the upward-ly mobile, competitive groups because of their disabilities and other-wise being low on social margin. Thus, they are not competitive in the marketplace and by analogy are considered unworthwhile, or "losers." In our society to be anybody is to be a "winner"! Indeed, most of the residents in adult foster homes do not fit the winner image. Even their choice in what, when, and where they will consume is curtailed, i.e., because most of their income is programmed to go to managers for their maintenance. They are low indeed in the winners' column in a society which worships winning. They are not usually programmed into the mainstream of societal thinking.

Those who do the programming are too frequently controlled by the monied interest groups, e.g., the marketplace and its partnership with organized industries whose prime law is to be winners in the race for making money. Some of the more blatant examples would be professional athletics, where the astronomical salaries paid to some star athletes no doubt feed the inflation mill. The tremendous impact of television may even determine who will be President, i.e., the first prerequisite is that the candidate must look good and be entertaining before the cameras. The planned obsolescence of automakers, who change models every 2–3 years, is well known. Thus, it seems these powerful interests may do more to shape our lives than even the social scientists. So, it may very well take dedicated people with rescue fanta-sies to save the three groups under consideration from social junk-yards. Perhaps the bonds between science, technology, and the market-place are so strong that we human service workers are predestined to remain comparatively low on the material wealth ladder because we have decided to serve as champions for some of the victims of the above alliance. However, we must not despair, and we must maintain the fight. Otherwise, our clientele may well be relegated to social junkyards.

Fromm-Reichmann (1959) thought that loneliness was perhaps one of the most important, yet least conceptualized, psychological phenomena, and that better comprehension of the concept may help pave the way for better communication with the mentally ill. In essence, recognizing and relating to loneliness could be a powerful therapeutic tool with which to begin to impart empathy to adult foster homes residents.

With the exception of authoritarianism, alienation, and self-esteem, the other theoretical concepts referred to in this book have not been very well-operationalized instrumentally. Certainly, there is a great need to improve measurement in the social sciences, particularly in adult foster care.

The literature search revealed that the Brief Psychiatric Rating Scale has been used in research with residents (Murphy et al., 1976; Whorley, 1978). Also from the clinical use of that instrument, I think it is relevant for research use, especially for schizophrenic residents. The Katz Community Adjustment Scale was also used by researchers on residents (Murphy et al., 1976). Apparently little used by researchers in adult foster care, the Hamister Post Hospital Adjustment Scale and the Departure Index (see Chapter 2), would seem to be of benefit for research. In addition to its usefulness as a diagnostic clinical tool for residents, the MMPI would seem to have considerable utility for research with managers, not to mention as a screening device for their selection. Also a good case history on managers might serve a similar purpose in manager selection.

Clinical Practice

To be therapeutic, social workers and other human service professionals must have empathy for their clientele. However, many people have difficulty in relating to the three groups under consideration. For this reason, only professionals having this ability (or good potential for developing it) should be assigned to adult foster care. Professionals should visit the homes monthly as a minimum. For each visit, the worker should have an objective in mind, even if it is no more than helping to build a trusting relationship with residents and managers. If the residents and managers are reasonably verbal and intelligent, group sessions should be held with both groups simultaneously. If they are not, or if the professional is inexperienced, simulation-type games along the lines of Johnson (1972) and Johnson and Johnson (1975) would help to stimulate interaction between residents and managers. Workers should leave managers their home telephone numbers for emergencies and to help in building relationships with them. Professionals should also become involved in community education projects, e.g., workshops and public speaking engagements with various community organizations to help enlighten them on the problems and issues of adult foster care. Residents should not only be linked with professional therapeutic community programs but also with self-help groups. Some of these could be Schizophrenics Anonymous, Recovery, Inc., Associations for Retarded Citizens, senior citizens, and church groups, to name but a few of many such organizations. Whenever possible, residents should attend sheltered workshops so that they might supplement their meager incomes. Also of potential value for residents are therapeutic social clubs. These sometimes have professional leadership, but sometimes they have indigenous leadership with professional advisors. Within the latter type, I have had some experience as a volunteer professional advisor and found the experience quite rewarding except that some of my professional colleagues chided me over working for no pay.

Clinicians also need knowledge, courage, and a strong conviction to humanitarian values. These qualities are essential for serving in the advocate role for clients and managers in their battles with federal, state, and local bureaucracies. Too often, residents and managers are treated disrespectfully by petty, and sometimes not so petty, empire-building bureaucrats who act as if the agency is the client. Continuous input from residents and managers should be sought, especially in any decision-making processes which affect them. Clinicians should keep current with the literature on adult foster care and related issues, especially research. Single-subject research is currently in vogue in social work research and is recommended as a tool to monitor and evaluate clinical practice (Thomas, 1978).

Policy Makers

A unified national policy on community-based shelter care for the three categories under consideration is sorely needed. Current federal and state policies are so cumbersome that many residents and managers fall through the cracks between bureaucracies. Often there are overlapping and duplication of effort. Accountability should be required of policy makers and administrators, not just clinicians, residents, and managers. Also on the national level, policy makers need to reexamine the SSI program, especially in relation to adult foster care. Too often states cannot or will not supplement SSI incomes for residents. Some states are financially penalized for transferring residents from nursing homes to adult foster homes. From both the state and national levels, more dynamic leadership is needed in adult foster care. Some federally funded demonstration projects in the past 15 years have been a step in the right direction but more are needed.

Administrators

Mental health and social agency administrators should give adult foster care equal priority with other services. Otherwise, how can they avoid criticism, by humanitarians, of being caught up in the social Darwinian ethic of favoring the "fittest"? As a minimum, a subsection on protective services for adults should be established to mitigate against resident exploitation and abuse and to investigate complaints as they arise. Administrators should require social workers to visit the homes at least monthly and to give managers their home telephone numbers. Also, administrators need to ensure the careful selection of workers for adult foster care. Also ongoing in-service training programs are needed for them and managers so as to encourage self-renewal and diminish the tendency toward burnout in such demanding work. Also, middle-management personnel sometimes do not appear to have had firsthand experience with adult foster care. They, and even experienced middle-management personnel, should be required to stay familiar with the homes' location and to know the managers and residents. Special incentives and awards should be provided to managers with exceptional motivations and abilities. Managers should be encouraged to form local and state organizations so as to enhance their effectiveness, morale, and esprit de corps. Finally, much more emphasis is needed on selecting managers of high quality.

Epilogue

It is hoped that this book will cast the die for substantial improvement in adult foster care, or if not, that a more suitable alternative can be located and quickly developed. At this time, however, I believe that adult foster care is a reasonably humane and viable system for providing an alternative to prolonged institutionalization. However, many improvements are needed. To bring about these changes, the dedication of national and state leaders not to mention the rest of us, is sorely needed.

Social work, the heir apparent to the unwanted stepchild of adult foster care, also has growing pains. It seems that we share much in common with our stepchild. Some of our mutual problems are slowness (or absence in some cases) of official state regulation and sanction and the concomitant low pay that the lack of such recognition fosters. Not only does this affect our pocketbooks but also our prestige, in other words, our social margin. Some of the wealthier siblings of social work are good examples, i.e., psychiatrists and psychologists. However, those professions seem to have advanced themselves prestige-wise and materially by following the roads toward science, technology, and politics. Are we as social workers and other human service professionals willing to pay that price at the expense of our humanitarian ideals, or can we still be scientific without sacrificing our humanitarian values? It seems that we are now heavily engaged in the battle to do just that, but we need more allies. Only the future holds the answer to the future of social work and the outcome of a 1200–1300-year-old unwanted stepchild—adult foster care.

REFERENCES

CHAPTER 1

American Psychiatric Association. *Diagnostic and statistical manual of mental disorders* (2nd ed.). Washington, D.C.: American Psychiatric Association, 1968.

Butterfield, E. Some basic changes in residential facilities. In R. B. Kugel & A. Shearer, (Eds.), *Changing patterns in residential services for the mentally retarded*. Washington, D.C.: Presidents Committee on Mental Retardation, 1976.

Deutsch, A. *The mentally ill in America*. New York: Columbia University Press, 1949.

Henry, J. *Culture against man*. New York: Random House, 1963.

Kaufman, R. J. *A social ecological study of Veterans American community placement settings*. Unpublished doctoral dissertation, Brandeis University, 1976.

McCoin, J. M. *A study of the association between community care home sponsors' personalities and alienation patterns of long-hospitalized schizophrenic male veterans*. Unpublished doctoral dissertation, University of Minnesota, 1977.

McCoin, J. M. *Adult foster homes: An empirical study*. Unpublished manuscript, 1979.

Miller, D., & Blanc, E. Concepts of 'moral treatment' for the mentally ill: Implications for social work practice with posthospital mental patients. *Social Service Review,* 1967, *41,* 66–74.

Miller, M. C. A program for adult foster care. *Social Work,* 1977, *22,* 275–279.

National Association of Social Workers. *Encyclopedia of social work.* New York: National Association of Social Workers, 1971.

Pincus, A., & Minahan, A. *Social work practice: Model and method.* Itasca, Ill.: F. E. Peacock, 1973.

Pumphrey, R. E., & Pumphrey, M. W. (Eds.). *The heritage of American social work.* New York: Columbia University Press, 1961.

Segal, S. P., & Aviram, V. *The mentally ill in community based shelter care: A Study of community care and social integration.* New York: John Wiley, 1978.

Webster's New Collegiate Dictionary. Springfield, Mass.: Merriam, 1953.

Webster's New Collegiate Dictionary. Springfield, Mass.: Merriam, 1977.

Wolff, K. *The emotional rehabilitation of the geriatric patient.* Springfield, Ill.: Thomas, 1970.

Zweben, A. *Family care: An exploratory study.* Unpublished doctoral dissertation, Columbia University, 1977.

CHAPTER 2

Albright, E. S. Personal communication with social services specialist, Bureau of Alternate Care, Wisconsin Department of Social Service, Madison, Wisconsin, March 30, 1978.

de Alvarado, C. R. *An experiment in community living for mental patients: Family care in Springfield State Hospital, Maryland.* Unpublished doctoral dissertation, University of Pennsylvania, 1955.

Anderson, J. Ex-mental patients abandoned. *Oshkosh Daily Northwestern,* Oshkosh, Wisconsin, February 18, 1978.

Aptekar, H. H. Foster and home care for adults. *Encyclopedia of Social Work,* 1965, *15,* 351–357.

Arnhoff, F. N. Social consequences of policy toward mental illness. *Science,* 1975, *188,* 1277–1281.

Barton, W. E. Family care and outpatient psychiatry. *American Journal of Psychiatry,* 1959, *115,* 642–645.

Barton, W. E., & St. John, W. T. Family care and out-patient psychiatry. *American Journal of Psychiatry,* 1961, *117,* 644–646.

Barton, W. E. Family care and outpatient psychiatry. *American Journal of Psychiatry*, 1963, *119*, 665–669.

Bernstein, R. Personal communication with Chief, Bureau of Long Term Care, Texas Department of Health, Austin, Tex., August 14, 1979.

Bigelow, N. J. T., & Schied, E. M. The therapeutic promise of foster family care for the mentally ill. *Psychiatric Quarterly*, 1939, *13*, 16–31.

Birenbaum, A., & Re, M. A. Resettling mentally retarded adults in the community. *American Journal of Mental Deficiency*, 1979, *83*, 323–329.

Bowen, W. T., & Fischer, G. J. Community attitudes toward family care. *Mental Hygiene*, 1962, *46*, 400–407.

Brody, E. M. Comments on Sherman/Newman paper. *Gerontologist*, 1977, *17*, 520–521.

Brook, B. D., Cortes, M., March, R., & Sundberg-Stirling, B. A. Community families: An alternative to psychiatric hospital intensive care. *Hospital and Community Psychiatry*, 1976, *27*, 195–197.

Brown, S. J., Windle, C., & Stewart, E. Statistics on a family care program. *American Journal of Mental Deficiency*, 1959, *64*, 535–542.

Butterfield, E. Some basic changes in residential facilities. In R. B. Kugel & A. Shearer (Eds.), *Changing patterns in residential services for the mentally retarded.* Washington, D.C.: Presidents Committee on Mental Retardation, 1976, 15–23.

Buxbaum, C. B. Second thoughts on community mental health. *Social Work*, 1973, *18*(3), 24–29.

Cautley, P. W., & Aldridge, M. J. Predicting success for new foster parents. *Social Work*, 1975, *20*, 48–53.

Cherry, M. S. *Factors related to the voluntary or mandatory closing of family care homes.* Unpublished masters thesis, University of Southern California, 1963.

Crockett, H. M. Boarding homes as a tool in social casework with mental patients. *Mental Hygiene*, 1934, *18*, 189–204.

Crutcher, H. B. *Foster home care for mental patients.* New York: Commonwealth Fund, 1944.

Cunningham, M. K., Botwinik, W., Dolson, J., & Weickert, A. A. Community placement of released mental patients: A five-year study. *Social Work*, 1959, *14*(1), 54–61.

Dumont, M. P., & Aldrich, C. K. Family care after a thousand years—a crisis in the tradition of St. Dymphna. *American Journal of Psychiatry*, 1962, *119*, 116–121.

Edelson, M. B. Alternative living arrangements. In H. R. Lamb & Associates, *Community survival for long-term patients.* San Francisco: Jossey-Bass, 1976, 33–55.

Evans, E. B. *The interpersonal relationships formed between sponsors and psychiatric patients in community-family care.* Unpublished doctoral dissertation, Brandeis University, 1976.

Federal Register, January 31, 1978, *43,* 4020.

Fenske, V., & Roecker, M. Finding foster homes for adults. *Public Welfare,* 1971, *29,* 404–410.

Giovannoni, J. M., & Ullman, L. P. Characteristics of family care homes. *International Journal of Social Psychiatry,* 1961, *7,* 299–306.

Goldenson, R. M. *Encyclopedia of Human Behavior: Psychology, Psychiatry and Mental Health.* Vol. 1. Garden City, N.Y.; Doubleday, 1970, 445–446.

Joint Commission on Mental Illness and Health. *Action for mental health: Final Report.* New York: Basic Books, 1961.

Kaufman, R. J. *A social ecological study of Veterans Administration community placement settings.* Unpublished doctoral dissertation, Brandeis University, 1976.

Keskiner, A., & Zalcman, M. Returning to community life: The foster community model. *Diseases of the Central Nervous System,* 1974, *35,* 419–426.

Kilgour, A. J. Colony Gheel. *American Journal of Psychiatry,* 1936, *92,* 959–965.

Lamb, H. R. Preface. In H. R. Lamb & Associates. *Community survival for long-term patients.* San Francisco: Jossey-Bass, 1976, xi–xiii.

Lamb R., & Goertzel, V. Discharged mental patients—are they really in the community? *Archives of General Psychiatry,* 1971, *21,* 29–34.

Lee, D. T. Family care: Selection and prediction. *American Journal of Psychiatry,* 1963, *120,* 561–566.

Linn, M. W., & Caffey, E. M. Foster placement for the older psychiatric patient. *Journal of Gerontology,* 1977, *32,* 340–345.

Lyle, C. M., & Trail, O. A study of psychiatric patients in foster homes. *Social Work,* 1961, *6*(1), 82–88.

Magner, G. W. *Placement of mental patients in family care.* Unpublished doctoral dissertation, University of Chicago, 1961.

McCoin, J. M. *A study of the association between community care home sponsors' personalities and alienation patterns of long-hospitalized schizophrenic male veterans.* Unpublished doctoral dissertation, University of Minnesota, 1977.

McCrary, L., & Keiden, B. Reporters from: *Philadelphia Inquirer,* appeared on "Good Morning, America" television program, October 26, 1978.

McNeel, B. H. Family care. *American Journal of Psychiatry,* 1965, *121,* 701–703.

Michaux, W. W., Katz, M. M., Kurland, A. A., & Gansereit, K. H. *The first year out*. Baltimore: Johns Hopkins Press, 1969.

Miller, D. H. Who are the family caretakers? *California Mental Health Research Digest*, 1964, *2*, 5–6.

Miller, M. C. A program for adult foster care. *Social Work*, 1977, *22*, 275–279.

Molholm, H., & Barton, W. Family care, a community resource in the rehabilitation of mental patients. *American Journal of Psychiatry*, 1941, *98*, 33–41.

Morrissey, J. R. Family care for the mentally ill: A neglected therapeutic resource. *Social Service Review*, 1965a, *39*, 63–71.

Morrissey, J. R. Family care research: A methodological note. *Community Mental Health Journal*, 1965b, *1*, 181–183.

Morrissey, J. R. *The case of family care for the mentally ill*. New York: Behavioral Publications, 1967.

Muncie, W. Foster homes for adults. *Journal of Nervous and Mental Diseases*, 1945, *102*, 477–482.

Murphy, H. B. M., Pennee, B., & Luchins, D. Foster homes: The new back wards? *Canada's Mental Health Supplement No. 71*, 1972, 1–17.

Murphy, H. B. M., Engelsman, N. F., & Tcheng-Laroche, F. The influence of foster home care on psychiatric patients. *Archives of General Psychiatry*, 1976, *33*, 179–183.

Newman, E. S., & Sherman, S. R. A survey of caretakers in adult foster care. *Gerontologist*, 1977, *5*, 436–439.

O'Connor, G., Justice, R. S., & Warren, N. The aged mentally retarded: Institution or community care? *American Journal of Mental Deficiency*, 1970, *75*, 354–360.

Overall, J. E., & Gorham, D. R. The brief psychiatric rating scale. *Psychological Reports*, 1962, *10*, 799–812.

Parks, J. M. *Characteristics of family care sponsors Veterans Administration Hospital, Salt Lake City, Utah, 1959*. Unpublished masters thesis, University of Utah, 1959.

Pollock, H. M. A brief history of family care of mental patients in America. *American Journal of Psychiatry*, 1945, *102*, 351–361.

Pumphrey, R. E., & Pumphrey, M. W. (Eds.) *The heritage of American social work*. New York: Columbia University Press, 1961.

Redding, R. A. Importance of early-family experience in placement of psychotic patients. *Social Work*, 1963, *8*(2), 72–76.

Richmond, C. Therapeutic housing. In H. H. Lamb & Associates. *Rehabilitation and community mental health*. San Francisco: Jossey-Bass, 1971, 114–135.

Richter, M. H., & Ostlund, L. M. Part-time social workers in a community care program. *NASW News,* 1970, *15,* 10, 23.

Sandy, W. C. Boarding out of mental patients. *Pennsylvania Medical Journal,* 1935, *35,* 155–158.

Schrader, P. J., & Elms, R. R. *Guidelines for family care home operators.* New York: Springer, 1972.

Schwartz, M. J., & Schwartz, C. *Social approaches to mental patient care.* New York: Columbia University Press, 1964.

Segal, S. P., & Aviram, V. *The mentally ill in community-based shelter care: A study of community care and social integration.* New York: John Wiley, 1978.

Segal, S. P., Baumohl, J., & Johnson, E. Falling through the cracks: Mental disorder and social margin in a young vagrant population. *Social Problems,* 1977, *24,* 387–400.

Segal, S. P. Shelter are needs of the mentally ill. *Social Work and Health Care,* 1979, *2,* 42–55.

Shadoan, R. A. Making board and care homes therapeutic. In H. R. Lamb and Assoc. *Community survival for long-term patients.* San Francisco: Jossey-Bass, 1976, 56–73.

Sherman, S. R., & Newman, E. S. Foster-family care for the elderly in New York State. *Gerontologist,* 1977, *17,* 513–520.

Sherman, S. R., & Newman, E. S. Role of the caseworker in adult foster care. *Social Work,* 1979, *24,* 324–328.

Simon, J. L. The effects of foster care payment levels in the number of foster children given homes. *Social Service Review,* 1975, *49,* 405–411.

Smitson, W. S. *The foster mother's relationship with the mental patient.* Unpublished doctoral dissertation, Smith College, 1967.

St. Cloud Veterans Administration Hospital. *Community placement: The family care program, St. Cloud, Minnesota.* Unpublished, n.d.

Steffy, A. O. *A study of the characteristics of sponsors in a psychiatric family care program: Their relationship to patient adjustment.* Unpublished masters thesis, University of Illinois, 1963.

Stycos, J. M. Family care: A neglected area of research. *Psychiatry,* 1951, *14,* 301–306.

Taylor, D. A., & Starr, P. Foster parenting: An integrative review of the literature. *Child Welfare,* 1967, *46,* 371–385.

Titmuss, R. M. Forward. In R. Z. Apte, *Halfway houses.* London: G. Bell & Sons, Ltd., 1968a.

Titmuss, R. M. *Commitment to welfare.* New York: Pantheon Books, 1968b.

Ullman, L. P., Berkman, V. C., & Hamister, R. C. Psychological report related to behavior and benefit of placement in home care. *Journal of Clinical Psychology*, 1958, *14*, 254–259.

Ullman, L. P., & Berkman, V. C. Types and outcomes found in the family care placement of mental patients. *Social Work*, 1959, *4*(2), 72–78.

U.S. Veterans Administration. *Program guide, social work service, community care.* Department of Medicine and Surgery, Washington, D.C., 1971.

Williams, J. F., & Neilson, J. Success and failure of patients in family care. *California Mental Health Research Digest*, 1964, *2*, 6–8.

Winnebago County Department of Social Services. *Adult foster care handbook.* Unpublished document, Oshkosh, Wisconsin, n.d.

Wohlford, M. Adult foster care: A unique answer. *Public Welfare*, 1968, *26*, 224–226.

Zeil, H. A. Personal communication with Chief, Bureau of Health Care Administration, Michigan Department of Public Health, Lansing, Mich. August 9, 1979.

Zweben, A. *Family care: An exploratory study.* Unpublished doctoral dissertation, Columbia University, 1977.

Chapter 3

Aaronson, L. S., Paranoia as a behavior of alienation. *Perspectives in Psychiatric Care*, 1977, *1*, 27–31.

Adorno, T. W., Frenkel-Brunswick, E., Levinson, D., & Sanford, R. N. *The authoritarian personality.* New York: Harper, 1950.

American Medical Association. *Mental retardation: A handbook for the primary physician.* Chicago: American Medical Association, 1964.

American Psychiatric Association. *Diagnostic and statistical manual of mental disorders* (2nd ed.). Washington, D.C.: American Psychiatric Association, 1968.

Babcock, C. G. Some psychodynamic factors in foster parenthood—Part I. *Child Welfare*, 1965, *44*, 485–493.

Bernard, H. W. *Human development in western culture* (5th ed.). Boston: Allyn & Bacon, 1978.

Christie, R., & Jahoda, M. (Eds.). *Studies in the scope and method of the authoritarian personality.* Glencoe, Ill.: Free Press, 1954.

Cupaiuolo, A. W. *Community interaction with V. A. family care homes for the mentally ill: A comparative study of conflict and nonconflict.* Unpublished doctoral dissertation, Columbia University, 1979.

Dean, D. C. Alienation: Its meaning and measurement. *American Sociological Review,* 1961, *26,* 753–758.

Deykin, E., Jacobson, S., Klerman, G., & Solomon, M. The empty nest: Psychosocial aspects of conflict between depressed women and their grown children. *American Journal of Psychiatry,* 1966, *122,* 1422–1426.

Dollards Illustrated Medical Dictionary, 1957 ed., s. v., alienation and alienist.

Ellenberger, H. F., Zoological garden and mental hospital. *Canadian Psychiatric Association Journal,* 1960, *5,* 136–149.

Ellman, N. K. *Degree of bureaucracy as related to sense of power and authoritarianism among teachers.* Unpublished doctoral dissertation, New York University, 1972.

Goldenson, R. M. *Encyclopedia of Human Behavior: Psychology, Psychiatry, and Mental Health.* Vol. 2, Garden City, N.Y.: Doubleday, 1970.

Evans, E. B. *The interpersonal relationships formed between sponsors and psychiatric patients in community-family care.* Unpublished doctoral dissertation, Brandeis University, 1976.

Fanshel, D. *Foster parenthood.* Minneapolis: University of Minnesota Press, 1966.

Field, M., & Bluestone, E. M. *Aging with honor and dignity.* Springfield, Ill.: Charles C Thomas, 1968.

Glaser, B. G., & Strauss, A. L. *The discovery of grounded theory: Strategies for qualitative research.* Chicago: Aldine, 1967.

Glickman, E. *Child placement through clinically oriented casework.* New York: Columbia University Press, 1957.

Gregory, E. W. The orothodoxy of the authoritarian personality. *Journal of Social Psychology,* 1957, *45,* 217–222.

Hajda, J. Alienation and integration of student intellectuals. *American Sociological Review,* 1961, *26,* 758–777.

Henry, J. *Culture against man.* New York: Random House, 1963.

Hoffer, A., & Osmond, H. *How to live with schizophrenia.* London: Morrison and Gibb, 1966.

Jones, E. E. Authoritarianism as a determinant in first impression formation. *Journal of Personality,* 1954, *23,* 107–127.

Kates, S. L., & Diab, L. N. Authoritarian ideology and attitudes. *Journal of Abnormal and Social Psychology,* 1955, *51,* 13–16.

Kaufman, R. J. *A social ecological study of Veterans Administration community placement settings.* Unpublished doctoral dissertation, Brandeis University, 1976.

Lastrucci, C. L. *The scientific approach: Basic principles of the scientific method.* Cambridge, Mass: Schenkman, 1967.

Levinson, P. Chronic dependency: A conceptual analysis. *Social Service Review,* 1964, *38,* 371–381.

Lidz, T. *The person: His and her development throughout the life cycle.* New York: Basic Books, 1976.

Lukes, S. *Essays on social theory.* New York: Columbia University Press, 1977.

Lukton, R. C. Current views on the etiology of schizophrenia. *Health and Social Work,* 1976, *1,* 70–84.

Marcus, E. S. Ego breakdown in schizophrenia: Some implications for casework treatment. In F. J. Turner (Ed.), *Differential diagnosis and treatment in social work* (2nd ed.). New York: The Free Press, 1976, 322–340.

McBroom, E. Socialization and social casework. In W. W. Roberts & R. H. Nee (Eds.), *Theories of social casework.* Chicago: University of Chicago Press, 1970.

McCoin, J. M. *A study of the association between community care home sponsors' personalities and alienation patterns of long-hospitalized schizophrenic male veterans.* Unpublished doctoral dissertation, University of Minnesota, 1977.

McCoin, J. M. *Effects of income on hospitalized veterans.* Unpublished manuscript, Oshkosh, Wisc., 1978.

McCoin, J. M. *Adult foster homes: an empirical study.* Unpublished manuscript, Grand Rapids, Mich., 1979.

Miller, M. C. A program for adult foster care. *Social Work,* 1977, *22,* 275–279.

Morrissey, J. R. *The case of family care for the mentally ill.* New York: Behavioral Publications, 1967.

Murphy, H. B. M., Engelsmann, F., & Tcheng-Laroche, F. The influence of foster-home care on psychiatric patients. *Archives of General Psychiatry,* 1976, *33,* 179–183.

Murphy, H. B. M., Pennee, B., & Luchins, D. Foster homes: The new back wards? *Canada's Mental Health* Supplement # 71, 1972.

Robinson, J. P., & Shaver, P. R. *Measures of Social psychological attitudes.* Ann Arbor, Mich.: Institute of Social Research, 1973.

Segal, S. P. Shelter care needs of the mentally ill. *Social work and Health Care,* 1979, *2,* 42–55.

Segal, S. P., Baumohl, J., & Johnson, E. Falling through the cracks: Mental disorder and social margin in a young vagrant population. *Social Problems,* 1977, *24,* 387–400.

Selltiz, C., Wrightsman, L. S., & Cook, S. W. *Research methods in social relations,* New York: Holt Rinehart, & Winston, 1976.

Sheerin, E. J., & Sheerin, J. L. *Adult foster care training program evaluation.* Lansing, Mich.: State Department of Social Services, 1977.

Smalley, R. The significance of the family for the development of personality. *Social Service Review,* 1950, *24,* 59–66.

Smitson, W. S. *The foster mother's relationship with the mental patient.* Unpublished doctoral dissertation, Smith College, 1967.

Steffy, A. O. *A study of the characteristics of sponsors in a psychiatric family care program.* Unpublished masters thesis, University of Illinois, 1963.

Teeter, R. B. *A study of community tenure, social participation, and patterns of alienation as related to continuity of service for formerly hospitalized mental patients.* Unpublished doctoral dissertation, University of Minnesota, 1972.

Torrance, J. *Estrangement, alienation, and exploitation: A sociological approach to historical materialism.* New York: Columbia University Press, 1977.

Turner, F. J. Some considerations on the place of theory in current social work practice. In F. J. Turner (Ed.), *Social Work Treatment.* New York: Free Press, 1974, 3–16.

Wax, J. Developing social work power in a medical organization. *Social Work,* 1968, *14*(4), 62–71.

Whorley, L. W. *Social exchange patterns in the psychiatric foster home.* Unpublished doctoral dissertation, University of Maryland, 1978.

Wolff, K. *The biological, sociological and psychological aspects of aging.* Springfield, Ill.: Charles C Thomas, 1959.

Wolff, K. *The emotional rehabilitation of the geriatric patient.* Springfield, Ill.: Charles C Thomas, 1970.

Zweben, A. *Family care: An exploratory study.* Unpublished doctoral dissertation, Columbia University, 1977.

CHAPTER 4

Adorno, T. W., Frenkel-Brunswick, E., Levinson, D., & Sanford, R. N. *The authoritarian personality.* New York: Harper, 1950.

Berger, R., & Piliavin, I. The effect of casework. *Social Work,* 1976, *21,* 205–208.

Campbell, D. T., & Staneley, J. C. *Experimental and quasi-experimental designs for research.* Chicago: Rand-McNally, 1966.

Christie, R., & Jahoda, M. (Eds.). *Studies in the scope and method of the authoritarian personality.* Glencoe: Ill.: Free Press, 1954.

Cupaiuolo, A. D. *Community interaction with V.A. family care homes for the mentally ill: A comparative study of conflict and non-conflict.* Unpublished doctoral dissertation, Columbia University, 1979.

Dean, D. C. Alienation: Its meaning and measurement. *American Sociological Review,* 1961, 26, 753–758.

Fanshel, D. Parental visiting of foster children: A computerized study. *Social Work Research & Abstracts,* 1977, *13,* 2–10.

Fischer, J., & Hudson, W. W. An effect of casework: Back to the drawing board. *Social Work,* 1976, *21,* 347–349.

Fromm, E. *The sane society.* New York: Rinehart, 1955.

Gregory, E. W. The orthodoxy of the authoritarian personality. *Journal of Social Psychology,* 1957, *45,* 217–222.

Kahn, A. J. The design of research. In N. A. Polansky (Ed.), *Social Work Research.* Chicago: University of Chicago Press, 1960.

Kim, J., & Kohout, F. J. Multiple regression analysis: Subprogram regression. In N. H. Nie, C. H. Hull, J. G. Jenkins, K. Steinbrenner, & D. H. Bent (Eds.), *Statistical package for the social sciences.* New York: McGraw-Hill, 1975.

Kogan, L. S. Principles of measurement. In N. A. Polansky (Ed.), *Social work research.* Chicago: University of Chicago Press, 1960.

Labovitz, S. The assignment of numbers to rank order categories. *American Sociological Review,* 1970, *35,* 515–524.

McCoin, J. M. *A study of the association between community care home sponsors' personalities and alienation patterns of long-hospitalized schizophrenic male veterans.* Unpublished doctoral dissertation, University of Minnesota, 1977.

McCoin, J. M. *Adult foster homes: An empirical study.* Unpublished manuscript, Grand Rapids, Mich:, 1979.

Miller, D. C. *Handbook of research design and social measurement.* New York: David McKay, 1970.

Nie, N. H., Hull, C. H., Jenkins, J. G., Steinbrenner, K., & Bent, D. H. *Statistical package for the social sciences.* New York: McGraw-Hill, 1975.

Robinson, J. P., & Shaver, P. R. *Measures of social psychological attitudes.* Ann Arbor, Mich.: University of Michigan, 1973.

Selltiz, C., Wrightsman, L. S., & Cook, S. W. *Research methods in social relations.* New York: Holt, Rinehart & Winston, 1976.

Sullivan, H. S. *Schizophrenia as a human process.* New York: Norton, 1962.

Teeter, R. B. *A study of community tenure, social participation, and patterns of alienation as related to continuity of services for formerly hospitalized mental patients.* Unpublished doctoral dissertation, University of Minnesota, 1972.

Tessler, R. B., & Polansky, N. A. Perceived similarity: A paradox in interviewing. *Social Work,* 1974, *20,* 359–362.

Whorley, L. W. Social exchange patterns in the psychiatric foster home. Unpublished doctoral dissertation, University of Marryland, 1978.

Chapter 5

Abell, D. F. Personal communication with Staff Development Coordinator, Division of Licensing, State Department of Welfare, Richmond, Va., 1979.

Albright, E. S. Personal communication with Social Services Specialist, State Department of Health and Social Services, Madison, Wisc., 1978.

Anderson, J. Ex-mental patients abandoned. *Oshkosh Daily Northwestern,* Oshkosh, Wisc., February 18, 1978.

Barquin, K. Personal communication with employee, D.C. Office on Aging, Washington, D.C., 1979.

Bays, W. Personal communication with Health Facilities Program Administrator, State Department of Health, Charleston, W. Va., 1979.

Bernstein, R. Personal communication with Chief, Bureau of Long Term Care, State Department of Health, Austin, Tex., 1979.

Borland, M. Personal communication with Acting Chief, Bureau of Housing Policy and Development, Division of Mental Health, Department of Human Services, Trenton, N.J., 1980.

Bratka, C. Personal communication with Program and Planning Specialist, Division of Social Services, State Department of Public Welfare, Lincoln, Nebr., 1980.

Cain, E. Personal communication with Director, Division of Aging, Department of Health and Social Services, New Castle, Del., 1980.

Cashaw, E. Personal communication with Manager, Residential Licensure Bureau, Department of Mental Health/Mental Retardation, Columbus, OH., 1979.

Cate, C. W. Personal communication with Regulatory Administrator, Office of Community Residential and Resource Development, State Department of Mental Health, Mental Retardation and Hospitals, Cranston, R.I., 1979.

Clifford, P. M. Personal communication with State Coordinator, Supportive Living Program, Mental Health Services Section, State Division of Mental Health and Mental Retardation, Atlanta, GA., 1979.

Clifford, P. M. Personal communication with State Coordinator, Supportive Living Programs, Mental Health Services Section, State Division of Mental Health and Mental Retardation, Atlanta, GA., 1980.

DiCenso, R. D. Personal communication with Chief, Division of Facilities Regulation, Community Health Services, State Department of Health, Providence, R.I., 1979.

Donnelson, L. Personal communication with Employee, State Department of Mental Health and Retardation, Austin, Tex., 1979.

Engquist, C. L. Personal communication with Director, Social Work Service, Veterans Administration Central Office, Washington, D.C., 1979.

Fish, J. Personal communication with Social Service Specialist, Welfare Division, State Department of Human Resources, Carson City, Nev., 1980.

Florida, "Residential Facilities Rules of the Department of Health and Rehabilitative Services, Chapter 10F-6, Licensure of Residental Facilities, n.d.

Folkemer, D. C. Personal communication with Long Term Care Coordinator, State Office on Aging, Baltimore, MD., 1979.

Fowler, J. R. Personal communication with Chief, Bureau of Adult and Child Development, Division of Community Rehabilitation, State Department of Health and Welfare, Boise, Ida., 1979.

Fuller, D. R. Personal communication with Director, Division of Evaluation and Services, Office of Human Development, State Department of Health and Human Resources, Baton Rouge, La., 1980.

Fuller, E. E. Personal communication with Program Manager, Bureau of Maine's Elderly, State Department of Human Services, Augusta, ME., 1979.

Garcia, A. A. Personal communication with Chief, Mental Health Bureau, State Behavioral Heath Services Division, Santa Fe, N.M., 1979.

Garrett, B. D. Personal communication with Director, Adult Services Division, State Department of Social Services, Columbia, S.C., 1979.

Gersten, E. Personal communication with Coordinator, Community Support Project, Division of Behavioral Health, State Department of Health Services, Phoenix, Ariz., 1980.

Ginsberg, L. H. Personal communication with Commissioner, State Department of Welfare, Charleston, W. Va., 1979.

Hall, W. S. Personal communication with State Commissioner of Mental Health, Columbia, S.C. 1979.

Hammer, V. Personal communication with Social Service Planning Specialist, Division of Adult Residential Care, State Department of Social Services, Albany, N.Y., 1980.

Harmon, R. E. Personal communication with Chief, Policy and Administrative Support Branch, State Department of Social Services, Sacramento, Calif., 1980.

Hartwick, D. Personal communication with Chief, Domiciliary Facilities Service, State Department of Health, Oklahoma City, Okla., 1979.

Hartze, M. Personal communication with Director of Community Services, State Social Service Board, Bismarck, N.D., 1980.

Headrick, C. H. Personal communication with Psychiatric Social Worker Supervisor, Lakeshore Mental Health Institute, Knoxville, Tenn., 1980.

Heighway, G. F. Personal communication with Director, Division of Health Facilities, State Board of Health, Indianapolis, Ind., 1979.

Inouye, W. H. Personal communication with Head, Clinical Services Standards, Program Support Services, Mental Health Division, State Department of Health, Honolulu, HI., 1979.

Jiménez-Colón, S. Personal communication with Auxiliary Secretary for Institutional Services, Puerto Rico Department of Health, San Juan, P.R., 1979.

Kaplan, M. M. Personal communication with Chief, Program Analyst, Division of Program Operations, State Office of Mental Health, Albany, N.Y., 1979.

Kellow, F. S. Personal communication with Assistant State Administrator, State Department of Health and Social Services, Cheyenne, Wyo., 1979.

Kemp, C. P. Personal communication with Chief, Central Referral Bureau, Department of Human Resources, Social Rehabilitation Administration, Government of the District of Columbia, Washington, D.C., 1979.

Kentucky, *Department for Human Resources, Bureau of Health Services, Health Facilities and Health Services Certificate of Need and Licensure Board*, State Department for Human Resources, Frankfort, KY., 1977.

Kinsinger, F. L. Personal communication with Director of Licensing, State Department of Public Welfare, Harrisburg, Pa., 1979.

Kott, M. G. Personal communication with Director, Division of Mental Retardation, State Department of Human Services, Trenton, N.J., 1979.

Larsen, J. G. Personal communication with Program Development Specialist, Division of Mental Retardation, State Department of Mental Health, Jackson, Miss., 1980.

Lawry, D. M. Personal communication with Planning Coordinator, State Department of Elder Affairs, Boston, Mass., 1979.

Lindren, D. Personal communication with Research Analyst, Mental Health Bureau, State Department of Public Welfare, St. Paul, Minn., 1980.

Lizon, R. H. Personal communication with Director, Bureau for Children, Youth, and Families, Division of Community Services, State Department of Health and Social Services, Madison, Wisc., 1979.

Long, W. R. Personal communication with Program Specialist, State Department of Social Services, Salt Lake City, UT., 1979.

Massachusetts, Division of Mental Health Services, *Northampton Consent Decree, Civil Action No. 76–4423–F*, United States Court, District of Massachusetts, Boston, Mass., 1976.

McCurdy, R. W. Personal communication with Supervisor, Adult Services Programs, State Department of Social Services, Denver, Colo., 1979, 1980.

Michigan, Department of Social Services, *Administrative Rules for Adult Foster Care Facilities,* Lansing, Mich., 1977.

Miller, L. Personal communication with Administrative Assistant, Office of Long Term Care, Division of Social Services, State Department of Human Services, Little Rock, Ark., 1979.

Monroe, P. Personal communication with Adult and Child Care Coordinator, State Department of Health and Social Services, Juneau, Alas., 1979.

Montana, Department of Social and Rehabilitation Services, *Adult Foster Family Care Policy,* 1976.

Moore, R. L. Personal communication with Chief, Bureau of Long Term Care Facilities, Division of Health Resources, State Department of Health Services, Phoenix, Ariz., 1979.

Morrissey, J. R. *The case of family care for the mentally ill.* New York: Behavioral Publications, 1967.

Morrissey, R. J. Personal communication with Director, Health Resources, State Department of Health and Environment, Topeka, Kans., 1979.

Nebraska, Department of Public Welfare, *A Guide for Adult Family Home Sponsors,* Lincoln, Nebr., n.d.

Nelsen, L. H. Personal communication with Program Coordinator, Division of Aging, State Department of Social Services, Salt Lake City, UT., 1979.

New Mexico, Department of Health and Social Services, *Adult Residential Shelter Care Homes Regulations and Standards,* Santa Fe, N.M., n.d.

New York, Department of Mental Hygiene, *Family Care Manual for Staff and Part 87 Standards for Family Care Homes,* Albany, N.Y., 1977.

Noë, G. Personal communication with Administrator, Division of Community Programs, State Department of Health and Social Services, Cheyenne, Wyo., 1979.

North Carolina, Division of Social Services, Department of Human Resources, *Family Care Homes: Minimum and Desired Standards and Regulations*, Raleigh, N.C., 1977a.

North Carolina, Division of Social Services, Department of Human Resources, *Homes for the Aged and Infirm: Minimum and Desired Standards and Regulations*, Raleigh, N.C., 1977b.

North Carolina, Division of Social Services, Department of Human Resources, *Minimum and Desired Standards and Regulations for Group Homes for Developmentally Disabled Adults*, Raleigh, N.C., 1978.

Ohio, Department of Mental Health and Mental Retardation, Division of Mental Health, *Rules for Licensure of Residential Facilities for the Mentally Ill*, Columbus, OH., 1979a.

Ohio, Department of Mental Health and Mental Retardation, Division of Mental Retardation, *Facilities Licensed to Care for the Mentally Retarded and Developmentally Disabled*, Columbus, OH., 1979b.

Ohio, Division of Social Services, Department of Public Welfare, *Ohio Laws Governing the Licensing of Adult Foster Care Facilities*, Columbus, OH., n.d.

Oregon, Adult and Family Services Division, State Department of Human Resources, *Oregon Administrative Rules, Chapter 461, Adult and Family Services Division*, Portland, Oreg., 1979.

Oregon, Adult Residential Care Homes, State Department of Human Resources, *Oregon Administrative Rules*, Chapter 410, Portland, Oreg., n.d.

Orton, R. E. Personal communication with Assistant Commissioner for Social Services, State Department of Human Resources, Austin, Tex., 1979.

Palmer, B. Personal communication with Administrator, Specialized Adult Services, State Department of Health and Rehabilitative Services, Tallahassee, Fla., 1979.

Parker, R. C., & Pettee, L. M. Personal communication with Mental Retardation Adult Services Specialist and Consultant, Adult Foster Care Services, State Department of Human Resources, Raleigh, N.C., 1979.

Pettee, L. M. Personal communication with Consultant, Adult Foster Care Services, State Department of Human Resources, Raleigh, N.C., 1979.

Proctor, J. Personal communication with Housing Development Specialist, Division of Mental Health and Developmental Services, State Department of Health and Welfare, Concord, N.H., 1979.

Puerto Rico, Assistant Secretariat of Family Services, Department of Social Services, *Regulation Number 1 for the Licensing and Supervision of Institutions for the Aged in Puerto Rico,* San Juan, P.R., 1979.

Richards, D. G. Personal communication with Bureau of Adult Services Employee, Division of Welfare, State Department of Health and Welfare, Concord, N.H., 1979.

Rose, R. Personal communication with Private Care Consultant, Division of Developmental Disabilities, State Department of Mental Health and Developmental Disabilities, Springfield, Ill., 1980.

Roy, D. Personal communication with Adult Services Coordinator, State Division of Social Services, Wilmington, Del., 1979.

Sanna, R. Personal communication with Employee, State Department of Mental Health Services, Boston, Mass., 1980.

Schmit, J. Personal communication with Administrative Aide, Office of Adult Services and Aging, Division of Human Development, State Department of Social Services, Pierre, S.D., 1979.

Schuler, L. T., & Kamakawiwoole, C. Personal communication with Nursing Consultants for Care Homes, Hospital and Medical Facilities Branch, State Department of Health, Honolulu, HI., 1979.

Scott, G. V. Personal communication with Chief, Licensing Evaluation and Support Bureau, State Department of Social Services, Sacramento, Calif., 1979.

Sekora, D. Personal communication with Consultant, Social Services Bureau, State Department of Social and Rehabilitative Services, Helena, Mont., 1979, 1980.

Sewell, J. R. Personal communication with Director, Community Placement, Pinecrest School, Office of Mental Retardation, Pineville, LA., 1980.

Sherman, S. R., & Newman, E. S. Foster family care for the elderly in New York State. *The Gerontologist,* 1977, *17,* 513–520.

South Dakota, Office of Resource Development, Division of Human Development, *Chapter 67:42:02 Adult Foster Care,* Pierre, S.D., n.d.

Steinhauer, M. B. *Family Home Care Program: A Study of Geriatric Foster Care Services as an Alternative Housing Environment in Illinois.* Illinois Department on Aging, Springfield, Ill., 1978.

Stern, A. J. Personal communication with Assistant Director, Division of Developmental Disabilities, State Department of Social and Health Services, Olympia, Wash., 1980.

Stevens, C. J. Personal communication with Director, Licensing and Certification Section, State Department of Mental Retardation, Hartford, Conn., 1980.

Surles, R. C. Personal communication with Commissioner, State Department of Mental Health, Waterbury, VT., 1980.

Tennessee, Department of Public Health, *Rules of Tennessee Department of Public Health Care Facilities*, Nashville, Tenn., n.d.

Treleaven, J. H. Personal communication with Administrator for Mental Health, Department of Human Resources, Salem, Oreg., 1980.

Turner, W. Personal communication with Bureau of Family Support Services Employee, Division of Community Programs, State Department of Social Services, Des Moines, IA., 1979.

Vaughn, R. Personal communication with Chief, Non-Institutional Care and Services, State Department of Mental Health, Montgomery, Ala., 1979.

Walker, J. C. Personal communication with State Ombudsman, State Department of Aging, Hartford, Conn., 1979.

Washington, Department of Health and Social Services, *Minimum Licensing Requirements for Foster Family Homes for Children, Expectant Mothers, Developmentally Disabled Adults and Other Adults in Need of Protection*, Olympia, Wash., 1978.

Watson, G. C. Personal communication with Chief, Health Care Facilities, Division of Health Care Facilities, State Department of Public Health, Nashville, Tenn., 1979.

Zanella, P. F. Personal communication with Administrator, Community Services, Department of Mental Health, Retardation and Hospitals, Cranston, R.I., 1980.

Zdanowicz, D. Personal communication with Chief, Bureau of Field Services, State Division of Mental Retardation, Trenton, N.J., 1980.

Zinnikas, J. D. Personal communication with Director, Bureau of Community and Residential Care, State Department of Social and Health Services, Olympia, Wash., 1979.

Zuckerberg, I. Personal communication with Administrative Assistant, Policy, Planning, and Evaluation, Adult Foster Care Licensing Division, State Department of Social Services, Lansing, Mich., 1980.

CHAPTER 6

American Psychiatric Association. *Diagnostic and statistical manual for mental disorders*. Washington, D.C.: American Psychiatric Association, 1968.

Folkemer, D. C. Personal communication with state Long Term Care Coordinator, Office of Aging, Baltimore, MD., 1979.

Grand Rapids, Michigan, Chamber of Commerce. Personal communication with employee, 1980.

McCoin, J. M. *A study of the association between community care home sponsors' personalities and alienation patterns of long-hospitalized schizophrenic male veterans.* Unpublished doctoral dissertation, University of Minnesota, 1977.

McCoin, J. M. *Adult foster homes: An empirical study.* Unpublished manuscript, Grand Rapids, Michigan, 1979.

McCurdy, R. W. Personal communication with State Supervisor, Adult Services Programs, Division of Social Services, Denver, Colo., 1979.

Nelsen, L. H. Personal communication with Coordinator, Adult Foster Home Programs, State Department of Social Services, Salt Lake City, UT., 1979.

Sheerin, E. J., & Sheerin, J. L. *Adult foster care training program evaluation.* Lansing, Mich.: State Department of Social Services, 1977.

Stahl, G. Personal communication with Home Finder, Kent County, Michigan Department of Social Services, 1979.

Statewide Home Care Association, Inc. *Newsletter,* 1979, 7, Livonia, Michigan.

Thiele, D. Personal communication with Adult Community Placement Supervisor, Kent County, Michigan Department of Social Services, 1979, 1980.

Treleaven, J. H. Personal communication with Administrator for Mental Health, State Department of Human Resources, Salem, Oreg., 1980.

CHAPTER 7

Borland, M. Personal communication with Acting Chief, Bureau of Housing Policy and Development, Division of Mental Health, Department of Human Services, Trenton, N.J., 1980.

Bratka, C. Personal communication with Program and Planning Specialist, Division of Social Services, Department of Public Welfare, Lincoln, Nebr., 1980.

Brierland, D., & Lemmon, J. *Social work and the law.* St. Paul, Minn.: West Publishing Co., 1977.

Cain, E. Personal communication with Director, Division of Aging, Department of Health and Social Services, New Castle, Del., 1980.

Clifford, P. M. Personal communication with State Coordinator, Supportive Living Program, Mental Health Services Section, State Division of Mental Health and Mental Retardation, Atlanta, GA., 1979.

Cupaiuolo, A. D. *Community interaction with V.A. family care homes for the mentally ill: A comparative study of conflict and non-conflict.* Unpublished doctoral dissertation, Columbia University, 1979.

Denny, L. W. Personal communication with Director, Licensing Unit, State Department of Social Services, Columbia, S.C., 1980.

Fish, J. Personal communication with Social Service Specialist, Welfare Division, State Department of Human Resources, Carson City, Nev., 1980.

Hall, W. S. Personal communication with State Commissioner of Mental Health, Columbia, S.C., 1979.

Harmon, R. E. Personal communication with Chief, Policy and Administrative Support Branch, State Department of Social Services, Sacramento, Calif., 1980.

Headrick, C. H. Personal communication with Psychiatric Social Worker Supervisor, Lakeshore Mental Health Institute, Knoxville, Tenn., 1980.

Iwan, M. J. Personal communication with Adult Social Services Administrator, State Division of Social Services, Lincoln, Nebr., 1979.

Kane, D., & Sanders, M. Personal communication with Director of Community Services, State Social Service Board, Bismark, N.D. and forwarded to me by the latter, 1980.

Kimber, C. M. Personal communication with Director, Developmental Services Program Office, State Department of Health and Rehabilitative Services, Tallahassee, Fla., 1980.

Lindren, D. Personal communication with Research Analyst, Mental Health Bureau, State Department of Public Welfare, St. Paul, Minn., 1980.

Massachusetts, Division of Mental Health Services. *Northampton Consent Decree, Civil Action No. 76-4423-F,* United States Court, District of Massachusetts, Boston, Mass., 1976.

Miller, M. C. A program for adult foster care. *Social Work,* 1977, *22,* 275–279.

Nebraska, Department of Public Welfare. *A guide for adult family home sponsors.* Lincoln, Nebr., n.d.

Nelsen, L. H. Personal communication with Program Coordinator, Division of Aging, State Department of Social Services, Salt Lake City, Ut., 1979.

Parker, R. C., & Pettee, L. M. Personal communication with Mental Retardation Adult Services Specialist and Consultant, Adult Foster Care Services, State Department of Human Resources, Raleigh, N.C., 1979.

Payne, D. Personal communication with Assistant Commissioner, State Department of Mental Health and Mental Retardation, Richmond, VA., 1980.

Pennsylvania, Office of Mental Retardation. *Implementation packet community living arrangements program for citizens who are mentally retarded.* State Department of Public Welfare, Harrisburg, Penn., 1978.

Proctor, J. Personal communications with Housing Development Specialist,

Division of Mental Health and Developmental Services, State Department of Health and Welfare, Concord, N.H., 1980.

Rose, R. Personal communication with Private Care Consultant, Division of Developmental Disabilities, State Department of Mental Health and Developmental Disabilities, Springfield, Ill., 1980.

Schrader, P. J., & Elms, R. R. *Guidelines for family care home operators*. New York: Springer, 1972.

Schuler, L. T., & Kamakawiwoole, C. Personal communication with Nursing Consultants for Care Homes, Hospital and Medical Facilities Branch, State Department of Health, Honolulu, HI., 1979.

Stevens, C. J. Personal communication with Director, Licensing and Certification Section, State Department of Mental Retardation, Hartford, Conn., 1980.

Vermont, Vermont Association for Mental Health, Inc. *The Vermont story: Community care of the mentally ill*. Montpelier, VT., 1976.

Whorley, L. W. *Social exchange patterns in the psychiatric foster home*. Unpublished doctoral dissertation, University of Maryland, 1978.

Zanella, P. F. Personal communication with Administrator, Community Services, State Department of Mental Health, Retardation, and Hospitals, Cranston, R.I., 1980.

Zdanowicz, D. Personal communication with Chief, Bureau of Field Services, State Division of Mental Retardation, Trenton, N.J., 1980.

CHAPTER 8

Aptekar, H. H. Foster and home care for adults. *Encyclopedia of Social Work*, 1965, *15*, 351–357.

Avis, D. W. Personal communication with Program Services Director, State Department of Mental Retardation, Hartford, Conn., 1980.

Boettcher, R. E., & Vander Schie, R. Milieu therapy with chronic patients. *Social Work*, 1975, *20*, 130–134.

Bogen, H. Personal communication with Director, Division of Foster Homes for Adults, New York City Human Resources Administration, 1980.

Brown, S. J., Windle, C., & Stewart, E. Statistics on a family care program. *American Journal of Mental Deficiency*, 1959, *64*, 535–542.

Cain, E. Personal communication with Director, Division on Aging, State Department of Health and Social Services, New Castle, Del., 1980.

Clifford, P. M. Personal communication with State Coordinator, Supportive

Living Program, Division of Mental Health and Mental Retardation, Atlanta, GA., 1979.

Cunningham, M. K., Botwinik, W., Dolson, J., & Weickert, A. A. Community placement of released mental patients: A five-year study. *Social Work,* 1959, *14*(1), 54–61.

Garcia, A. Personal communication with Chief, Mental Health Bureau, State Behavioral Health Services Division, Santa Fe, N.M., 1979.

Hall, J. C., & Bradley, A. K. Treating long-term mental patients. *Social Work,* 1975, *20,* 383–386.

Hall, W. S. Personal communication with State Commissioner of Mental Health, Columbia, S.C., 1979.

Harmon, R. E. Personal communication with Chief, Policy and Administrative Support Branch, State Department of Social Services, Sacramento, Calif., 1980.

Headrick, C. M. Personal communication with Psychiatric Social Worker Supervisor, Lakeshore Mental Health Institute, Knoxville, Tenn., 1980.

Inouye, W. H. Personal communication with Head, Clinical Services Standards, Program Support Services, Mental Health Division, State Department of Health, Honolulu, HI., 1979.

Iwan, M. J. Personal communication with Adult Social Services Administrator, Division of Social Services, State Department of Public Welfare, Lincoln, Neb., 1979.

Kane, D., & Sanders, M. Personal communicatiin with Stutsman County, North Dakota, Social Workers and forwarded to me by Director of Community Services, State Social Services Board, Bismark, N.D., 1980.

Levy, C. S. *Social work ethics.* New York: Human Sciences Press, 1976.

Levy, C. S. Values and ethics for social work practice. Continuing Education Series #11. Washington, D.C.: National Association of Social Workers, 1979.

Lindren, D. Personal communication with Research Analyst, Mental Health Bureau, State Department of Public Welfare, St. Paul, Minn., 1980.

McCoin, J. M. *A study of the association between community care home sponsors' personalities and alienation patterns of long-hospitalized schizophrenic male veterans.* Unpublished doctoral dissertation, University of Minnesota, 1977.

Morrissey, J. R. *The case of family care for the mentally ill.* New York: Behavioral Publications, 1967.

Murphy, H. B. M., Engelsman, N. F., & Tcheng-Laroche, F. The influence of foster home care on psychiatric patients. *Archives of General Psychiatry,* 1976, *33,* 179–183.

National Association of Social Workers. Working definition of social work practice. *Social Work,* 1977, *22,* 344–346.

National Association of Social Workers. Special issue on family policy. *Social Work,* 1979, *24,* 447–570.

National Association of Social Workers. The NASW code of ethics. *N.A.S.W. News,* 1980, *25,* 24–25.

Nebraska, Department of Public Welfare. *A guide for adult family home sponsors.* Lincoln, Neb., n.d.

Nelsen, L. H. Personal communication with Program Coordinator, Division on Aging, State Department of Social Services, Salt Lake City, UT., 1979.

Parker, R. C., & Pettee, L. M. Personal communication with Mental Retardation Adult Services Specialist and Consultant, Adult Foster Care Services, State Department of Human Resources, Raleigh, N.C., 1979.

Payne, D. Personal communication with Assistant Commissioner, State Department of Mental Health and Mental Retardation, Richmond, VA., 1980.

Pilsecker, C. Values: A problem for everyone. *Social Work,* 1978, *23,* 54–57.

Proctor, J. Personal communication with Housing Development Specialist, Division of Mental Health and Developmental Services, State Department of Health and Welfare, Concord, N.H., 1979.

Schuler, L. T., & Kamakawiwoole, C. Personal communication with Nursing Consultants for Care Homes, Hospital and Medical Facilities Branch, State Department of Health, Honolulu, HI., 1979.

Sewell, J. R. Personal communication with Director, Community Placement, Pinecrest School, Office of Mental Retardation, Pineville, LA., 1980.

Soyer, D. Reverie on working with the aged. In F. J. Turner (Ed.), *Differential diagnosis and treatment in social work.* New York: Free Press, 1976, 150–155.

Stevens, C. J. Personal communication with Director, Licensing and Certification Section, State Department of Mental Retardation, Hartford, Conn., 1980.

Surles, R. C. Personal communication with Commissioner, State Department of Mental Health, Waterbury, VT., 1980.

Vaughn, R. Personal communication with Chief, Non-Institutional Care and Services, State Department of Mental Health, Montgomery, Ala., 1979.

Willetts, R. J. Cross cultural training in operating community care homes. *Social Work,* 1978, *23,* 31–35.

Wohlford, M. Adult foster care: A unique answer. *Public Welfare,* 1968, *26,* 224–226.

Zanella, P. F. Personal communication with Administrator, Community Services, Department of Mental Health, Retardation and Hospitals, Cranston, R.I., 1980.

Zdanowicz, D. Personal communication with Chief, Bureau of Field Services, State Division of Mental Retardation, Trenton, N.J., 1980.

CHAPTER 9

Aigner, S. M., & Simons, R. L. Social work and economics: Strange bedfellows. *Social Work*, 1977, *22*, 305–308.

Anderson, J. Ex-mental patients abandoned. *Oshkosh Daily Northwestern*, Oshkosh, Wisconsin, February 18, 1978.

Anderson, R. E., & Carter, I. *Human behavior in the social environment: A social system approach.* New York: Aldine, 1978.

Avis, D. W. Personal communication with Director, Program Services, State Department of Mental Retardation, Hartford, Conn., 1980.

Barbardo, F. The case against family policy. *Social Work*, 1979, *24*, 455–458.

Barquin, K. Personal communication with employee, Office on Aging, Washington, D.C., 1979.

Berger, R., & Piliavin, I. The effect of casework: A research note. *Social Work*, 1976, *21*, 205–208.

Bogen, H. Personal communication with Director, Division of Foster Homes for Adults, City Human Resources Administration, New York, N.Y., 1980.

Brierland, D., & Lemmon, J. *Social work and the law.* St. Paul, Minn.: West Publishing Company, 1977.

Buxbaum, C. B. Second thoughts on community mental health. *Social Work*, 1973, *18*(3), 24–29.

Cain, E. Personal communication with Director, Division on Aging, State Department of Health and Social Services, New Castle, Del., 1980.

Clifford, P. M. Personal communication with State Coordinator, Supportive Living Program, Mental Health Services Section, State Division of Mental Health and Mental Retardation, Atlanta, GA., 1979.

Cupaiuolo, A. D. *Community interaction with V. A. family care homes for the mentally ill: A study of conflict and non-conflict.* Unpublished doctoral dissertation, Columbia University, 1979.

Denny, L. W. Personal communication with Director, Licensing Unit, State Department of Social Services, Columbia, S.C., 1980.

Donnelson, L. Personal communication with Employee State Department of Mental Health and Retardation, Austin, Tex., 1979.

Fish, J. Personal communication with Social Service Specialist, Welfare Division, State Department of Human Resources, Carson City, Nev., 1980.

Galper, J. *The politics of social services.* Englewood Cliffs, N.J.: Prentice-Hall, 1975.

Garcia, A. A. Personal communication with Chief, Mental Health Bureau, State Behavioral Health Services Division, Santa Fe, N.M., 1979.

Glassner, B., & Freedman, J. A. *Clinical sociology.* New York: Longman, 1979.

Gordon, W. E. Knowledge and value: Their distinction and relationship in clarifying social work practice. *Social Work,* 1965, *10*(3), 32–39.

Hall, W. S. Personal communication with State Commissioner of Mental Health, Columbia, S.C., 1979.

Harmon, R. E. Personal communication with Chief, Policy and Administrative Support Branch, State Department of Social Services, Sacramento, Calif., 1980.

Headrick, C. H. Personal communication with Psychiatric Social Worker, Lakeshore Mental Health Institute, Knoxville, Tenn., 1980.

Heraud, B. J. *Sociology and social work.* New York: Pergamon, 1970.

Horejsi, C. J. Developmental disabilities: Opportunities for social workers. *Social Work,* 1979, *24*, 40–43.

Inouye, W. H. Personal communication with Head, Clinical Service Standards, Program Support Services, State Division of Mental Health, Honolulu, HI., 1979.

Iwan, M. J. Personal communication with Adult Social Services Administrator, State Division of Social Services, Lincoln, Nebr., 1979.

Kane, D., & Sanders, M. Personal communications with Director, Community Services, State Social Services Board, Bismark, N.D., 1980.

Kaufman, A. Social policy and long-term care of the aged. *Social Work,* 1980, *25*, 133–137.

Killian, E. C. Effect of geriatric transfers on mortality rates. *Social Work,* 1970, *15*(1), 19–26.

Knickmeyer, R. A Marxist approach to social work. *Social Work,* 1972, *17*(4), 58–65.

Lichtenberg, P. Radicalism in casework. *Journal of Sociology and Social Welfare,* 1976, *4*, 258–276.

Lindren, D. Personal communication with Research Analyst, Mental Health Bureau, State Department of Public Welfare, St. Paul, Minn., 1980.

McCrary, L., & Keiden, B. Good morning, America. Nationwide television program, October 26, 1978.

McCurdy, R. A. Personal communication with Supervisor, Adult Services Programs, State Department of Social Services, Denver, Colo., 1979.

Murphy, H. B. M., Pennee, B., & Luchins, D. Foster homes: The new back wards. *Canada's Mental Health*, Supplement No. 71, September 1972, 1–17.

Murphy, H. B. M., Engelsmann, F., & Tcheng-Laroche, F. The influence of foster-home care on psychiatric patients. *Archives of General Psychiatry*, 1976, *33*, 179–183.

Nelsen, L. H. Personal communication with Program Coordinator, Division of Aging, State Department of Social Services, Salt Lake City, UT., 1979.

Nooe, R. M. Toward independent living for the mentally retarded. *Social Work*, 1975, *20*, 286–290.

Osmond, H. The medical model in psychiatry. *Hospital and Community Psychiatry*, 1970, *21*, 275–281.

Page, A. N. Economics and social work: A neglected relationship. *Social Work*, 1977, *22*, 48–53.

Parker, R. C., & Pettee, L. M. Personal communication with Mental Retardation Adult Services Specialist and Consultant, Adult Foster Care Services, State Department of Human Resources, Raleigh, N.C., 1979.

Payne, D. Personal communication with Assistant Commissioner, State Department of Mental Health and Mental Retardation, Richmond, Va., 1980.

Plant, R. *Social and moral theory in casework*. Boston: Routledge & Kegan Paul, 1970.

Proctor, J. Personal communication with Housing Development Specialist, Division of Mental Health and Developmental Services, State Department of Health and Welfare, Concord, N.H., 1980.

Scheff, T. *Being mentally ill*. Chicago: Aldine, 1966.

Schneiderman, L. Against the family. *Social Work*, 1979, *24*, 386–389.

Schuler, L. T., & Kamakawiwoole, C. Personal communication with Nursing Consultants for Care Homes, Hospital and Medical Facilities Branch, State Department of Health, Honolulu, HI., 1979.

Segal, S. P. Community care and deinstitutionalization: A review. *Social Work*, 1979, *24*, 521–527.

Sewell, J. R. Personal communication with Director, Community Placement, Office of Mental Retardation, State Department of Health and Human Services, Pineville, La., 1980.

Sherman, S. R., & Newman, E. S. Role of the caseworker in adult foster care. *Social Work,* 1979, *24,* 324–328.

Skarnulis, E. Noncitizen: Plight of the mentally retarded. *Social Work,* 1974, *19,* 56–62.

Solomon, J. R. Insanity in the mental health system. *Social Work,* 1975, *20,* 236–237.

Stern, A. J. Personal communication with Assistant Director, Division of Developmental Disabilities, State Department of Health and Social Services, Olympia, Wash., 1980.

Stevens, C. J. Personal communication with Director, Licensing Certification Section, State Department of Mental Retardation, Hartford, Conn., 1980.

Surles, R. C. Personal communication with Commissioner, State Department of Mental Health, Waterbury, VT., 1980.

Szasz, T. *The myth of mental illness.* New York: Harper & Row, 1961.

Vaughn, R. Personal communication with Chief, Non-Institutional Care and Services, State Department of Mental Health, Montgomery, Ala., 1979.

Walker, J. C. Personal communication with State Ombudsman, State Department of Aging, Hartford, Conn., 1979.

Willetts, R. J. Cross cultural training in operating community care homes. *Social Work,* 1978, *23,* 31–35.

Wink-Basing, C. Personal communication with Director, Adult Protective Services Project, School of Social Work, Western Michigan University, Kalamazoo, Mich., 1980.

Wood, K. M. Casework effectiveness: A new look at the research evidence. *Social Work,* 1978, *23,* 437–458.

Zanella, P. F. Personal communication with Administrator, Community Services, State Department of Mental Health, Retardation, and Hospitals, Cranston, R.I., 1980.

Zdanowicz, D. Personal communication with Chief, Bureau of Field Services, State Division of Mental Retardation, Trenton, N.J., 1980.

Zweben, A. *Family care: An exploratory study.* Unpublished doctoral dissertation, Coumbia University, 1977.

CHAPTER 10

Aptekar, H. H. Foster and home care for adults. *Encyclopedia of Social Work,* 1965, *15* 351–357.

Bogen, H. Personal communication with Director, Division of Foster Homes for Adults, City Human Resources Administration, New York, N.Y., 1980.

Brook, B. D., Cortes, M., March, R., & Sundberg-Stirling, M. Community families: An alternative to psychiatric hospital intensive care. *Hospital and Community Psychiatry*, 1976, 27, 195–197.

Cain, E. Personal communication with Director, Division of Aging, Department of Health and Social Services, New Castle, Del., 1980.

Clifford, P. M. Personal communication with Coordinator, Supportive Living Program, Mental Health Services Section, State Division of Mental Health and Mental Retardation, Atlanta, GA., 1979.

Denny, L. W. Personal communication with Director, Licensing Unit, State Department of Social Services, Columbia, S.C., 1980.

Fuller, E. E. Personal communication with Program Manager, Bureau of Maine's Elderly, State Department of Human Services, Augusta, ME., 1979.

Garcia, A. A. Personal communication with Chief, Mental Health Bureau, State Behavioral Services Division, Santa Fe, N.M., 1979.

Gersten, E. Personal communication with Coordinator, Community Support Project, Division of Behavioral Health, State Department of Health Services, Phoenix, Ariz., 1980.

Hall, W. S. Personal communication with State Commissioner of Mental Health, Columbia, S.C., 1979.

Harmon, R. E. Personal Communication with Chief, Policy and Administrative Support Branch, State Department of Social Services, Sacramento, Calif., 1980.

Headrick, C. H. Personal communication with Psychiatric Social Worker, Lakeshore Mental Health Institute, Knoxville, Tenn., 1980.

Herrick, H. D. Forward. In P. J. Schrader, & R. R. Elms (Eds.), *Guidelines for family care home operators*. New York: Springer, 1972.

Inouye, W. H. Personal communication with Head, Clinical Service Standards Program Support Services, Mental Health Division, State Department of Health, Honolulu, HI., 1979.

Iwan, M. J. Personal communication with Adult Social Services Administrator, State Division of Social Services, Lincoln, Neb., 1979.

Kane, D., & Sanders, M. Personal communication with county social workers and forwarded to me by Director of Community Services, State Social Services Board, Bismark, N.D., 1980.

Lindren, D. Personal communication with Research Analyst, Mental Health Bureau, State Department of Public Welfare, St. Paul, Minn., 1980.

Linn, M. W., & Caffey, E. M. Foster placement for the older psychiatric patient. *Journal of Gerontology*, 1977, *32*, 340–345.

McCurdy, R. W. Personal communication with Supervisor, Adult Services Programs, State Department of Social Services, Denver, Colo., 1979.

Miller, M. C. A program for adult foster care. *Social Work*, 1977, *22*, 275–279.

Morrissey, J. R. *The case of family care for the mentally ill.* New York: Behavioral Publications, 1967.

Nelsen, L. H. Personal communication with Program Coordinator, Division of Aging, State Department of Social Services, Salt Lake City, UT., 1979.

O'Connor, G., Justice, R. S., & Warren, N. The aged mentally retarded: Institution or community care? *American Journal of Mental Deficiency*, 1970, *75*, 354–360.

Parker, R. C., & Pettee, L. M. Personal communication with Mental Retardation Adult Services Specialist and Consultant, Adult Foster Care Services, State Department of Human Resources, Raleigh, N.C., 1979.

Payne, D. Personal communication with Assistant Commissioner, State Department of Mental Health and Mental Retardation, Richmond, VA., 1980.

Perlmutter, F., & Silverman, H. A. CMHC: A structural anachronism. *Social Work*, 1972, *17*(2), 78–84.

Proctor, J. Personal communication with Housing Development Specialist, Division of Mental Health and Developmental Services, State Department of Health and Welfare, Concord, N.H., 1980.

Rose, R. Personal communication with Private Care Consultant, Division of Developmental Disabilities, State Department of Mental Health and Developmental Disabilities, Springfield, Ill., 1980.

Schrader, P. J., & Elms, R. R. *Guidelines for family care home operators.* New York: Springer, 1972.

Schuler, L. T., & Kamakawiwoole, C. Personal communication with Nursing Consultants for Home Care, Hospital and Medical Facilities Branch, State Department of Health, Honolulu, HI., 1979.

Segal, S. P. "Shelter Care Needs of the mentally ill". *Social Work and Health care*, 1979a, *2*, 42–55.

Segal, S. P. Community care and deinstitutionalization: A review. *Social Work*, 1979b, *24*, 521–527.

Sherman, S. R., & Newman, E. S. Role of the caseworker in adult foster care. *Social Work*, 1979, *24*, 324–328.

Spence, W. R. Who needs the institution: Client or professional? *Social Work*, 1978, *23*, 511–512.

Vaughn, R. Personal communication with Chief, Non-Institutional Care and Services, State Department of Mental Health, Montgomery, Ala., 1979.

Vermont, Vermont Association for Mental Health, Inc. *The Vermont story: Community care of the mentally ill.* Montpelier, VT., 1976.

Washington, Department of Social and Health Services. *Adult foster homes: Change in program, payment rate, payment method.* Notice #G-35, July 1979.

Zanella, P. F. Personal communication with Administrator, Community Services, State Department of Mental Health, Retardation, and Hospitals, Cranston, R.I., 1980.

Zweben, A. *Family care: An exploratory study.* Unpublished doctoral dissertation, Columbia University, 1977.

CHAPTER 11

American Medical Association. *Mental retardation: A handbook for the primary physician.* Chicago: American Medical Association, 1965.

Cupaiuolo, A. W. *Community interaction with V.A. family care homes for the mentally ill: A comparative study of conflict and nonconflict.* Unpublished doctoral dissertation, Columbia University, 1979.

Evans, E. B. *The interpersonal relationships formed between sponsors and psychiatric patients in community-family care.* Unpublished doctoral dissertation, Brandeis University, 1976.

Fenske, V., & Roecker, M. Finding foster homes for adults. *Public Welfare,* 1971, *29,* 404–410.

McCoin, J. M. *A study of the association between community care home sponsors' personalities and alienation patterns of long-hospitalized schizophrenic male veterans.* Unpublished doctoral dissertation, University of Minnesota, 1977.

Morrissey, J. R. *The case of family care for the mentally ill.* New York: Behavioral Publications, 1967.

Schrader, P. J., & Elms, R. R. *Guidelines for family care home operators.* New York: Springer, 1972.

Wisconsin Chapter, National Association of Social Workers. *Licensing social workers: Toward better service for people.* Milwaukee, Wisconsin, approximately 1978.

Whorley, L. W. *Social exchange patterns in the psychiatric foster home.* Unpublished doctoral dissertation, University of Maryland, 1978.

Wohlford, M. Adult foster care: A unique answer. *Public Welfare,* 1968, *26,* 224–226.

Zweben, A. *Family care: An exploratory study.* Unpublished doctoral dissertation, Columbia University, 1977.

CHAPTER 12

Evans, E. B. *The interpersonal relationships formed between sponsors and psychiatric patients in community-family care.* Unpublished doctoral dissertation, Brandeis University, 1976.

Fromm-Reichmann, F. On loneliness. In D. M. Bullard & E. V. Weigert (Eds.), *Psychoanalysis and psychotherapy: Selected papers of Frieda Fromm-Reichmann.* Chicago: University of Chicago Press, 1959, 325–336.

Henry, J. *Culture against man.* New York: Random House, 1963.

Johnson, D. W. *Reaching out: Interpersonal effectiveness and self-actualization.* Englewood Cliffs, N.J.: Prentice-Hall, 1972.

Johnson, D. W., & Johnson, F. P. *Joining together: Group therapy and group skills.* Englewood Cliffs, N.J.: Prentice-Hall, 1975.

Kaufman, R. J. *A social ecological study of Veterans Administration community placement settings.* Unpublished doctoral dissertation, Brandeis University, 1976.

McCoin, J. M. *A study of the association between community care home sponsors' personalities and alienation patterns of long-hospitalized schizophrenic male veterans.* Unpublished doctoral dissertation, University of Minnesota, 1977.

Murphy, H. B. M., Pennee, B., & Luchins, D. Foster homes: The new back wards. *Canada's Mental Health,* Supplement No. 71, September 1972, 1–17.

Murphy, H. B. M., Engelsmann, F., & Tcheng-Laroche, F. The influence of foster-home care of psychiatric patients. *Archives of General Psychiatry,* 1976, *33,* 179–183.

Robinson, J. P., & Shaver, P. R. *Measures of social psychological attitudes.* Ann Arbor, Mich.: Institute of Social Research, 1973.

Sherman, S., & Newman, E. Foster family care for the elderly in New York State. *Gerontologist,* 1977, *17,* 513–520.

Thomas, E. J. Research and service in single-case experimentation: Conflicts and choices. *Social Work Research and Abstracts,* 1978, *14,* 20–31.

Townley, R. Talk shows seek the fountain of youth. *TV Guide,* July 5, 1980, *27,* 2, 4–5.

Whorley, L. W. *Social exchange patterns in the psychiatric foster home.* Unpublished doctoral dissertation, University of Maryland, 1978.

AUTHOR INDEX

234

SUBJECT INDEX

237